P9-CRJ-951

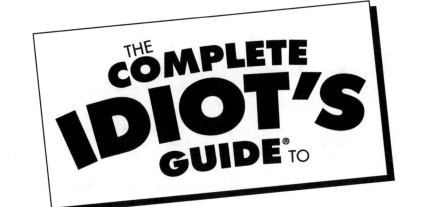

THE COMPLETE IDIOT'S GUIDE® TO

Rock and Water Gardening

Illustrated

by Carlo A. Balistrieri and Bill Gutman

ALPHA

A member of Penguin Group (USA) Inc.

Copyright © 2004 by Carlo A. Balistrieri and Bill Gutman

All rights reserved. No part of this book shall be reproduced, stored in a retrieval system, or transmitted by any means, electronic, mechanical, photocopying, recording, or otherwise, without written permission from the publisher. No patent liability is assumed with respect to the use of the information contained herein. Although every precaution has been taken in the preparation of this book, the publisher and authors assume no responsibility for errors or omissions. Neither is any liability assumed for damages resulting from the use of information contained herein. For information, address Alpha Books, 800 East 96th Street, Indianapolis, IN 46240.

THE COMPLETE IDIOT'S GUIDE TO and Design are registered trademarks of Penguin Group (USA) Inc.

International Standard Book Number: 1-59257-159-X
Library of Congress Catalog Card Number: 2003116926

    04   8   7   6   5   4   3   2   1

Interpretation of the printing code: The rightmost number of the first series of numbers is the year of the book's printing; the rightmost number of the second series of numbers is the number of the book's printing. For example, a printing code of 04-1 shows that the first printing occurred in 2004.

Printed in the United States of America

Note: This publication contains the opinions and ideas of its authors. It is intended to provide helpful and informative material on the subject matter covered. It is sold with the understanding that the authors and publisher are not engaged in rendering professional services in the book. If the reader requires personal assistance or advice, a competent professional should be consulted.

The authors and publisher specifically disclaim any responsibility for any liability, loss, or risk, personal or otherwise, which is incurred as a consequence, directly or indirectly, of the use and application of any of the contents of this book.

Most Alpha books are available at special quantity discounts for bulk purchases for sales promotions, premiums, fund-raising, or educational use. Special books, or book excerpts, can also be created to fit specific needs.

For details, write: Special Markets, Alpha Books, 375 Hudson Street, New York, NY 10014.

Publisher: *Marie Butler-Knight*
Product Manager: *Phil Kitchel*
Senior Managing Editor: *Jennifer Chisholm*
Senior Acquisitions Editor: *Renee Wilmeth*
Development Editor: *Tom Stevens*
Senior Production Editor: *Christy Wagner*
Copy Editor: *Nancy Wagner*
Cartoonist: *Richard King*
Cover/Book Designer: *Trina Wurst*
Indexer: *Angie Bess*
Layout/Proofreading: *John Etchison, Rebecca Harmon*

For Emily, Eric, and Eva—already the crowning achievement of my life and getting better every day, and for all my family and friends who've known I was a complete idiot all along.

—Carlo A. Balistrieri

For do-it-yourselfers everywhere. Good luck.

—Bill Gutman

Contents at a Glance

Contents

Foreword

American gardeners were once obsessed with neatly edged sweeps of green lawns where the occasional mulched tree was the only relief. For most gardeners, the thought of having rocks or water in your garden meant you had problems or at best obstacles to overcome or remove. Rocks were hazards for the lawnmower, and water equated to a dead lawn or, at best, a muddy one. As we have become more sophisticated about plants and gardens, we realize that these once-hated obstacles can become assets. What is more soothing and relaxing than the sound of water? What is more natural than rock to give a garden character? The authors, Carlo A. Balistrieri and Bill Gutman, believe that "every yard can benefit from the addition of rock and water features." They also understand that building these types of gardens can be a very scary proposition to the average person.

In *The Complete Idiot's Guide to Rock and Water Gardening Illustrated*, the authors, drawing on years of experience, relate the techniques they use in their own gardens, recommending the steps that will make the process easy to understand and accomplish. They understand that the basis for successful gardening is not only having an attractive garden but that gardening should be fun, and that the right way to proceed is almost always the easiest way. They believe, as do most gardeners, that if you find yourself in a project that is over your head, you will soon tire of it. This book places a special emphasis on starting small and working your way up to larger rock or water features. But the authors are careful to note that there is a workable-size rock or water feature for every situation and garden size. Scale to them is very important.

As a teenager, I worked under the late T. H. Everett, who designed and built the rock garden at The New York Botanical Garden. I gained an appreciation of how the proper use of rocks and cascading water, although artificially placed by man, gave one the feeling that the garden was a creation of nature and not of man. The authors agree that using rocks native to your area, or at least using only one type of rock and placing them to look as if they have been there forever, is very important.

The authors illustrate many different types of rock or water features that can highlight every garden. Stone projects range from large hillside rock gardens to small trough gardens that can rest on an outdoor table or that would be perfect for a deck. Water features projects range from still ponds of all sizes to cascading waterfalls, streams, fountains, or containers of all sizes and types. There are ideas here to fit every situation and, just as important, every budget. Throughout the chapters you will find quick tips and warnings that relate to the task at hand. I particularly like the tip about putting your garden hose in the sun for a while to soften it and take the kinks out of it and then using it to outline the curves in your layout. Quick lists of tools and materials are highlighted for each project, followed directly by numbered step-by-step instructions that are precise and easy to follow. In fact, the only thing that is missing would be the authors coming to your home and performing the work themselves.

Michael A. Ruggiero
Senior Curator (Retired)
The New York Botanical Garden

Introduction

How would you like to have a bubbling oasis in your backyard or a natural rock garden with a variety of low-growing and colorful alpine-type plants? If not that, how about the sound of a small waterfall in which the water cascades over a bed of well-placed rocks 24 hours a day? Maybe your choice is a natural dry-stone wall built against a hillside to prevent erosion, with small, flowering plants growing out between cracks in the rocks.

All these features and more are possible additions to your own yard, and many of them are projects you can do yourself. Rock and water features aren't for everyone. If you don't use your yard, don't spend time there, and really don't want or enjoy maintenance, then maybe you should just keep the grass cut and let it go at that. But if you want more, you can make your backyard a special place with the judicious use of rock and water.

The installation of rock and water features takes work, sometimes pretty heavy work—moving and lifting rock, digging holes, or laying cable for an electrical source. It takes knowledge and patience to do the job correctly. But if you install your own rock garden or pond, or build a rock wall, or lay out a stream, you will have accomplished something that will make you proud, that you can enjoy for years, and that will undoubtedly get compliments from friends and neighbors for a job well done.

In this book, you will learn just how to go about installing your own rock and/or water features. There are step-by-step instructions to take you through basic projects, with more than enough information on how to be creative and change the projects to suit your needs and tastes. There are descriptions of the tools and equipment you'll need and ways to maintain your features, as well as how to adorn them with a variety of plants. This book can take you from start to finish, make your ideas become reality, and show you just how rock and water features can become a permanent part of your lifestyle.

There are also dozens of sidebars including tips, warnings, related information, and terms to aid you in preparing and planning so that you do it right and keep the project in perspective.

The Right Stuff

These sidebars give a variety of general advice regarding the planning, preparation, installation, planting, and maintenance of various types of rock and water features. They are geared to help the reader make the correct decisions in all aspects of rock and water feature development in the backyard.

Backyard Lingo

Backyard Lingo sidebars define and explain terms you're likely to encounter when learning about rock and water features.

Quick Tip

Quick Tip sidebars will give the reader a little extra here and a little extra there, suggestions that will make the job easier and make sure it is done right the first time.

A Word of Warning

These sidebars will highlight various pitfalls the do-it-yourselfer might encounter when installing and planting features in the yard. The best way to avoid mistakes is to be aware of them before they happen and these warnings are geared to serve that purpose.

Acknowledgments

The authors would like to thank the following people and institutions for their generous help in providing information, photographic sites, and materials needed to aid in the preparation of this book:

The Matterhorn Nursery, the Innisfree Foundation and Petronella Collins, Margaret and John Falk, Iggie and Gloria Balistrieri, Steve and Denise Balistrieri, Mike Ruggiero, Aquascape Designs, Inc., Jack Ferreri, Lynden Miller, and people who garden everywhere, making the world a more beautiful place and providing grist for photographers and writers everywhere.

Illustrations

Unless otherwise credited, all photographs are by Carlo A. Balistrieri.

All sketches are by Marsha Richter.

Trademarks

All terms mentioned in this book that are known to be or are suspected of being trademarks or service marks have been appropriately capitalized. Alpha Books and Penguin Group (USA) Inc. cannot attest to the accuracy of this information. Use of a term in this book should not be regarded as affecting the validity of any trademark or service mark.

In This Part

Part 1

Rock and Water

Rock and water have been basic elements of the earth since the beginning of time. Both were essential for the survival of early man and have continued to play a functional role as civilizations evolved. Slowly, man began to find ways to use both rock and water in more artistic and decorative ways, ultimately bringing them into the backyard for his personal satisfaction and pleasure.

Rock can easily become part of the landscape, with dry-stone walls, paths and patios, and rock borders giving backyards a natural character and look. The rock garden added beauty, and plants were used to soften and adorn rock. Natural water gardens, ponds, streams, and waterfalls also found their way onto private grounds, adding a soothing and relaxing presence, an escape from the stress of the everyday world. Plan wisely, and these features can add to almost any yard.

In This Chapter

- ◆ Enhance your yard with rock and water features
- ◆ Plan features that work
- ◆ Know your limits
- ◆ Learn the features available to you

You can almost feel the sound and movement of
the water in this picturesque backyard feature.

Using Rock and Water in Your Yard

Mention landscaping or gardening, and the first things that pop into most homeowners' minds are trees, shrubs, and flowers. While these elements are critical aesthetic additions to a yard, many people forget about rock and water, two essential features for the complete yard. You're missing the boat if you don't include these in your gardening compositions.

There is little doubt that every yard can benefit from the addition of rock and water features. Regardless of size, *topography*, and existing plantings, the addition of rock or water features makes the terrain more interesting, beautiful, and tranquil. There are many types of rock and water features to build, either on their own or in combination. Before you decide what to include in your design, it might help to learn a little about how these projects can benefit your landscape and how to build them yourself.

It helps at the outset to consider the kind of yard you have and how you want it to look. Finally, you'll have to weigh the cost of adding these features, the time it takes to install them, and the work required to keep them well maintained and in tip-top condition. We hope we can help make your yard the enchanted setting for your home that it ought to be. Our goal is to give you the information, knowledge, and instruction you need to get going in the right direction. It's only a start, but making the right choices about rock and water in your yard will result in many years of enjoyment of the magical oasis you'll create. This chapter is the beginning of the story.

Backyard Lingo

Topography is the detailed features of a yard or tract of land, whether it is flat, sloped, or contains small hills, trees, existing rocks, manicured lawn, or high-grassed fields.

"But I Just Want a Pretty Yard"

For generations we've been obsessed with removing rock and water from our yards. We've pulled out rock, tilled to drain water, rolled, seeded, weeded, fed, cut, and edged. The Sisyphean task of maintaining the urban lawn was a given, neighbor competing with neighbor to have the flattest, greenest, most weed-free lawn on the block.

If you are lucky enough to have a naturally rocky area in your yard, you are well on your way to creating a beautiful rock garden.

Times, however, have changed, and the tight, skinny flower and "green meatball" strips around the house have evolved into wonderful, flowing borders with island gardens out in the yard and complete environments being manufactured for our enjoyment. Bringing rock and water back into the yard completes the process of creating a sense of place for your home—making it feel as if it belongs where it is.

Backyard Quick Tip

Even if you live on a block where all the lawns are flat and green, you have the option to change. There is no reason not to be the first one in your neighborhood to build a rock wall, install a pond and waterfall, or create a slope for a rock garden. If you see something you would like for your yard, go ahead and do it. You may be surprised at how many of your neighbors follow suit.

Create a Setting for Your Home

You may be thinking, "But my yard looks great. I've got nice flowerbeds, so why should I bring in rock?" Putting rock and water features in your backyard, even if you already have the flowerbeds you want, is like putting the finishing touches on an incomplete painting. Adding these brushstrokes to your masterpiece will bring the whole composition into balance and completeness.

Many projects are the do-it-yourself kind, which can give you quite a sense of accomplishment and save a little cash for the important things—like more plants. If you have a big yard and the money to bring in professionals, you can have larger, more complex features installed. Either way, if the job is done right, you'll realize tangible and intangible benefits and increase the enjoyment and value of your property.

This sturdy-looking natural stone bench set alongside a rock path can serve as an anchor for the style of your yard.

Rock features tend to anchor your entire landscape, creating the feeling of permanence. Stone creates a sense of timelessness and the stability that comes with age. A well-installed rock feature, if it's made to look natural, will seem like it's been there since the dawn of time.

Adding water features heightens the sense of enchantment. Sound, rhythm, and movement are the perfect counterparts to the solid presence of stone. The gurgle and splash of moving water is soothing and tranquil, allowing you to escape from the noisy chaos of the outside world. Water features attract wildlife, can become a home for fish, and are always a focal point in the yard.

Planning Quick Tip

If your lifestyle includes the enjoyment of water, whether it be relaxing at the beach, canoeing on a lake, or even swimming at a local pool, you should think about adding a water feature to your yard. It will enable you to bring a little bit of the beach or lake home with you and enjoy it full-time.

Before you begin installing rock paths, building walls, creating a rock garden, making a backyard pond or stream, or even building a waterfall, you need to consider many things. Projects can get complex and costly, but don't have to be. All involve some level of maintenance. They must also serve their intended purpose. Sometimes people see or read about a rock or water feature and rush to put something similar in their yard. Without careful planning, your new addition can be a millstone around your neck—a far cry from the original idea.

Be Sure to Inventory Your Yard

Prior to making any decisions about the addition of a rock or water feature, you should make a careful inventory of your yard. In some cases, the physical size and layout of your property may limit your additions. And the surest road to disappointment is to simply plop features around your yard without thinking about the overall effect. Planting a rock garden here, digging a small pond there, slapping up a retaining wall, and laying a path willy-nilly leads to a jumbled, busy, unhappy mess. If you're going to do the work, the end result should make you happy. A job well done is the most satisfying of exercises.

You must consider the natural landscape of your yard before deciding upon the size and kind of rock or water features you want to add.

Consider these things before planning for rock and water features:

- What are the size, topography, and existing features of your yard?
- Is your yard flat or sloped?
- Is your yard already heavily planted with bushes, gardens, and large trees?
- Are there rocks already in place?
- Will you keep what is already there?

Once you have checked out what you have, think about how you and your family use the yard. Do you entertain frequently? Do you or your kids use the yard for recreation? Consider traffic patterns for family, guests, and even your pets. All these elements will factor into your ultimate choice of rock or water features.

Views Are Important

Another essential component of your inventory should be visual. Think about what you see when you look at your yard from various locations within it and from the windows of your home.

If you stand at a single point in your yard and make decisions about where to add a rock or water feature, you are forgetting an important element. How will the feature look from the places where you normally relax and look out over your yard? What about the view from your living room? Do you have a window or sliding glass doors overlooking the yard from another heavily used room? Take time to look at the setting from several perspectives. Try to envision the feature in several possible places and decide which would be most pleasing to your eye. Then make maximum use of your views to install your feature where you'll get the most bang for your effort.

Always check the views of your yard from several angles before deciding on the placement of a new rock or water feature.

Views are important but aren't the only criteria for placement. The layout and physical nature of your yard may make the location of your new feature a moot point. Nevertheless, the only reason to add such a feature to your landscape is the pleasure and enjoyment you'll get from it, so maximize the upside. The location must be practical, but should be one that is attractive from any angle, inside and out in the yard.

Kids, Pets, Traffic, and Houseguests

Lifestyle is another, often overlooked, factor. Think about the way you use your yard. If you enjoy entertaining and regularly have large groups of people in your yard, be sure to leave enough open space to accommodate your guests and their activities. A large rock or water feature may not be practical or may have to be moved to an area where it doesn't conflict with your uses of the yard.

Don't forget some consideration for your children. Everyone remembers that special yard in the neighborhood where all the kids came to play. Carefully tended swards of grass become trampled, and bare ovals of mud gradually indicate the high-impact areas. Backyards are natural locations for fun and games, so you should not discount their value for such uses. Swimming pools, volleyball nets (remember horseshoe pits?), and many other recreational needs may create additional priorities for the center of the yard. Aesthetics must then be moved to the sides and corners for safety and sanity! Although the location may not be ideal, you can still indulge yourself, and after all, the pool you sink into the ground for your kids can be made into an amazing pond when they've flown the coop.

Planning Quick Tip

If it seems that every spot in your yard has a use, don't fret. You can still find ways to add rock or water features. You can always miniaturize them, making small container water gardens or small rock gardens in troughs. Bigger isn't always better, and the small features can be both beautiful and charming.

Like recreational uses, traffic patterns are often forgotten in planning for yard improvements. Your children and pets are not likely to abandon their favorite paths and shortcuts just because you decide to beautify the yard. If you don't want them cutting through your project, plan with their needs and patterns in mind. You'll save yourself a headache or two. Maybe the route they take is the ideal solution for that garden path you've been thinking about.

These and other factors make up a family's lifestyle. Don't forget to think about them before you decide to do the work of adding rock and water features in the yard. A few minutes of thought at the beginning can save lots of blood, sweat, and tears.

Planning Quick Tip

Careful planning is important. When you decide to place a rock or water feature, think not only of today but also the future. Anticipate your family's needs down the road. It's much less work to build these features once. Taking them apart and moving them is excruciating, not only physically but mentally. If you're not certain what your grand plan for the yard is, try one or two of the smaller, portable features before committing to more permanent additions. You'll save a lot of familial angst.

Consider Space and Budget

Once you've inventoried your yard and decided where to put your new rock or water feature, you should consider size and budget. Before you act, strike a balance with both your available space and the money you can spend. Rock and water features can vary from a small rock border and a container water garden to very large and elaborate tableaus. These complex features can be striking and beautiful, but they aren't for every yard.

Scale is important. If you have a small yard, it's smart to start with one or more small features. If you want a larger feature, it's even more important to site it carefully so it doesn't overwhelm the yard. Medium-size yards give you greater flexibility. You may want to keep features on the small side, but you have the luxury of using larger features without making things look out of proportion. If you want to install two or more features, you will still have the space to do it. For bigger yards, the sky is the limit. But be careful. Don't bite off more than you can chew.

This beautiful setting in a concrete trough is a rock garden in miniature and doesn't take up much space.

Even with limited space you can create a small, planted water garden with several goldfish swimming inside.

Cost considerations also come into play. It is one thing to use that pile of rocks you pulled out of the lawn to make a border, small wall, or even a rock garden. It's another matter entirely to recreate a scale model of the Matterhorn. Water features, on the whole, tend to be more expensive. You must consider liners, electricity, pumps, filters, and more complicated construction. An elaborate waterfall or fountain project can easily cost more than $5,000 for a professional to plan and install. Even do-it-yourselfers will run up a sizable bill. And don't forget maintenance costs. A little homework ahead of time will keep your pocketbook plump.

The Right Stuff

Are you a little nervous about putting in rock or water features? If that's the case, start simple and go slowly. There's less chance of making a costly mistake, and you can always add more later on. Unless you have a huge yard, a similar-size budget, and are certain that you want a large feature, it's best to begin with something basic and small. In that way, if it doesn't work, it's easier to change or remove. If you get the bug and have to have more, you can always add to what you've got and have your yard evolve with your lifestyle and budget. Starting small doesn't mean you neglect the future. It's always a good idea to think about what you might add later, even if it is years down the road. Planning ahead helps avoid a yard that looks like it was together higgledy-piggledy without much consideration. In addition, if you love your new feature and enjoyed putting it together, then you have more to look forward to in years to come.

With space and a big budget you can have a feature such as this huge terraced garden adorned by formal columns as an added touch.

Rock and Water Features You Can Add

Rock and water features come in a wide variety of shapes and sizes and can be very useful, functional additions to the backyard. You can add a simple artistically placed boulder near a container filled with water and a small water lily or construct a complex array of rock and water built to look like a mountain stream. Lay a stepping-stone path to a paved boulevard or add a landing outside the back door leading to the patio for entertaining. Or consider a small planted wall versus castlelike retaining walls. There is no end to the wide variety of features you can construct to add value and enjoyment to your backyard.

Rock

Rock features can be as simple as using stone to highlight an existing flower garden or a stepping-stone path between plantings. Easy but effective, these basic features will enhance the overall look of the yard. A small dry-stone wall can serve as a border or divider, and a simple set of stone steps can make walking up a hill or slope a lot easier while giving the terrain a gentrified, country look. These kinds of projects are functional and also improve the look of the yard.

Existing flower gardens benefit greatly from the addition of rock features. Rock is the perfect foil to set off the beauty of plantings, and you'll find over time that the plantings perform the same service for the rock.

Not to be lost in all this discussion of rock features is the rock garden itself. As with other rock features, gardens can be simple or elaborate and made to look completely natural—as if they have been in place for many years—or more formal. You can construct rock gardens on any terrain. If you have flat land, you can build up, using berms and rock to create a realistic-looking outcropping to fill with special plants. Using rock creatively on flat land, you can make terracelike raised beds to form different planting levels to fill with your favorite plants.

You can also use rock to create stone patios or decorative, flowing borders around already-existing trees. With the unlimited sizes and shapes of rocks, the possibilities for creative placement are endless. The more of these features that you can see personally, on your travels or at a garden center that specializes in their construction, the more ideas you will have about what will look best in your yard.

This large water feature with a fountain, terrace, and wooden bridge shows there is no limit to what you can create in your yard.

This natural stone walkway, made with Belgian pavers, is yet another way to add a functional feature with a natural look to your yard.

Planning Quick Tip

For those who don't have access to natural rocks and who don't want to have to transport them, believe it or not, there are other ways to go. You can find artificial rocks that are lighter than the real thing, use soft rocks in which you can drill holes for plants, or even make your own rocks (see Chapter 6).

Water

As with rock, water features also offer unlimited opportunities. In truth, water features tend to be a bit more complex in their construction and maintenance. Even small features require you to make decisions that you won't encounter in working with rock. Do you want to include plants or fish? What kind of filter or pump will you need? And what do you need to know to maintain an ecological balance, to keep the pond fresh and clean? Once you decide, a pond makes a great centerpiece in the yard, something around which you can plan gardens or additional rock features.

The sight and sound of water is soothing and tranquil. Ponds, small streams, waterfalls, fountains, and *burblers* are just some of the possibilities for bringing this benefit to your yard, providing you have the space, the budget, and the time. Professionals might have to construct and install some of the more elaborate features. This will definitely cost more, but the investment is often well worth it on many levels.

Gurgling water and soothing waves make this millstone burbler a great water feature for a deck or patio.

Backyard Lingo

A **burbler** is simply something that you can add to a small water feature, such as a container garden, that uses an air pump to produce a constant, soothing effect of air bubbling to the surface of the water. It can keep the water from becoming stagnant, as well.

Small water features can be placed close to the house, deck, or patio so they can be seen and enjoyed whenever you are sitting outside. Larger ones will be placed farther out in the yard to add a natural and majestic look, one that brings you close to nature, even if you live in a crowded suburb.

That's another upside of the water feature. You have the option of combining a pond, stream, or waterfall with both rocks and vegetation in a way that makes it look completely natural, as if nature itself was the creative force. If well done, the feature will look like it was there long before your home. Thus, both rock and water features present the opportunity to take your yard out of the ordinary. If you're not content with the traditional suburban yard, think about adding these unique and interesting adornments.

A Word of Warning

Even with the smallest of rock and water features, placement and planning are key. If you decide you want a small rock or water feature near your patio, be careful with the plants you choose. Nectar-producing plants attract bees, some plants produce irritants, and others have spines and thorns. It might be better to use these away from areas that are heavily used to avoid having family and friends stuck or stung.

By now you should have a good idea about what rock and water features are and what they can do for you and your yard. Read on to discover more about these fantastic features. We'll help you take the plunge and give you some ideas for your first project. It won't be your last.

The Least You Need to Know

◆ Rock and water features can add a beautiful finishing touch to your backyard.

◆ Careful planning is the key before beginning to place a rock or water feature in the yard.

◆ Check out your yard and examine your lifestyle before making changes to the terrain.

◆ Start simple, don't overcrowd the yard, and don't construct a feature that will have to be torn down or moved in a year or two.

◆ There is a variety of interesting rock and water features available to you. Be thoughtful and creative, and you will be amazed at what happens to your yard.

In This Chapter

- ◆ Rocks as ageless specimens
- ◆ Gardens and rock put together
- ◆ Rock features can be artistic and functional
- ◆ Styles of rock gardens

This natural rock outcropping is one of many on the East Coast of the United States. It's historic and beautiful at the same time, having stood the test of time.

Chapter 2

Rock Features

Rock is one of the fundamental elements of the earth. It supports the thin layer of soil that makes all life possible on our planet. Because of this, it's no surprise that rock has played a major role in man's existence since the beginning of time. Whether used as shelter, for defense, or as weapons, rock helped house early man, aided him in fending off enemies, and enabled him to hunt for food. Long before it was aesthetic, rock was fully functional. However, the utilitarian aspect of rock was soon joined by the artistic as early men painted on and piled rock to tell stories and enliven their dwellings. In today's world, rock continues to play multiple roles, being used functionally and artistically. In addition to supporting the surface of the earth, it can form the bedrock of a garden's look and feel.

Functional *rock features* and *rock gardens* can serve specific purposes and enhance your yard at the same time. A simple dry-stone wall or a small path of stepping-stones does a job but looks good at the same time. Rock gardens come in a variety of shapes and sizes and are beautiful additions to the look of a yard, but these gardens can also help with aesthetic and landscaping issues. Both rock features and rock gardens can hold a wide variety of plants. With a little imagination, almost anything is possible. This chapter will begin to tell you how.

Backyard Lingo

We use **rock feature** to mean a structure made of natural stone that may or may not be planted. Some are utilitarian, like patios, steps, paths, and walls. Others are more artistic, but all provide aesthetic additions to the yard.

A **rock garden** is a type of rock feature that is built to showcase rocks and plants. In a classic rock garden the plants are small and generally come from the mountainous areas of the world. Rock gardens are not usually utilitarian in the sense that they are not usually "used" by people. Their value is predominantly artistic.

Ageless Rocks

Rocks are everywhere. While we can find some sort of plant life in nearly every area of the earth's land surface, it is rock that predominates. It is always at or near the surface and many of our most awe-inspiring natural features are stone, thrust up from the earth's core. Our distant ancestors may not have realized how much they depended on these natural features. Rock caves probably first provided hiding places but soon became valued for shelter and warmth. Rocks could also be used as weapons and piled up to provide a safe barrier from enemies. The first rudimentary tools were also made from rock.

As civilization developed, the uses of rock began to expand. The Great Pyramids were constructed of stone. It's estimated that Stonehenge, the mysterious formation of large standing stones in England, was built between 1800 and 1400 B.C.E. Some of the stones are as long as 30 feet and weigh upward of 50 tons. The Easter Island monoliths, ziggurats in Asia, fabulous constructions in Central and South America, walls to retain soil for agricultural terraces around the world, and similarly amazing structures wherever man has lived are evidence of our close connection to rock and its use. Scientists remain baffled about how many of these huge features were constructed.

Decorative stone features, such as this one created in a Japanese style, were early manifestations of man's artistic bent.

Later, man used rock to make roads, build castles, and construct rudimentary dams to hold back water. Stone walls, a carryover from the earliest uses of rock, continue to be built to divide lands and hold back soil. Advanced civilizations, such as the Roman Empire, began using rock in both functional and decorative ways, constructing aqueducts to bring water to their cities and creating large, decorative fountains that adorned many of their large buildings, which were also built largely with rock.

Rock continues to be used in a wide variety of utilitarian and aesthetic ways. The timelessness and permanence of these structures from the past have inspired countless people to include rock in their landscapes. A simple rock wall built last week can be made to look similar to an ancient wall built in Wales by a craftsman or farmer hundreds of years ago. Using rock and building rock features connects us to our past and will allow the future to take a look back at us.

The First Rock Gardens

Considering our "beginning-of-time" relationship with rock, it's surprising that it took so long for rocks and plants to be used together. After our nomadic "hunter-gatherer" stage, the first agriculturists needed to concentrate on raising food to feed their families. No one was thinking about flowers and shrubs. The first use of rock in the garden was probably to ring the planting area, separating it from other parts of the landscape and protecting it from possible predators.

Only after civilization advanced to the stage where every waking moment of the day wasn't devoted to surviving could rock and plants be put together in a decorative scheme. Although the British of the mid-nineteenth century are generally credited with the first "rock gardens," stone had already been an integral part of many Asian cultures for centuries. The aesthetic traditions of China, Japan, Vietnam, and other cultures treat rock with reverence and have very specific rules about its use in the garden. The oldest gardening book in the world is *Sakuteiki* or *Records of Garden Making*. The first line of this 1,000-year-old work is translated as "The art of setting stones." Each of these Asian cultures has its own art form involving the use of rock and plants.

England is generally considered the home of the first "alpine garden," rock gardens built to mimic mountain habitats with plants from the mountains of other lands. In the early to mid-1800s, travel to the Alps became fashionable.

Enamored of the alpine scenery and the beautiful array of plants whose gemlike flowers glittered among the rocks, some mountain-lovers schemed to recreate that feeling at home. They began bringing the colorful plants back with them in an attempt to capture some of the beauty they had experienced on their holidays.

Early attempts failed because the travelers weren't aware of the special needs of these new plants and couldn't maintain them successfully. Some plants were put in formal settings, arches and bridges which didn't approximate the natural mountainous settings. The turn of the twentieth century brought increased understanding of the needs of the plants, but failures were still frequent with many rock gardens poorly constructed.

The Right Stuff

The first decade of the twentieth century probably saw the biggest improvement in the skills and knowledge of rock gardeners. Some of the influential books that helped greatly in early rock garden development were *My Rock Garden*, written by Reginald Farrer, who developed a famous garden in Yorkshire, England, and *Rock Gardens*, by Lewis Meredith, who learned the craft in County Wicklow, Ireland. Farrer then wrote a second book, *The English Rock Garden*, which was published in 1919 and soon became the bible of many rock gardeners in both Britain and later America. Yet another major publication was *Rock Garden and Alpine Plants*, by Henri Correvon, a Swiss pioneer in the cultivation of alpine plants. Correvon's book was published in English in 1930 and helped more people to understand and care for these special plants. All these early books provide fascinating reading for the modern rock garden enthusiast, and useful nuggets of information can still be gleaned from them.

It didn't take long for interest in rock gardening to cross the Atlantic. One of the first rock gardens in America was constructed in 1890 at the Smith College Botanic Garden in Northhampton, Massachusetts. It was modeled after Kew, the Royal Botanic Garden in England. Another was created in the 1920s at the Brooklyn Botanic Garden in New York City, and in 1932 construction was begun on a large rock garden at The New York Botanical Garden. Now nearly every major botanical garden in temperate climates around the world has a rock garden. Even tropical gardens use rock to beautify their holdings. Although alpine plants can't be grown because of their need for cold winters, small plants from warm areas of the world can be used with rock just as effectively.

Like Europe, American interest in rock gardening grew quickly as books about how to build these gardens and grow these plants from all over the globe began to be written. An early contribution was *The Rock Garden*, a 1923 book by Louise Beebe Wilder. In 1968, *Rock Gardening*, by H. Lincoln Foster and Laura Foster, helped enormously in bringing the hobby to many more people all over the country. It's still regarded as a modern-day "bible" by many gardeners.

This colorful *Erigeron Chrysopsidis*, or Grand Ridge, is a North American alpine plant used in many rock gardens.

Not every climate can grow the traditional alpine plants that grace European rock gardens. Once American rock gardeners realized this, they began selecting small plants native to their respective regions and putting them into traditionally constructed rock gardens. In this way, gardeners can achieve a rock garden look and feel using plants that have a much better chance of surviving. Because of these advances in horticulture today, rock gardening is available to you no matter where you are.

The *Campanula Orphanidea* is a European alpine that has found its way into many American rock gardens.

Sculptural/Artistic

Rock can be used purely for artistic reasons. Thousands of years ago glaciers covered much of the earth. Here and there "glacial erratics" have been left behind. Far different from natural rock outcroppings, these are large boulders, left seemingly in the middle of nowhere. Because of their size and imposing presence, they form natural focal points.

This 8-foot-tall glacial erratic, formed by nature, can stand alone as an imposing piece of stone sculpture.

Functional Rock Features

The ancient functions of rock—shelter, weapons, and protection—obviously no longer carry the same importance they once did, but there are many ways rock can be used in functional features in the backyard. The use of rock gives a yard a natural look, is fairly easy to maintain, and lasts for years.

Functional rock features can be constructed from natural rocks and stones that you look for and gather (with appropriate permissions if they aren't found on your own property), but in most cases with material that you purchase from a garden center or stone yard. It's physical work, especially if the stones are large, but the satisfaction of making your own feature is hard to beat. With a little ingenuity and some sweat, you can do the job yourself. Here are some features with function you can build.

We can use stone to create similar points of emphasis. Everyone has seen pictures of wide sweeping lawns with monolithic natural stones set almost as sculptures in their midst. On a smaller scale, uniquely shaped or colored stone can also be used to create interest. The Chinese and Japanese people are masters in the use of stone in this fashion. In many of their gardens, stone is the important element and plants just accents; much the opposite of Western gardens where flowers and plants are generally considered the focus. Some Eastern gardens are constructed entirely of stone and gravel.

Walls

Dry-stone walls are among the oldest of functional rock features. For thousands of years people have been stacking stone to mark boundaries and separate lands, crops, and livestock. A well-constructed dry-stone wall results from the proper selection and placement of the stone. Done right, such a wall can last for centuries. Stone walls are still used in many areas to separate farmers' fields. In residential settings they have long been used to mark property lines but also serve as barriers from the road or as a retaining wall to hold back soil.

The Right Stuff

Although this one isn't in the backyard, many tourists have seen The Old Man in the Mountain, a natural rock formation in New Hampshire that resembled the face of an old man. What nature created, nature finally destroyed in 2003 when part of the weathered formation broke away and fell off, destroying the aesthetic value of a natural rock landmark.

This close-up shows the character of this old, New England dry-stone wall complete with lichen-covered rock.

This rock border, made with symmetrical Belgian pavers with mortared joints, has a more formal look. A less-formal border will use natural rocks and no mortar.

If your yard doesn't have a stone wall, you can construct one that will serve a purpose and also stand the test of time. Whether you use your wall to divide property, to keep a hillside from eroding, to put a border around a patio, or to set off a garden, the beauty of stone will enhance the overall look and feel of your yard.

Borders

Do you have a flower garden that requires a constant spading of the edges to keep the grass from growing into the bed? Or would you like to set off a group of small shrubs to highlight their position in your yard? In either case, you can use a natural rock border to accomplish your goal. Placing stones around existing flower gardens sets them off from the rest of the yard and gives them a distinctive look. You choose the size of the stones and arrange them in a way that is pleasing to your eye. Your choice of stone and the way you construct your border determines whether it is effective or looks like a giant piece of costume jewelry. Properly setting the stone makes all the difference.

Paths and Stairways

Paths and steps may be the most overlooked opportunity in homeowner landscaping. Too often these necessary features are done in the quickest, cheapest manner so that attention can be focused on flowers, shrubs, and ornamental trees. By paying equal attention to the permanent additions to your yard, you can achieve an elegant solution to the problem of getting from here to there that also provides a beautiful frame for your plantings.

Stone or rock paths can be put almost anywhere they will serve a purpose. They can be simple stepping-stones through a garden, giving you a place from which to cultivate and weed. Paths can be put in high-traffic areas to replace worn-out grass and mud scrapes. These rock paths should lead from one place to another and where possible wind to create contour and the potential for mystery and surprise.

A quaint stone path leads to this natural stone stairway that winds its way up through a rock garden.

Rocks can be used in a variety of ways to create steps on a slope or hillside. They can be put in stepping-stone-style or as a natural stairway enabling you to safely walk up and down the grade even when it is wet and slippery. If you have a rock garden set on the slope, the natural stairway will allow you to move about the garden without trampling any of the plants. In addition, if the stairway is made with stone, it will create a natural look that will better blend with the rock garden.

Patios

Patios are often made of cement or pavers to provide a flat surface for entertaining and outdoor living. Natural stone like lannon stone, flagstone, slate, and others with flat surfaces can be used just as effectively and have the additional advantage of being made by nature. This continues the theme of a natural, timeless look, and when properly set, they will be as flat and sturdy as man-made material.

Natural stone patios also provide a unique planting opportunity because creeping plants and others of small stature can be used between the stones to add splashes of color. Many will also take light foot traffic so you don't have to play hopscotch to use your new outdoor area if you plant it properly.

As with many of these features, advance planning and preparation make the job easier and the finished product more beautiful and lasting.

You can take advantage of a natural stone patio by placing low-growing plants between the cracks in the rocks, adding color and beauty to the feature.

The Rock Garden

Rock gardens come in all shapes and sizes and can be crafted in many ways. With rock and a little imagination, you can have a rock garden. It can be made on a natural slope in your yard, built up on flat ground, or made in a container.

This basic rock garden, which is planted with thyme, lavender, and *Penstemon pinifolius*, isn't fancy, but it is very effective.

Rock garden purists insist on using only alpines. These are plants, usually shorter than 1 foot, which are found in the mountainous areas of the world above the timberline. Despite advances in horticulture and our understanding of the needs of these special plants, they are not easy to grow in many climates. Some alpines are very adaptable and will grow in places far removed from their mountain homes; others are nearly impossible to grow. The good news is that wherever you live, you can combine plants and rock in your landscape plans. The key is to understand your climate and choose plants that will survive whatever nature throws at you.

If you're not into plants in a big way and are interested only in beautifying your yard, talk to local nurserymen about what will work in your rock garden. Check out your local rock garden society to speak with others about what succeeds for them. Knowing what plants thrive in your area will greatly increase your chances of success.

If plants intrigue you, there is no harm in experimenting with those you've seen in books or magazines and just can't resist. Learn about the conditions in which they live in the wild, and see if you can provide them with an agreeable setting right in your own yard.

Some homeowners have natural rock outcroppings in their yards to form the backbone of their gardening efforts. If you can't move it, you may as well use it. Working with what nature provides makes the job that much easier. Those of us who don't have rock thrusting its way up through our backyard can, with creative thought and some hard work, build features that accomplish the same thing.

With larger rock specimens, this garden is planted with trees, shrubs, and perennials to keep the overall scale intact.

If you have a site with good topography, work with it. If your yard was scraped flat by developers, create your own topography, building up areas of the yard to provide additional structural appeal and a terrific starting point for your new garden. For much more on creating natural-looking rock gardens, see Chapters 5, 6, and 7.

Formal Alternatives

Rock can also be used in a more formal setting. Some homes and some gardeners require a more geometric and symmetrical arrangement of their landscapes. This is the main difference between the formal and natural styles. Here, instead of imitating the gentle chaos of nature, the goal is order, control, simplicity, and predictability. It's a different kind of elegance, a manufactured calm, and something you can certainly do yourself.

Planning Quick Tip

If you are moving into a new home and the backyard has some hilly areas with natural rocks jutting out of the earth, don't be so anxious to have your contractor remove them and level the yard. Think about what you might do with the natural topography you are inheriting. If you act too quickly, you could be destroying the perfect setting for a beautiful rock garden.

The Natural Look

The natural rock garden mimics formations found in nature. Making your garden look like a natural hillside, studded with rocks of various sizes and with plants growing in the cracks and crevices that nature has created over hundreds of years is a real art. Slavish imitation of nature is not a universal goal, but lessons can be learned, and the natural look is most effectively achieved if you adhere to the basic rules.

This raised, terraced rock garden, with dry-stone walls and stone stairway, is a beautiful structure enhanced by a combination of dwarf trees and alpine plants.

The use of an irregular natural product like stone in a formal, regulated setting may seem like a contradiction. Cut stone, shaped and contoured, may seem a more appropriate material and is often used to create the straight lines sought by those who opt for the formal alternative. Using natural stone in a formal design, however, melds the two worlds in a unique and wonderful way.

Planting Your Functional Rock Features

Rock features, functional or aesthetic, nearly always benefit from being planted. Many will look bare, hard, and cold if not decorated with plants to soften their edges and add form, life, and color to the picture. While groups of rocks can stand alone as sculptural features, it's often more difficult to make them look as if they belong unless they are married to the landscape with associated plantings.

You can add plants to almost every type of rock feature. Here a beautiful clump of *Thymus* springs into bloom in the crack of a stone patio.

Those features that are purely functional are especially easy to forget about, but they can be beautiful and still do their jobs. Stone walls, which might look cold and forbidding if bare, can be warmed and accented with colorful curtains of flowers and soft foliage. Smaller walls will benefit from plants strategically placed in their cracks and crevices.

A path of stepping-stones is a natural setting for low-growing and creeping plants. Stone patios are beautified by the same kind of treatment.

By now it should be obvious that plants make perfect companions for rock. Including them in your plans will enliven your rock features and help make them look as if they belong. Their addition adds color and life to your yard and will enhance your enjoyment of your home. And by doing it yourself, you're beginning a healthful, relaxing, ongoing, and even challenging hobby.

The Least You Need to Know

- Rock has a history that goes back to the days of prehistoric man.
- Some early man-made rock formations defy explanation or logic.
- Functional rock features can enhance your yard.
- You can construct many different rock features yourself.
- Plants are the perfect compliment to all rock features, big or small.

In This Chapter

- ◆ The joy of water in the yard
- ◆ The use of water down through the years
- ◆ Bringing water to the yard and garden
- ◆ Adding fish
- ◆ Matching water with rock

This elaborate man-made waterfall shows how natural beauty can be created by man's ingenuity.

Chapter 3

Water Features

No element is more essential to life than water. Every organism, plant and animal, needs water to survive. It's no accident that early civilizations developed near water. Later, when people began settling in areas farther from natural water sources, they had to find ways of getting water to their homes and communities. The ancient Romans used aqueducts to bring water to their cities, often over long distances. Then man learned to dig for water, finding ways to bring it up from under the ground. While water has always been a necessity, it soon evolved into becoming a source of enjoyment as well.

Now water is being moved into the backyard. There are many ways to bring water into your yard to be viewed and enjoyed. No matter where you live, you can use water. Whether you create a small burbler, a bubbling container, or opt for elaborate ponds and waterfalls, the tangible and intangible benefits of water are available to you. This chapter will serve to introduce you to the many different things you can do and the effects you can achieve when you add water to your backyard décor.

Burble, Trickle, and Splash—What Water Brings to the Yard

It's no secret why doctors and dentists have aquariums in their waiting rooms. The sight and sound of water, as well as the movement of the fish, have a calming, almost hypnotic effect on humans. It's relaxing, and the result of having water in the yard is very much the same. The sound of running water is soothing to the ears. Small streams and waterfalls are tranquil, enchanted reminders of another world. Including them in the garden gives you a place to go in order to escape everyday hassles without leaving home.

Water in the yard also has a cooling effect on hot days. Just running your hand through a backyard pond or feeling the spray from a fountain on a breezy summer afternoon takes the edge off. The sound and movement of the water is also an essential and interactive element of your garden. The simplest trickle of water creates a never-ending point of interest. It is constant, stabilizing, and reliable.

With water features, big isn't always better. Here is a simple frog fountain releasing its stream of water into a barrel garden.

![hummingbird] **Planning Quick Tip**

Don't let the idea of a water feature scare you off. Yes, elaborate ponds and waterfalls can be quite costly to install in the backyard. But you can still enjoy the movement and sound of water by having small fountains and spouts, with the water simply falling into basins, troughs, or containers filled with pebbles. The possibilities are endless.

If you have a backyard pond, you also have the option of adding fish. They bring color and life to the yard and add to the overall effect. Planting your water features carries the same benefit as planting rock features, contributing a more natural look and bringing color to the scene. And it is certainly possible to combine both plants and fish, putting all the elements of nature together for you to enjoy.

Planning ahead is especially important in constructing water features because they all require maintenance. Once you learn what is necessary to keep your features clean, healthy, and alive, maintaining water features is no more difficult than working in the garden and can be a source of great fun and satisfaction.

This section of a tranquil backyard pond shows a pair of healthy fish swimming among the Water Lilies.

Early Uses of Water

Without water, there is nothing. It's as simple as that, a fact the earliest men knew intimately. Water was a necessity and they had to be near it to live.

While the early inhabitants of Earth knew the survival value of water, they also discovered its joys. They found it to be cleansing to body and spirit. They knew it felt good to sit in a small stream or wade into a cool lake. The sound of water running over rocks was relaxing. Sustenance for body and soul comes in the form of fish to watch and eat, as well as from the water itself. Not surprisingly, it wasn't long before survival and enjoyment went hand in hand.

A Functional Necessity

The earliest uses of water were a simple matter of survival. Water was a functional necessity, providing drink, food from the organisms that lived in it, and a means of cleaning. Even though early people experienced the aesthetic pleasures of water, they knew first and foremost that they had to be near it to live. Once people began to grow their food, water for crops became another critical necessity. If there wasn't enough rain, water had to be carried to the fields, or the crops would wither and eventually die.

As people began to concentrate their dwellings and move farther from their own fields, the movement of water gained importance. Hauling water by hand was no longer enough, and aqueducts were built to bring a large and steady supply of water to cities. They were often huge and elaborate aboveground stone structures. Without them, there wouldn't be enough water and the city couldn't continue to thrive in that place. Once essential needs were met, water began to be used in other ways. Soon aqueducts were constructed more artistically to blend in with the architecture of the cities they serviced. At the same time, fountains and baths were built to utilize the aqueduct's water for recreational and aesthetic purposes. Owners of great estates constructed elaborate follies as part of their gardens, with hidden sprinklers and fountains to shock and delight guests. Reflecting pools, water stairs, and complicated constructions of stone and water were central to massive pleasure gardens.

Today, the importance of water remains undiminished. If anything, it has grown through the years as we've harmed the water supply. All life needs pure, fresh water to sustain it, and now it's a battle to keep the sources clean.

This raised water garden with timber sides shows just how elaborate some water features can be.

Strictly for Pleasure

Beyond its essential nature, water brings pleasure in many ways. For many years, the oceans, lakes, rivers, and streams have provided various means of recreation to countless numbers of people. Many naturally gravitate to their shores to relax and unwind, while others choose to structure their lives around a body of water. Many sporting activities continue to proliferate on or in the water. Surfing, for example, is a way of life as much as it is a sport. Many surfers find a spiritual side to being out in the ocean and riding large waves almost every day.

This small waterfall is made by setting two half-barrels at different levels and having the water recirculate with a pump.

The same relaxation and enjoyment of water can be brought to the places in which we live. The most common at-home water feature is the swimming pool, but the pleasurable uses of water in the backyard can go much further than that. Homeowners can build ponds, waterfalls, and small streams, install fountains, water and bog gardens, as well as construct fish ponds in virtually any size space. The growing popularity of these backyard features is further proof of the pleasure and enjoyment people find in having water nearby.

Adding Water to the Garden

Water in the garden is not a new idea. There is evidence of water gardens dating back thousands of years. Queen Hapshetset of Egypt grew lotus and papyrus at Luxor in 1480 B.C.E., and water lilies were often placed on the mummies of high priests as far back as 2000 B.C.E. The tradition has continued unabated. There are famous European water gardens dating back to the eighteenth century, and gardens all over the world feature water as an essential element of their design.

For many years water gardens were usually installed in and around natural lakes and ponds. There was an occasional bath, cistern, or other watertight feature to house a few lilies and fish, but not until the twentieth century did water gardening begin to make a splash on estates and in individual yards, constructed artificially by those living there.

The real explosion of interest occurred with the advent of the formed and flexible pond liners and accompanying pumps and filters. Before these, water features were typically lined with cement, a more complicated and difficult installation. Prior to the use of pumps and filters, many backyard ponds became dirty and stagnant, a difficult place for plants to thrive and a near impossible one for fish to live. In 1907, Reginald Farrer, already a foremost expert in rock gardening, was asked about the feasibility of creating water gardens. Farrer had a one-word answer: "Don't!"

The Right Stuff

Elaborate water gardens exist in almost every country of the world. No matter what kind of government or political philosophy pervades the land, there is always a special feeling about water. In England, there is a calmness in the tranquil lakes and the series of canals that are the trademark of the Studley Royal and Fountains Abbey at Yorkshire. The Bouchart Gardens on Vancouver Island in Canada feature water jets with elaborate patterns that are constantly changing shape and are beautifully illuminated at night by a variety of colored lights. A huge water jet that moves 3 tons of water at 125 miles per hour is a huge attraction at the War Memorial in Canberra, Australia, while waterfalls and cascades are the predominant feature of many Japanese Gardens. All these large-scale features attract a steady stream of visitors each year. It's no wonder so many people want to emulate these water features on a smaller scale in their own backyards.

This picturesque container water garden provides contrast amidst a conventional garden, yet another way to add a small water feature to the yard.

But all that has changed now. People install water gardens for many of the same reasons they build other water features in their backyards. They enjoy the soothing tranquility and the lively color water gardens provide. Water gardens have become more popular today than ever before. It now is a rewarding hobby that can keep the amateur horticulturist and fish keeper very busy and bring everyone involved beauty, pleasure, and relaxation in their own backyards.

Fish and Wildlife

Adding fish to a garden pond must be a conscious and careful decision. Keeping colorful koi or goldfish is a satisfying and pleasing occupation, bringing a new element of nature to the backyard garden. The addition of fish, however, involves specialized care, and knowing how to properly care for your fish is a necessity before you make the commitment.

This Northern Green Frog is just one of many animals that may be attracted to a pond or other water feature in your backyard.

Once you decide to add fish, they become the focus of the feature. You are creating the environment in which they will live and should plan every aspect of that environment with their needs in mind. For example, if you live where winters are cold, you will need to bring your fish inside or make sure that your pond will allow them to survive a deep freeze.

A Word of Warning _____

When considering any kind of pond or water feature for your yard, always think in terms of safety. If you have small children or your neighbor has small children with access to your yard, there should not be a deep water feature in the yard if it isn't fully protected. Natural ponds and those with fish won't look the same with a fence around them. So make sure you are not creating a potential hazard for the little ones.

Clean water and a healthy environment will attract a wide variety of additional wildlife to your yard. The environment you create determines the wildlife that will visit. Food and shelter are the keys. Floating plants, for example, protect wildlife in the pond from the sun and from overhead predators, such as herons. These same plants provide landing places for small birds, frogs, and insects. Dragonflies and other invertebrates use plants that emerge from the water for laying eggs and sunning. Grasses, shrubs, and other plants along the banks of the pond provide nesting places for birds and homes for small mammals, as well as protecting them when they come to drink.

A lazy Red-Eared Slider pokes his head out of the water of a backyard pond on a sunny afternoon.

It won't be long before your wild neighbors find your water. One of the most attractive features of including water in your garden is the

other life it brings to your yard. Birds, butterflies, frogs and toads, and many mammals will find their way to your yard in short order. Most of these guests are desirable additions to the landscape. Some are not.

A Word of Warning _____

While a healthy pond environment provides a haven for many forms of wildlife, an unhealthy environment with standing, stagnant water, can become a home for undesirables. Stagnant water is a breeding ground for mosquitoes, and these insects are not only pests but can also carry a variety of diseases. Always make sure the water is moving and healthy to reduce the likelihood of encouraging these insects.

Regardless of your decision about adding fish to your pond or water feature, you will attract animal neighbors. Keeping the water healthy and creating an environment in which wildlife can thrive makes the experience a better one for both man and beast.

A Painted Lady butterfly is another frequent visitor to a well-flowered pond or waterfall area. If you enjoy wildlife, a water feature can attract a host of different species to your yard.

Water and Rock, a Matching Pair

You can build rock features without water and water features without rock, but when constructing one, always be sure to consider the other. Rock and water are natural companions and go together splendidly to produce better-looking and more lively features.

Here is another formal water feature, with a stone stairway leading down to a rock landing overlooking a pond. There is no end to what you can do when you combine rock with water.

The match can be a simple one, as easy as having a trickle of water running downhill over a few rocks in the middle of a rock garden or a couple large rocks breaking the surface of the water in a pond or stream. More complex matches include a rock waterfall, where both elements are needed to make the feature work, or a formal-looking rock fountain spraying a cooling stream of water several feet into the air. A water feature alongside a rock garden or stone patio is one of the most effective uses of both, and each will serve to accentuate the other, building a unified and beautiful picture. The sound, look, and feel of water in and around rock brings the whole scene together and can make the entire yard seem enchanted.

The Least You Need to Know

- Water has been a staple of all life since the beginning of time.
- Though necessary for survival, water has also been a longtime source of pleasure.
- Water features in the yard are soothing, tranquil, relaxing, and fun.
- You can add a variety of water features to your yard.
- Combining water and rock gives you the best of both worlds—and a totally natural look.

In This Chapter

- ◆ Know what you want
- ◆ Consider your home and your entire yard
- ◆ Use what you already have
- ◆ Recognize features you can use and where
- ◆ Light it all up

You wouldn't see this formal stone paver walkway with pillars in a back-yard, but it does represent a style and motif that features natural stone.

Chapter 4

Choosing Your Own Style

Now it's time to make some hard decisions about how you want to improve your yard. Like any do-it-yourself home project, careful planning is more than half the battle. Whether you are making a rock feature, a water feature, or both, take your time and think things out. In other words, know what you want to accomplish before you start. Here's how to think through, in general and specific terms, your home, yard, and options you can realistically consider.

Take a close look at the shape, size, and overall setup of your yard as it currently exists. Consider the setting it provides for your home and how the buildings relate to the land. If you can use something that is already there—a rock, hill, or trees—as an element in your new design, that's a good way to start. From there, you can decide upon the type and size of the features you'd like to include.

What Kind of Yard Do You Want?

As mentioned in Chapter 1, it's important to recognize the way you use your yard before you begin adding rock and water features. Think about the number of people who normally use the yard, the games your kids like to play, and whether you use the yard to entertain. Then make a lifestyle list when thinking about creating changes in your yard. Start by asking yourself the following questions:

- ◆ How much time do you spend in your backyard?
- ◆ How much do you enjoy working in your backyard?
- ◆ Do you enjoy gardening as a hobby?
- ◆ Do you prefer an open look with uncluttered space?

◆ Do you mind having to maintain a feature that requires constant attention?

◆ Will the rest of your family support any decisions you might make regarding rock and water features?

This neatly constructed stone wall with stone pillar and pineapple finial sets the tone for a formal setting, yet still uses only natural rock.

Remember to consider your home. If you have a formal-looking home, very symmetric lines, or a modern home with lots of angles and glass, maybe something traditional with columns along the front, a formal garden and landscape is likely to be the most suitable solution. But if you've chosen a country cottage or informal home as suiting your tastes, then a natural-looking yard with rough stone features, such as walls, borders, stone paths, and informal plantings, may be just the ticket.

Planning Quick Tip

Before you decide on the installation of a rock or water feature in your yard, it may help to hold a family meeting. Explain what you want to do and why, and then ask other members of the family if they have any objections. If your kids feel the planned feature will hamper their ability to use the yard in a certain way, it may be time to rethink the size or location of the feature. Having unhappy family members can diminish the fun and excitement of creating your feature.

This is just a starting point, the first stage in your decision-making process. But there are other things to consider, as well.

The Look and the Feel

If you have decided to add rock or water features to your yard, the next step is to think about the end result. What kind of look and feel do you want to create when your work is done? Do you want your yard to have a distinctly natural look, with features that appear to have been there for years? How much open space are you willing to sacrifice to achieve that look? To create a more tranquil feeling, consider adding a water feature, whether pond, waterfall, stream, or fountain.

Though this looks elaborate, it is actually a mini-water feature with a pond and liner, natural rocks, and a boardwalk. It shows how much can be achieved in a small space only about 6 feet wide.

Backyard Quick Tip _____

Unless you're building a theme park, it's best to carefully choose a style and stick with it. Mixing styles and motifs is difficult to do successfully and a stylistic disaster when it can't be pulled off. Always remember that the most successful landscapes are often deceptively simple in design.

Rock, Water, or Both

Once you've decided that it's time to improve your yard, you need to decide how much you'd like to do and whether you'll add rock, water, or a combination of both. This decision also depends upon a number of factors. If you're looking for a natural look, rock features like dry-stone walls, rock borders, or rock gardens will get you started and provide plenty of planting opportunities to add color to the mix.

If the relaxing, cooling effect is your goal, consider a water feature—although rock can still be used in combination. Be prepared and aware that ponds and waterfalls take careful planning and constant maintenance. A rock feature without plants can remain in place with little or no change for years. Plants, of course, take care and some maintenance, especially in climates that feature seasonal changes. All but the simplest water features require the addition of electricity to run pumps and filters and constant attention to be sure the water is clean and healthy, whether or not you decide to add fish.

Planning Quick Tip _____

Rock and water work together very effectively. A pond sitting at the base or to the side of a colorful rock garden makes a beautiful marriage.

Consider Your Options

Once you are reasonably sure that you want to add rock and/or water features to your yard, you are ready for the final steps in the decision-making process. The final considerations are those that relate to how the proposed additions fit into what you already have. All the things you noted in the initial assessment of existing conditions should be brought back into play as you decide where to locate and how large to build your new features.

The Size and Shape of Your Yard

The size and shape of your yard can be limiting or liberating. If you have a large property, you can think big. The large yard can hold larger features or more of them. The features can be more complex without overwhelming the space available. The large yard allows you to develop the kind of features you want yet retain enough open space for recreational activities. On the other hand, a large space dictates that the features be bigger. It's hard to maintain a sense of scale if your 3-acre backyard garden has only a tiny fountain in it. If your features are too small, they will be swallowed up and lost in a large space.

In smaller spaces the equation changes. Homeowners with small yards should avoid busy designs jammed with features. On the whole, the size of the features and their elements should be reduced to remain in scale with the space. Features should be on the simple side, avoiding overly complex and elaborate layouts. A large formation in a small yard will simply overpower it and put everything out of perspective. What should be eye-catching can easily become an eyesore. Avoid overcrowding or overpowering the smaller yard.

The shape of the yard is important, too. If you have a long, narrow yard, you might consider a smaller feature near the house, but anything larger should be placed toward the rear of the yard. A large rock or water feature near the house in a narrow yard will cut you off from the rest of your yard. If the feature is toward the rear, you can enjoy its presence without losing all the open space you may need. Another option is to use a feature in the middle of the yard to create two distinct yard/garden spaces. A path could run to it, around it, and beyond it to unify the whole yard.

If the yard is wide, but not deep, you might consider putting your features off to the side in a back corner and keeping the middle open. This allows you to maximize open space. In a small yard, keep the features that are near the house or patio small, or use container water gardens, small rock gardens, or trough gardens.

A small feature for a small space can be a mini-water garden in a stone pot that can be set almost anywhere.

A Word of Warning

Always keep perspective and scale in mind when you plan your features, and the end result will always be a success. Some people become so enamored with rock and water features that they continue to add new things or go too big. Remember, when in doubt, simplicity is often the best way to go.

Topography

The lay of your land is also important. As challenging as hilly property can be for routine maintenance, it may make an ideal site for a rock garden. If you have a completely flat yard, it will be very difficult to make it appear that a rock outcropping or waterfall is natural.

This natural hill not only provided an area for a rock garden but was also a perfect place for this beautiful set of natural stone steps.

At the same time, level ground makes it easy to install ponds and fountains. Using the soil you excavate to build a small hill alongside the pond creates topography and is a great spot to make a rock waterfall for returning water to the pond, giving the feature a special look.

If you have a natural low spot that's continually wet, it might be a perfect place to put a bog garden or to use for digging a pond. In this way, using the natural attributes of the existing yard and dealing with what might be a problem area results in a most beautiful and favorable outcome.

A Word of Warning

It is possible to alter the natural topography of your yard. However, it isn't always easy to create a hill or rise where none exists, and you must be able to do it correctly so that the feature doesn't look contrived. The easiest way to begin is to use what you have and install features that will blend in naturally within the guidelines dictated by your existing yard. Anything more complex can come later.

Using Existing Rock, Vegetation, and Trees

Using what is there applies to things other than the dimensions and physical attributes of your space. Is there existing rock, either already set in a pleasing configuration or available for harvest and use as you wish? If you have existing rock, you have the makings of a rock garden or other rock feature. Don't waste them.

While having rock already in the yard can be an asset, existing vegetation can be a mixed blessing. Existing trees casting dappled shade can be a major asset in the blazing heat of summer. On the other hand, the shade they give may be so deep that nothing but moss will grow in it. Most rock gardens will appreciate near full-sun conditions, benefiting from shade in the heat of the afternoon. A rock garden can be constructed in the shade, but the plants selected will be very different. And it is not a good idea to locate a pond directly below a tree where roots will interfere and the feature will be choked with leaves in the fall and shaded in the summer. However, flowering trees and shrubs at the pond's edge are a lovely way of breaking up the outline of the pond and adding to your design.

Sometimes there is more existing vegetation than can be used. Then it's time to selectively clear, always saving plants that will fit into your plans for the site. If you dig the culled plants, try to get all roots so nothing grows back. The plants you keep may benefit from a pruning or *limbing up* to improve their shape and rejuvenate them. Small shrubs and perennial plants can be transplanted to a new location or reserved to be replanted in the new rock or water feature.

If you're lucky enough to have an area with existing rock already in place, you're more than halfway to having an exciting and interesting rock garden. This kind of topography is almost begging you to start planting.

Backyard Lingo _____

Removing the lower branches from large trees is called **limbing up.** This is often done to increase the amount of light that is let through and to allow more sun and bright light to reach your garden.

Here's What You Can Do

No matter where you live or what your property is like, there are rock and water features for you. Let's consider a few ideas for specific situations you may encounter. Remember, all these early evaluations are leading up to one thing, a decision to install a specific rock or water feature in your yard and to do it in the best way possible within the parameters with which you have to work. Learning, thinking, and planning should be a process, not a snap decision. So take it one step at a time.

Rock Features

It's not too difficult to make rock look natural. By its very nature, it has a great head start, and all you have to do is use it the right way to construct features that look as if Mother Nature had a hand in them. By now, you should already be aware that rock can be used in many ways. If there is an area on your property where rock already exists, an outcropping, natural hill, or rock-strewn field, the raw materials are in place for a rock garden. Some adjustments will likely be necessary, but you've got the kind of situation that makes rock gardeners green with envy.

The large boulder in the middle was already in place and served as a great focal piece of this dry-stone wall that was constructed around it.

Dry-stone walls are great options for retaining walls or dividers and can be paired with plants. Because mortar is not used in dry-stone construction, it is important to understand the basics of this method of building with stone before starting. If you want a small patio, you might consider using flat stones and setting them without cement. Cracks between the stones can be filled with sand or fine gravel and hold creeping plants.

Planning Quick Tip _____

Stepping-stones, paths, and a rock staircase can be used to help get from one part of the yard to another in style. An infinite variety of each is possible, and there is a way to include them in any garden. Always consider adding these features to heavily trafficked areas of the yard or where footing should be improved.

More manicured, formal settings require a different approach. Here you won't want any rough stone walls or random grouping of rocks. A formal rock garden might be built up in raised beds of cut stone or constructed in tiers. Formal stone borders can set off your plantings and help define the space. Stone can also be used to accent other garden art and statuary.

If you want a place to walk through your garden or even in another part of your yard, the natural stepping-stone path is an excellent way to go.

Paths and patios in formal gardens can be made with flagstones or brick to give a more ordered look. Small rock walls can be neatly constructed with brick instead of irregular stone, giving your yard a look in keeping with the house and general appearance of the property.

A Word of Warning

While there are infinite possibilities to consider when you are choosing which rock and/or water features to add, always remember that your home will always be the largest feature on your property. The look and style of the home and how it sits on your property should always be the first factor in determining what rock and water features fit best.

Water Features

The same basic rules apply for water features as for rock. For example, the size and appearance of your home and yard should figure in the choice. The threshold choice is whether you will use a formal or more free and natural style.

This rectangular pre-formed pool liner can be set in the ground as the cornerstone of a formal-looking water feature.

For a formal look, consider a rectangular reflecting pool or a round pool with a fountain in its middle. A neatly bordered pond with geometric plantings fits nicely into a well-manicured, austere setting.

On the other hand, a rock stream with adjoining bog garden can look just as much like a stream found running through a low-lying field in a natural setting. Rocks can be placed in the stream and on the land surrounding it, with bog and marginal plants and other natural-looking objects, such as a couple well-placed large tree branches that appear to have fallen into the water.

Because fountains are hard to find in nature, they work particularly well in the formal setting, while rock waterfalls can be formal or approximate the look found in nature. It depends on how you choose to construct them. When deciding, all the aforementioned factors should come into play.

This shallow stone bowl can be placed in a rock garden or among other plantings to add a touch of water. It, too, can be planted or decorated with surrounding vegetation.

Small water features like container water gardens and burblers can be used to bring the sight and sound of water to any setting, formal or natural, and put in many different locations around the home and yard. Once again, the rule of thumb is not to mix and match. Keep your style consistent throughout. There is still plenty from which to choose and combinations that will serve your style sense and improve the look and feel of your home. But as you can clearly see, there is something for everyone, the right choice for any setting or any size yard. Now, you should have much of the ammunition and knowledge so you can make the choice and do it right the first time.

Lighting

Lighting your rock and water features for safety and nighttime viewing is an increasingly popular option. There are many different styles of lights available and a number of different ways in which to light your yard. Besides showcasing your rock and water features, lighting allows you to see what is happening in the yard and makes it safer when going outside during nighttime hours.

Lighting any kind of rock or water feature should be subtle and unobtrusive, so it doesn't interfere with or overpower the feature itself.

A Word of Warning

In most situations involving electricity, a new line must be run into the yard near the features you wish to power or light. Always check local codes for proper installation, use a ground fault interrupter with your outlet, and have the installation checked by a professional if you install it yourself.

If you decide to light your features, make sure the hardware doesn't intrude on the real subject of all your work. It's hard to make features look natural if you've got bright bulbs and wires hanging everywhere. Always make lighting as unobtrusive as possible so it doesn't stick out like a sore thumb. A string of lights hanging above a rock garden or pond will seriously diminish the effect of the feature. So will a lamppost with a bright light on top or a spotlight aimed directly at the feature.

Lighting should be subtle, as if coming out of nowhere. The most effective way to light backyard features is to hide the fixtures around rocks or plants, so at night the light seems to just come right out of the ground. Ponds are commonly lit from within, the fixtures underwater and out of view.

Select your fixtures to avoid awkward situations. They must be outdoor fixtures and should have a color and finish that blend into the landscape. Then you will have lighting that is both subtle and effective and will enhance your features and extend your viewing hours.

The Least You Need to Know

◆ Decide early on just what kind of yard you want and how rock or water features will fit in.

◆ Choose a motif that will be consistent with your overall lifestyle and stick with it.

◆ Consider all your options, including the size of your yard and the overall topography that is already in place.

◆ Make careful decisions about whether you want rock or water features or a combination of both.

◆ It always helps to light your features, but only if you do it right.

In This Part

Part 2

Building and Maintaining Rock Features

There are a large variety of rock features that you can construct in your yard. Because it often isn't easy to move and place rocks, especially larger ones, careful planning is a necessity. You must make decisions about the look you want, the feature you want, the size and placement of the feature, all before the work begins.

Once you begin building, you should be sure not to take on more than you can handle. Learn the safest ways to lift and move rock, get help when necessary, and don't bite off more than you can chew. There are ways to both place and "plant" rocks so they will last a lifetime and ways to make sure your feature remains stable after deep-freeze winters and heavy rains. Then there are the plants that help bring rock features to life. Finally, if a project is just too ambitious for the weekend warrior, professionals are available who can design and build the features for you.

In This Chapter

- ◆ Planning for your installation
- ◆ Getting ready for functional rock features
- ◆ Organizing the rock garden
- ◆ Considering plants
- ◆ Planting the rocks

A stonemason constructed this stacked Cotswold stone wall with artistic care using the special stone imported from England. Note the way the larger and smaller stones mesh almost perfectly.

Planning and Preparation for Installing Rock Features

Stacking stone is a very quiet, intimate art form. It's just man and nature, working together to create a thing of lasting beauty. Artisans of this craft are connoisseurs, picking and choosing just the right stone for a particular spot. Years of experience makes their job a joy, albeit a sweaty one. You, too, can build with stone. Even the best of the professionals working with stone had to start somewhere.

Let's build a new rock feature. Obviously, this is something that you shouldn't do on a whim. Don't decide to build a wall, install a rock path, or create a rock garden without careful planning and preparation. The better you plan, the easier the actual job will be.

In this chapter, we will talk about smart preparation. There are some general rules that you should follow for any feature. Specific rules follow that ensure that your project is done correctly the first time. Think ahead, especially if you want to add plants or electricity to your feature.

One Thing at a Time

We've already discussed a number of steps in the decision-making process. You should know the feature you want, its size, and the best location for it in your yard. Once these preliminary decisions are made, it's time to plan, assemble, and execute. There's nothing worse than starting a project and not having everything ready to go. By following this simple procedure, you will have everything in place for the actual installation: all the materials you need on-site and the site ready for the work to begin.

Plan

You can't get from point A to point B without a roadmap, and the easiest way to make one for any project is to create a list containing each step along the way. The goal is a punch list that provides a clear-cut picture of exactly what you are going to do and how you are going to do it. To complete the project, simply check off the steps as you finish them.

Convinced you can do the work yourself? If you haven't done this kind of project before, look at similar features. Try to find one to visit at a friend's house or local garden center. Many finished projects can be viewed on the Internet, sometimes with helpful information about how they were constructed.

You don't have to be an artist to rough out a sketch of a prospective rock garden so you have an idea of what you want to do before you actually do it.

Some people are even more visually oriented. It may help to sketch the project out on paper, getting as detailed as you can. You don't have to be a draftsman to do this. Rough it out. It may not look perfect, but it will give you and your helpers a clearer idea of what it is you're trying to accomplish.

Next, mark off the area where you are going to build the feature. This can be done with something handy and flexible like a rope or garden hose. Some people sprinkle a border of sand to mark the boundaries.

Planning Quick Tip

Many people lay garden hose out to mark the outline of their projects. It helps to take the kinks out and make the curves in your layout if you put the hose in the sun for a while before starting. The heat softens the hose, making it more pliable and easier to work with.

In addition to your punch list of steps in the process, make a list of all the materials you'll need. Be sure you refer to your punch list as you put together the list of materials. It'll help to make sure you don't leave anything out.

Finally, it always helps to have a preliminary plant list available. Knowing what you'd like to plant ahead of time will save time when you visit the nursery. Just prepare to be flexible if it isn't easy to find your first choices.

Assemble

Building a rock feature is like putting a puzzle together. Step one in each process is making sure that you have all the pieces. Step two is laying them all out on the table/ground. Pull together everything you need *before you begin*. Make sure any tools you need are handy. If you don't have a tool you need for the job, borrow one or run to your local hardware store. A key to success for any home project is to have the right tool for the job.

Spread everything out in order to get a good look at what you have. This includes any rock being used in the feature. Just like people's faces, rock has a "good side." It's important to begin familiarizing yourself with the individual rocks early, so that you can set them with their best face forward.

Building a rock wall or other feature is often like putting together a puzzle. Get all the pieces together, then go to work.

Before starting any work, you should have all your materials on hand. A visit to a local nursery will give you a wide choice of materials. This one has bags of gravel and pebbles just waiting for prospective gardeners.

Sand, gravel, soil mix, and mulch should be ready before you start. It's not a bad idea to have your plants available as well. Setting the pots in full view will serve as a visual reminder to leave space for them as you put the feature together. You can add plants to almost any rock feature, even a dry-stone wall.

Once you've assembled your materials, set them in a nearby but out-of-the-way place, and taken a good long look at everything, then you're ready to execute.

A Word of Warning

Give yourself room to work. Don't lay everything out on your work site or just adjacent to it. Your job will go much smoother and faster if you don't do anything more than once. If your material is too close to where you need to work, you'll have to stop and move things around to create the proper space.

Execute

This is the final step in the planning stage and the preliminary stage in building your rock feature. In construction parlance it is known as "site work." It involves doing any work to the site that is necessary for construction to begin. The most common work is excavation, grading/shaping, and contouring the land. You should also do trenching for electrical and/or plumbing connections before construction of the feature begins.

Any stone feature must be put together step by step with great care and an eye to the next step. It's best if you only have to do it once.

Don't dig and build in little segments. The whole project should proceed at one time. This will avoid patchy-looking situations that require disassembling and fixing sections of the project. Excavating all at once ahead of time allows you to concentrate on building the feature without having to stop and go back.

Although it's not always as easy to see progress early in the day, following these suggestions will speed construction and make the job more enjoyable. It may take 3 or 4 days to complete the three stages of planning. But if you follow the steps and are thorough in your preparation, the actual construction of your feature will go smoothly and quickly.

Functional Features

The planning process is the same for all rock features. The goal is to do the job right the first time. There are some general rules to follow, along with specific suggestions for particular features.

The following tips will enable you to install modest backyard rock features without hiring a professional. You might be able to use some help from a friend or neighbor, but for the most part you can do the work.

A Word of Warning

Never take a chance building a rock feature that's bigger than you can handle or that has rocks bigger than you can move. Rock is dense and heavy. It hurts when it falls on you. There are ways to safely move rock that will be detailed in the following chapter, but big rocks should not be moved without machinery operated by a pro.

Walls

The dry-stone wall is one of the oldest functional rock features known to man. As mentioned earlier, well-built walls can survive for hundreds of years. These walls can be built for purely aesthetic reasons but are still used for boundaries between owners or property uses, for raised planting beds and terraces, and as retaining walls. Dry-stone stacking is among the most satisfying of do-it-yourself projects.

Your wall may be only 1 foot high or much taller. Its height will depend on its function and the particular design needs of your plan. Building the wall as a do-it-yourself project may save you up to 75 percent of the cost of having it professionally installed. You can save even more if you have access to the rocks and don't have to purchase them.

The most important aspect of building a wall yourself is whether you can do the work safely, alone or with help. Once you take a chance, you are opening both yourself and your helpers to possible injury.

A Word of Warning

Be careful with the size of the stones you use to build your wall. Stone is heavy. Granite and limestone, two of the kinds of stone you're likely to encounter, weigh more than 160 pounds per cubic foot. At the light end of the scale, sandstone weighs in at about 143 pounds per cubic foot. At this rate a rock does not have to be very large before it is impossible to move without mechanical help. As a rule of thumb, placing 250-pound stones will prove strenuous, but not impossible, for 2 men working together and using hand tools like pry-bars. Never try to lift and place stones that are too heavy. A healthy body is a terrible thing to waste.

Unless they are free-standing, dry-stone walls should lean slightly backward against their backfill. The angle of this lean is called the wall's "batter" and prevents the wall from being pushed forward and falling down.

It's advisable from a design standpoint to use only one kind of stone for your wall. Don't mix and match. More than one makes the finished wall look busy and unnatural. For example, if you are using field stone, a common stone left by glaciers in many parts of the country, it's unwise to put hard-edge stone with them. Not only should you use the same kind of stone, but consider shape, color, and texture as well. Cracks can be left as they are, used as planting pockets, or filled with small pieces of stone used as wedges to steady each layer.

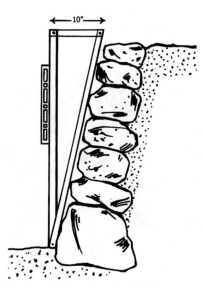

By using an angle board when building a retaining wall, you can not only keep the face of the wall straight but also make sure the slight backward angle is maintained as you build upward.

The Right Stuff

An angle board will ensure that your dry-stone wall is flat-faced and maintains its batter. You can make one by nailing two boards together. Use 2×2s or 2×4s as long as the wall is high. One of the boards will be used in a vertical position. The second, which begins in the same position at the bottom, is then set at the angle of the wall. A third, smaller board nailed across the top will hold the vertical and angle boards together. To use the angle board, set it at the base of the wall with the vertical board in an upright position. The board set at the angle shows if each rock is placed appropriately to preserve the wall's batter. This is a simple way to keep your wall growing in the right direction.

In general, the largest stones should be placed at the bottom of the wall. This initial layer should be set into the ground at least 6 inches deep to provide stability. Excavate a trench the entire length of your wall before you start to stack stone. It's advisable, especially in areas where winter weather involves frost in the ground, to layer 3 to 6 inches of gravel or sand in the trench and pack it down to form a foundation. This helps to steady the stone but also allows water running down the wall to drain, keeping it out of the ground at the base of the wall. This will help minimize frost heaving, the ground's way of upsetting your carefully laid rock.

Try to make rows roughly the same size. As you gain experience, you can experiment with using different-size stones throughout the wall to create a puzzle effect. While this can be very exciting to do, it's best to do your first walls simply.

As you build each row upon the previous one, tilt the rock slightly backward so that the stone's weight rests partially against the soil it's holding back. Continue doing this as you go up until you place the final stone.

Building Quick Tip

Most stone walls are built with rock laid horizontally rather than on end. Because this is the way most stones lie naturally, it produces a more stable wall. Stones placed on end are not as stable and can become unsafe if not handled very cautiously.

This sketch shows how rocks are set to make a stepped-back stone wall on a slope. Each rock is set into the ground to make it look more like a natural outcropping, and the addition of plants gives you, in essence, a rock garden.

The stepped-back stone wall is generally used on slopes and is essentially a formalized rock outcropping. These walls are easier to build than the foregoing and easier to combine with plantings. If you want to put a stepped-back wall on a gentle slope in your yard, it's better to set the stones more deeply in the ground and to organize them as an outcropping.

The degree of formality in your plans determines whether you will set the stones symmetrically or use a more random look. In either case, when dug into the ground the stones will stay in place. The spacing of the stone in this arrangement allows more flexibility to add plants, and, in essence, you are creating a type of rock garden even if the stone is performing a functional service.

Borders

Borders can be used in many different situations and help to create definition in your space.

A border is basically a small wall. Even a single row of rocks around a flower garden, a patio, or a pond serves the purpose of a wall, dividing the feature from the rest of the yard. Borders are relatively simple to place but one of the hardest rock features to make look good. Too many people plop bowling-ball-size rocks on the ground in a perfect ring, and the resulting feature looks like a prehistoric pearl necklace.

This small, undulating rock border is actually a small wall constructed with natural rock of varying sizes.

Borders look much more realistic and natural if they undulate. Unless you're building a formal wall, the rock will look better if its size varies. The advice about sticking to one type of rock still applies. Dig them into the ground for stability and a more natural appearance. You should be able to stand on any of them and not have the rock move. Many gardeners prefer to bury from half to two thirds of the rock.

Another common mistake made by many gardeners involves the planting after the border is made. Too many people set up their border and then plant well inside of it. This contributes to the necklace effect. It's better to plant just inside the border, allowing selected flowers to billow over the edge. This softens the entire feature and makes a difference that can only be described as magical.

Depending on the location of the border and the use of the land outside it, some gardeners plant the same plant inside and outside the border to make it look as if the plant is spreading. This also helps soften the boundary, reducing the harshness that might otherwise result.

Stairs

Rock or stone stairs are often used in gardens and rock features to provide access from one level to another. Stairs make it easier to negotiate hills or slopes. You can build stone stairs in two ways. You can use a wood form, pour concrete, and set flat rocks into it before it dries, mortaring between the stones to finish. Or you can set the stone directly into the ground on a pad of gravel.

It you want a slightly more formal look and still use natural rock, these level stairs with mortar in between the joints will fill the bill.

Because safety and ease of access are the primary goals of step making, be sure that with whatever method you use, the stone is well set and stable. A wobbly stone is a bad stone.

To build steps, you need to know something about the size of your slope. This will aid in deciding how many stairs you will need. Here is a method that works:

1. Place a board at the slope's highest point and parallel to the ground. Support it with another that stands vertically between the spot where the bottom step will be and the horizontal board. Make sure the horizontal board is level.

2. Next, measure the distance from the horizontal board to the spot at the bottom of the slope where the first step will be.

3. Assuming a 6-inch height (rise) is ideal between stairs, allow 16 inches from front to back (tread) for each stair. These measurements will vary depending on the height and angle of the slope. Some treads are much wider and function almost like platforms or landings.

4. Now calculate the number of steps you will need.

Excavating for your stairway depends on the thickness of your projected steps and where you want the surface of your step to be in relation to the ground around it. As with other stone features, you should put in a 3- to 6-inch layer of crushed stone under your stone. This helps to drain water away and keeps your stone from moving. Remember to allow for this base of stone when you dig.

Regardless of method and materials, always start your stairs at the bottom and work your way up. In most cases, each step on the way up will overlap the one below it to some extent, and bottom-up is really the only way to go.

If it's possible, have your material arranged at the bottom of the slope. Although it's easier to slide stone downhill than struggle to bring it up, safety dictates that the latter is the way to work with this project. Control is much easier to maintain working from the bottom of the hill to the top, and runaway stones are less likely to crush hapless gardeners.

Lay out your stone before you begin so you can see which ones go together the best. If at all possible, use a single large stone for each step. In many cases, you'll have to use two stones on each level. Make sure they are a pleasing pair. Use the fewest number of stones per step. This increases stability and safety because there are fewer joints between the stones and, therefore, less likelihood of tilting, heaving, and otherwise separating.

Wherever you are going uphill, you have an opportunity to beautify your landscape and make it easier to move in by creating stone stairways. They are functional and beautiful and can combine with rock gardens to provide a stunning addition to your yard.

Paths and Stepping-Stones

Paths and stepping-stones are among the most basic functional rock features. With appropriate plantings, they are the most attractive way to get from here to there. Because they dictate where foot traffic should go, they help to direct and move people through the yard.

Raised stepping-stones can create an interesting walking path, especially if plants are set alongside and between the stones. Just be sure they aren't in an area where people might trip over them.

There are two ways to set paths and stepping-stones. The usual way is for the tops of the stones to be flush with the ground. This style makes for the easiest walking. The second way is to have the stones raised, each set two to four inches above the ground. Although stepping-stones are often set this way, save raised walks for gardens. You have to be a bit more careful walking over raised stones, and in the middle of the yard they would be a hazard for people and your mower. Within the garden's boundaries, they are a nice way to move about your plants, stay out of the mud, and provide a foil for a variety of low-growing and colorful plants.

While paths and stepping-stones are not difficult to install, they need to be designed with thought and care. Paths can set a style and mood. Designed well, they will lead your guests to special areas in the yard safely and with a sense of adventure. Walks that are poorly designed make no sense, are superfluous, and can actually be dangerous.

Material and design for paths and stepping-stone walks can reflect either a formal or informal preference. As mentioned previously, it's a good idea not to mix styles. It's better to remain consistent so the overall picture is unified and coherent.

Make your choice of material and design follow the style of your home and yard. In a formal setting, it's usually more attractive to use cut, straight-edge stone and construct your paths with straight runs and angles. Cut flagstone is a common material for a formal path. Mortared joints heighten the effect. You can use slate, blue stone, Belgian pavers, and other flat, uniform stone for the same purpose.

Brick, cast concrete pieces, and decorative stepping-stones are not as natural-looking but are readily available and easy to use.

Pebbles and cobbles, not ordinarily considered for walkways because they aren't flat, can be used to create colorful mosaic patterns. These walkable pieces of art should be set in concrete for safety and permanence.

For informal, natural-looking walks, nothing beats raw rock. This is stone that is uncut, unpolished, and irregular. Not surprisingly, these rocks have the most character when used in natural-looking yards and rock gardens. Natural paths should not be straight and should avoid hard angles. Their design should be organic, curvy, and undulating. Bends should hide vistas so that around each curve is a new surprise.

Regardless of the style of your yard, stones for paths will vary greatly in size. Many homeowners make the common mistake of using stones that are too small. As a general rule, unless you are trying to achieve a special fine-textured effect or creating a pebble mosaic, use the largest stones you can safely handle. Not only will they look more in scale, but also, once settled, they will be less likely to shift or tip.

Once again, you must decide what you can handle safely and get help if you need it. Consider the use of hired machinery if you'd like the added benefits of large stone.

To lay out the area for your path, we return, once again, to considerations of style. A formal path must be measured, marked out, and staked. Lines need to be straight, with angles and measurements precise. Natural paths, because of their flowing lines, are more forgiving in this respect, and the use of the warm garden hose or rope from the previous chapter is all that is necessary.

Have a large rubber mallet, shovels, a couple pieces of scrap 2×4s, and a pry-bar handy. If you're really brave, a mason's hammer, chisel, and safety goggles are handy for pinging off corners and oddball protrusions that make it difficult to set one rock next to another. Use a level to determine how flat the finished product is.

Once you lay out the area for your path, calculate the amount of stone you'll need to build it. A rough estimate is all that's necessary because you should always order more than you need. Stone is sold by the ton, but your figure will need to be measured in square feet. Calculations are much easier for formal paths, where straight lines make it simple to multiply length times width to get the number of square feet. Because natural paths are not easy to measure without advanced mathematics, make your best guess. It's always a good idea to order 10 to 15 percent more stone than you need. Some pieces just won't work, and you will soon find a use elsewhere for any leftovers.

You'll also need sand or gravel to form a base for the stone. These materials are usually sold by the cubic yard. There are formulas to determine how many cubic yards are needed to fill an area of a certain number of square feet to a depth of X inches. Again, it's best to order more than you calculate you will need. The excess will disappear quickly as you find other uses for it.

Here's how to proceed:

1. Spread your stone on a flat area near your new path but out of the way of your work zone.

2. Look them over as a group with a view toward figuring out which you will put next to each other for the best look.

3. After marking out your walk and taking a break to look at all your stone, the next step is to excavate for your stones. The depth of your excavation should take into account two factors: the thickness of the stone you're using and the gravel/sand base that you'll be laying the stone on.

4. Allow at least 2 to 4 inches for the tamped-down base, more if you live in an area where the ground freezes in winter. Excavate the entire walk at once. Stepping-stones can be done one at a time.

5. Next, pour the sand or gravel into the excavated area and level it off by pulling the 2×4 toward you with both hands. Once level, tamp the base with a tamper or by walking over it.

6. You'll need to re-level with the 2×4 after tamping. Your goal is to have a firm base upon which to set the stone.

Now comes the fun part. Like the great European cathedral builders, there is always a first stone.

7. Starting at a corner, make your pick for number one and put it into place by setting it on top of your firmed base. The stone should be just above the level you'd ideally like the walk to be.

8. Next, grab the stone with both hands and wedge it into place, pressing and twisting it into the base so it sinks to the proper level, making sure it has full contact with the sand or gravel.

9. Grab your rubber mallet and give it a few whacks around its perimeter like you're resealing a can of paint. This will help settle it and ensure that it isn't wobbly.

Now you're ready for stones 2 through 4,563. As you proceed, choose each new stone for how it relates and fits with the stones set before it. Repeat the process for setting each stone as you put your puzzle together.

This procedure is no different for a formal walk. Here, however, the shape of the material is standardized, so measurement and exacting placement are important. This is even more true if you're making a geometric pattern.

Now, let's consider just a few more things before you start planting at the edges of your walk. Once all your stone is in place and firmed, it's a good idea to fill the cracks between them to help keep them in place. Here's where some

of that extra sand comes in handy. Simply throw sand over the walk and then sweep it into the cracks. When you think you're done, lightly sprinkle the cracks with water to settle the sand. Then refill the cracks until there is no more settling. Set leftover sand on the side; over time the sand will settle again and you'll need it.

A Word of Warning

Even if you opt for a raised path, you should excavate and set the stones on a firmed bed of sand or gravel. Simply placing stones on top of the ground is a recipe for trouble. They'll be difficult to keep level and far more likely to tilt and move. Remember, a wobbly stone is a bad stone.

Patios

Patios are extensions of your living space, areas where you're taking the inside out and bringing the outside in. Properly made, they add years of enjoyment to your home and are perfect for relaxing and entertaining.

There are many different styles of stone patios. This one shows the decorative use of stone pavers, which can also be used to create a much more natural look.

There are many ways to build a patio and a variety of styles and materials to use. As with the other features discussed here, you make the choice to go formal or free and natural. A wide variety of pavers, bricks, and slabs will give you diverse looks. Because here we are talking about rock features, we will deal with a patio made from natural rock and stone.

Like paths, patios are often surrounded by or connected to gardens and other stone features. This helps unify the whole design and avoids the uncomfortable isolated feeling of a feature in the middle of nowhere. The process for building patios is exactly like that described for paths. The major difference is that patios generally abut the house and because of this, drainage of water away from the foundation of your home becomes a prime concern. To alleviate drainage concerns, you must pay special attention to having a slight drop in the level of the patio from the house to its outer edge.

The Right Stuff

A simple way to gauge whether you are maintaining the proper slope is to run a string from the house to the edge of the proposed patio. Set a stake in the ground at the foundation of the house. Tie a string to it at the level the patio will be when finished. Run the string to the outside edge of the patio, and tie it to another stake in the ground. Make sure the string is level. Now you'll be able to judge whether you're creating the slight slope you need by looking at the distance between the ground and the string. At the house the space between string and ground should be the thickness of your stone. At the outer edge it should be greater to ensure your slope. The idea behind the slope is that it will guide water away from the foundation of the home. It doesn't need to be a big drop. Your finished patio should still feel and appear flat.

You can use short stone walls (see, there are plenty of uses for that extra stone), to set off the patio from the surrounding yard, or to make small retaining walls to keep the patio level if your yard drops off.

Patio Quick Tip

Since patios are really extensions of your living area, choose flat stone with a minimum of irregularities. Set them as close together as possible to avoid large cracks into which chair legs can drop. Decide where you'll set your table and other furniture pieces and level them up once in place.

Rock Gardens

It doesn't take much imagination to realize the benefit of using rock and plants together. Close your eyes for a minute, and imagine either one of these two essential garden elements without the other. Now close them again and add plants to the rock or rock to the plants. The reason that people *ooh* and *aah* when they visit a good rock garden is because stone and plants just go together really well and because too few gardeners, for inexplicable reasons, use stone in their gardens.

Anyone who can make a garden or plant a container can build a rock garden. Each rock garden is unique, and the options are unlimited. Like other rock features, some guidelines and suggestions will help in the planning and construction of this most beautiful of all projects.

With large rock already in place, all that had to be added was plants.
Rock gardens can be made with any size rock and in either large or
small spaces, just like in nature.

Like other gardens, rock gardens are always unfinished works of art. When you deal with living things, continual change and flexibility are constants. Even the rock itself, although often used to create a feel of age and permanence, can be redone or changed. A small to mid-size garden is challenging but not excessively demanding. Using rock to create the perfect backdrop and setting for a collection of plants is the most satisfying of garden arts.

The Right Stuff

Classic rock garden plants are true alpines, miniature gems that occur in nature on mountains above the timberline. The most accepted definition of rock garden plants is generally much broader and includes any small growing plant in scale with the rocks amongst which it is planted. In gardens constructed of large pieces of stone, larger plants can be used. While purists disparage these gardens as "rockeries" and not true rock gardens, we include them in our definition. It's all a matter of scale and preference.

A Feeling of Randomness

Almost all rock gardens are created in the natural style, even if they are incorporated into a formal setting. A natural rock garden should always appear as if it's a creation of nature. Some lucky gardeners already have existing outcroppings of rock to use as a starting point for a rock garden. Regardless of whether you start with a mountain or a plain in your backyard, the art of rock gardening is to make the rocks appear as if they were positioned by nature, not by man.

Having a little topography in the yard gives you a leg up on others who'd like to try this form of gardening. Rocks look more natural set into a slope than they do erupting from flat land. While effective rock gardens can be built on flat land, you may want to consider creating your own topography by digging holes to create small valleys and using the excavated soil and/or additional soil brought in to make small hills adjacent to the excavation.

This heavily planted rock garden retains that much-desired feeling of randomness with the same kind of rock clusters that often appear in nature.

Rocks generally lie with their broadest side down, the so-called "angle of repose." Not surprisingly, placing rocks in your garden this way will help with their stability. To make them look as if they've been in the ground forever, bury one third to half the rock. This iceberg-like state of affairs is another aid to solidity in rock garden construction. The feature as a whole should suggest the emerging end of a massive underground rock structure exposed by weathering and erosion. We will deal more with rocks, finding and moving them as well as their placement, in the next chapter.

If you're creating more than one rock formation, make them different sizes to avoid sameness. Try to use the same stone for each and, whenever possible, use stone indigenous to your own area for the most realistic look.

The Right Stuff

If you decide to build an area up so you can put in a rock garden, make sure you allow the ground to settle before planting rocks. You'll naturally be anxious to put in your rocks and plants, but be patient. It may take several weeks for the soil to subside, but it's important to let this happen. If the soil isn't allowed to settle, it will sink. Even after settling, some additional sinking will occur, but if the initial settling doesn't happen, the end result will be more dramatic. Rocks set in loose soil will shift and move out of position. Formations may fall apart. Soil will sink between the rocks, leaving holes and taking plants too deep for their survival. Always allow the ground to stabilize before setting rocks. Because the ground will settle, it's important that any area you are building up is initially set 10 to 20 percent higher than your projected final height.

Size matters. The size of your property and the scale of your home limits your project. Your rock garden shouldn't stick out like a sore thumb or disappear from view entirely because it's too small. In a large area, use large stones for most of the feature with medium- and smaller-size rocks as dressing. You may need to have the largest rocks professionally placed.

In a smaller area, smaller stones are the natural design choice. You may still consider using a large rock or two as a focal point, but you should scale down the garden proper to fit the space.

Every rock garden should reflect the size of the yard or property on which it is built. Small gardens belong in small yards; large ones on much bigger tracks. This beautiful large garden allows for colorful planting without crowding and plenty of open space in between.

In situations with no yard or balconies, townhouse patios, or rooftops, don't overlook the possibility of building a small rock garden in a container. Many fabulous plants will thrive in such a setting, extending the joys of rock gardening to anyone.

Rock Garden Quick Tip

Before starting out, it pays to visit other gardens and look at photos in books and magazines for inspiration. Make a pilgrimage to mountainous areas for the ultimate in rock garden idea generation. Never slavishly copy what you see, but take the best ideas and make them your own.

What About the Rocks?

In a perfect gardening world, all the rocks you need would be sitting in the yard just waiting to be arranged and planted in your garden. This rarely happens, of course, so you have to take the initiative. Most experts feel rock that is native to your area lends the most natural look to the garden. They also recommend using only one type of rock.

No matter what size rocks you have or bring in for a rock garden, don't overplant. Complement your rocks with your plants, but never lose the fact that it is a rock garden and the rocks should be seen and showcased by the plants.

Avoid using newly quarried rock. These rocks, newly broken, have cut surfaces that will take a long time to weather to match the rest of the surfaces. In addition, recently quarried rock may display drilling marks, scrapes from equipment, or other undesirable blemishes.

While rules should never get in the way of creativity in the garden, there are some helpful tips for setting rocks in your yard:

- Use the largest rocks you can handle to form the bones of your rock garden.

- Accent the bones of your garden with different-size rock.

- Don't distribute the rock evenly throughout the garden. An asymmetrical arrangement is more natural and pleasing to the eye.

- Make a more massive use of your rock in some areas of the garden and use it more sparingly in others to accent the main feature.

- Partially bury most of the rock to make it look as if it has always been there.

- All stones have a good side or face. Highlight the best-looking part of the rock by facing it forward.

- To achieve the look of a natural outcrop, face the rock in the same direction.

- If you're using stratified stone (stone with lines created by the layers of sediment that created it), position the rocks so the lines go in the same direction.

- Mulch with gravel to unify the entire structure. Try to match the gravel's color to that of the stone used to construct the feature.

- Don't be afraid to leave an area or two bare. The rockless, gravel-mulched areas will give some relief to the eye, provide interesting contrasts, and allow an opportunity to vary your planting.

Use these principles to set your rocks, and you'll have a fine-looking garden and the opportunity to grow an outstanding selection of the world's finest flowers. In subsequent chapters, we will discuss the refinement of the rock garden, the soil mix that is necessary for the proper drainage and plant growth, and the amazing plants you can grow.

The Least You Need to Know

- Always plan your features first, assemble your materials, and then execute the construction when all else is done.

- Build dry-stone walls carefully, and never exceed your limits when handling large stone.

- Always stabilize a stone staircase so the stones don't wobble or shift.

- Always build patios with a slight slope running away from the house for the best drainage.

- The rock garden is the most beautiful of all the rock features and a great project to undertake.

In This Chapter

- ◆ Using rock correctly
- ◆ Finding or buying rocks
- ◆ Making the rock yourself
- ◆ Moving rock the safe way
- ◆ Placing rock within your feature

Many people cannot always gather large stone. An option is to buy it from a nursery or stone yard. Piles of stacked stone at a nursery such as this one will eventually find their way to various kinds of rock and water features.

Choosing, Finding, and Using Rock

Building with rock can be extremely satisfying when you do it yourself. That doesn't mean it's an easy task. Before you begin, you must know all you can about using rock the correct way. This means knowing how to select the rock you need, how to move the individual pieces safely, and finally how to place each stone within the feature you are building.

In this chapter, we cover all these aspects about working with rock, including the option of making your own rocks right in your yard. Many of you who have been trying to rid your yard of rocks for years probably never thought you would be reading about using rock. Now, however, you know how the beauty of rock features can enhance your yard, and it's time you know just how to handle this valuable resource.

The Rock Can Make or Break the Feature

The character and beauty of the rock you choose will make a huge difference in the finished appearance of your rock features. Choosing well is another of the keys to creating a successful illusion in your yard. Handling and placing the stone correctly will ensure that you accomplish your dream in a safe manner. Working with stone, especially the larger pieces, can be daunting, and if not handled with care, dangerous.

Learn what you can about choosing, handling, and placing rock before you begin. While the work can be difficult, the results are eye-popping and will make all the difference in the world in your yard.

This segment of a dry-stone wall is build entirely with natural rock of various sizes, found locally. Note the gaps and crevices of various sizes, all potentially perfect for planting.

Rock Building Quick Tip

Don't make the mistake of thinking that bigger is better with any rock feature. Some people use huge boulders as rock sculptures in their yard, but in the garden, scale is crucial. Remember that other rocks and plants will have to coexist with your major rock placement. Rock size depends on the size of the feature and the nature of the buildings and other features of the site. Small features look better with smaller rocks, and large features benefit from bigger stones.

Types of Rock

The backbone of any rock feature is its stone. Choose the wrong stone, align them poorly, stack them incorrectly, match them badly, use too many or not enough, and your feature will lose much of its appeal and effectiveness.

In the previous chapter, we touched briefly on the types of rock used in rock gardens. We suggested you use rock native to your area to give your garden a natural look. In doing this, many options are still available. Here are some tips on choosing the right kind of rock for your feature and your garden.

Sometimes the kind of plants you want to grow will dictate the nature of the rock you use. Limestone and water-worn limestone is beautiful rock, but not the best choice for acid-loving rock garden plants like heaths, heathers, and rhododendrons because small amounts of alkaline lime leach out of it over time.

If you choose to use limestone for your rock feature, you can find it at a nursery or stone yard. These large slabs of limestone are just waiting to be bought for use in a finished feature.

Tufa, a soft, lightweight, porous rock formed by calcium carbonate deposited in springs and streams, is easy to handle and very compatible with a wide variety of plants. It is an ideal choice for many high-alpine plants because its porosity allows perfect drainage. In addition, tufa can be drilled to create planting holes so that flowers will literally spring from the rock. It's ideal for use in containers because of its light weight, but its unique appearance isn't always easy to accommodate in larger features.

Sandstone ranges in color from a light yellowish-gray to a dark reddish-brown and is a great choice for many areas. It's considered a strong rock but is soft enough to weather into interesting shapes and porous enough to retain a little moisture, which benefits plants growing around it in hot, dry weather.

Other rocks that are suitable for gardens include gneiss, which is a layered rock usually of a striking gray color with lighter bands running through it, shale, and schist. These rocks, however, can be brittle and may break and crumble around the edges.

Granite is hard and fine-grained, weathers slowly, and is nonporous. As opposed to the alkaline nature of limestone, granite tends to be acidic. In areas where it's available, it can be used in rock gardens. Because of its structure, however, it tends to be rounded rather than flat. This makes it a little more challenging to work with in the garden and to keep it solid and stable in your feature.

Basalt, a dark volcanic rock, is also available commercially and provides a pleasing background for the small jewels you'll be planting. Other types of rock may be available depending on where you live. It helps to look at specimens of different rocks so you can determine which will look best with your rock feature or garden. In Japan, where rock has a cultural importance that goes back centuries, they have stone nurseries, where you can go to view and purchase rock just as you do plants in other parts of the world. You can find information on the rocks in your area at garden centers, rock garden societies, and rock, stone, and gravel dealers.

Where You Can Find and Buy Rocks

For many years, rock gardeners in search of stone for their gardens only had to drive to the countryside to locate a farmer more than willing to unload the rocks pulled from his field. They were free for the taking. As the farmers realized the desirability of this resource, once a nuisance to them, they made it an additional revenue stream. Now, like the stone yards, the farmers are charging for their stone. The big difference is that most of the time, buying from a private source means that you handle delivery.

If you know someone with a large tract of land and get permission to take rock from a section of the property, be sure you are prepared. Know the sizes and numbers you need. Be sure your vehicle can carry the load. If not, prepare to make multiple trips. Have a friend help so you don't overburden yourself as well. Get yourself and your vehicle home in one piece.

If you want specialized stone for a project, you have to buy it. These Belgian pavers are an excellent choice for patios and walks and are quite easy to use.

If you have your own rocky property, you may have all the stone you need right in your backyard. In rural areas rocks often seem to be everywhere, especially where you don't want them. Anyone who's tried to dig a vegetable garden has encountered rocks in the wrong place. If this is you, stockpile that rock. Then all you have to do is pick over the pile and choose those rocks that fit in your feature.

For those who need to leave the friendly confines of their own property to find stone, suppliers in nearly every area have a wide variety of choices. Except for specimen boulders, stone is usually priced by the ton. Much of this cost reflects the transportation of the chosen rock to your site, but always be sure to find out whether there is a separate charge for delivery. Knowledgeable suppliers will be able to help with selection of the stone and the amount needed if you give them an idea of the type of feature you're building and its dimensions.

Regardless of whether you cart the rock home or have it delivered, try to have it staged as close to the work area as possible so you don't have to move it more than once. This will save considerable wear and tear on your back, arms, and legs.

These long, flat stone slabs are perfect for patios or terraces. The different sizes can still give you a natural look.

The Right Stuff

You may see usable rocks on the roadside, wooded areas, or construction sites. Before you pick up a stone, be sure to *get permission* from the landowner or public authority. If you don't, you are trespassing and stealing. You rarely get something for nothing, so don't assume that the rock you desire is waste to its owner. Take the extra step of getting permission and you'll avoid a lot of trouble. In some areas you can apply for permits to harvest rock from government land and roadsides. This is a great way to get stone from rockfalls and other areas where it might otherwise be a hazard. Just be sure to get the permit first. Keep in mind that harvesting your own rock is a lot of work and takes time.

Fake Rocks

The best way to build a rock feature or rock garden is by the use of natural, weathered stones. Where an adequate supply of natural rocks cannot be found, you may be well advised to consider fake or homemade rocks.

One of the alternatives is to use fake rock, called *faux stones*. A number of manufacturers now produce these artificial rocks, and these stone imposters can do the job, albeit a bit differently. Some faux stones are made from cement, then stained to look natural. Like real rocks, they will weather over time and support the growth of moss and lichens, which just makes them appear more realistic.

While these stones can be used in the same way as real rock, the big knock on them is that the shape is not random enough and they tend to look alike. They also tend to be a bit lighter than real stone and are generally sold by the piece as opposed to by weight. Fake rocks come in a variety of shapes and sizes, but should be carefully selected so that they don't look artificial when they're used.

Faux stones are more useful when your feature needs a formal look. They can be molded into precise dimensions very predictably and can be made in whatever shape is required. Manufacturers can dye them with different colors, and the surface can be imprinted with natural or formal patterns or inset with gravel or other small stone. Faux stones also come as cement squares, stained and scored to resemble mortared brick. Some are made to look naturally weathered. These are an excellent alternative when the real thing is not readily available.

Homemade Rocks

For small projects, you can even make your own rocks. Making them look real is an art, and if you master it, you'll be able to make a variety of realistic-looking rocks to surprise your friends and neighbors.

Here's how it's done:

1. Mound a pile of sand on the garage or patio floor.
2. Push in the center of the pile to create your mold. Shape the bottom of the hole the way you'd like the top of your stone to look. Leave ridges and some rough areas to create a realistic-looking rock.
3. Next, place a large plastic bag over the sand. Spread it open over the sides of the depression in the sand pile.

4. Make your dry cement mix in a separate tub. Use Portland cement. Include peat moss, dried grass clippings, or plant material to help reduce weight and give the resulting stone a little texture. Sand can be added for additional realism. Add only enough water to wet down the mix to the stage where you can form a ball in your hand and not have it slop through your fingers.

5. Pack the wet mix into the depression, making sure there are no air spaces.

6. Pull the corners of the bag shut at the top to prevent sharp edges at the bottom of the rock (which is the top surface of the mix). Taking this step will round off the bottom edges.

7. Allow the mix to cure but not dry totally. It should set in 12 to 24 hours. Next, unwrap the rock and flip it over. This is your nearly finished piece. You may need to attack it with a wire brush to eliminate any sharp edges. You can use a screwdriver to score the rock in strategic places, creating the character you'd expect from a real rock.

8. Now leave it outside, exposed to the weather, for a month or two to age. This helps leach any lime that might not be appreciated by plants.

9. Change the shape or size of the depression in your sand pile and make another.

Make no mistake—it takes time and work to make rocks, but it's an option if natural rocks aren't available or if you just want the satisfaction of saying "I did it all myself."

Moving Rock

Moving rock isn't the same as moving small stones. Unless you're a professional or have help, huge boulders that must be moved by machine, pushed by bulldozers, lifted into buckets of front-end loaders, or lifted by a chain hoist and a winch aren't realistic alternatives.

There are, however, a number of ways to maneuver rocks larger than you can lift.

If you are going to be handling heavy rocks, you should take these basic precautions:

◆ Wear heavy gloves with leather palms for maximum protection of the hands.

◆ Wear boots or work shoes that have reinforced steel toes.

◆ If you are going to be lifting heavy rocks, it is advisable to wear a protective belt, similar to those worn by competitive weight lifters. These give extra support to the lower back.

◆ When you are lifting a heavy rock, always squat in front of it, grasp it firmly, pulling it into your body, then stand up using your legs with your back held straight. This puts the brunt of the load on your legs and will help you avoid a possible back injury.

 Rock Quick Tip

Because you want your rocks to look natural and weathered, you don't want to scrape, scar, or chip them in handling. One trick is to wrap choice pieces of rock in burlap while you're handling them. This may be necessary if you are using pry-bars or similar implements.

There are a number of ways to move rocks heavier than you can lift. If you use any of these methods, practice with lighter rocks first before you move up to the heavy stuff.

◆ With long pry-bars and a little effort, 2 men can roll a 500-pound boulder over level ground or downhill. Take extra caution when moving any stone downhill so that the stone doesn't get away and roll down on its own.

◆ Stones up to about 300 pounds can be moved with industrial wheelbarrows that have rubber tires. The trick is to lay the wheelbarrow on its side. Then roll the stone onto it and tip the wheelbarrow upright. It helps to have one or two people to assist.

◆ You can use hand trucks for moving fairly heavy stones if their loading arms are long enough to fit under the stone. This method is for stones that are relatively flat. If you are doing this regularly, you might have a steel plate welded to the arms to extend them.

One man can usually move a rock weighing 100 pounds or more by using a homemade dolly. You can make one from a 3×4 foot piece of ¾-inch plywood laid on top of several 3-foot pieces of 4-inch PVC pipe. Make a rope pull by drilling two holes through the lead edge of the plywood and tying on a thick nylon rope.

You can move rocks weighing more than 100 pounds by pushing them on a homemade dolly using plywood and PVC pipe. If you don't want to push, another trick is to attach a rope to the front of the plywood and pull the dolly over the pipes.

Begin your rock move by placing a single piece of pipe at the front end of the board. Roll the rock onto the middle of the plywood. Then pull the plywood and rock forward onto the additional lengths of pipe.

Now use the pipes as rollers, pulling the rock along the ground. When the rear pipe is free at the back end of the board, pick it up and place it in front of the dolly. Just continue the process until you get where you want to go. It's slow work, but it will get the job done, and it's safer than some other alternatives.

A Word of Warning

No matter what method you choose to move rock, there is one condition you must avoid. Never work on soft, wet ground. You need a solid base for you and the stone, whether you are rolling the rock or using a wheelbarrow or a homemade dolly. It's much more difficult on wet ground, and the chances of an injury increase. Always wait until the ground is dry and hard before you move your rock.

Never be afraid to ask for help. You can always return the favor. Using these tips will help you move large stone, but if you have any doubt in your mind, get a friend to help. Don't try doing it by yourself, and never attempt to move a rock that is too big or heavy.

Building With Rock

Building with rock is an art. Ancient stone walls, which are still standing today, were built by stonemasons, men who studied rock and knew how to stack it so it would last. They found stone in rocky fields and chose the best specimens with which to build their walls. One modern-day stonemason says the stones themselves tell him how to build a wall. He uses wider, larger rocks at the bottom, then tapers the rock, making it thinner as the wall gains height.

The free-standing stone wall is still built using these principles. Small stones are often wedged between large ones to fill in cracks and add stability. Retaining walls, which lean slightly into the ground they hold back, are built the same way but are not usually tapered at the top because the rocks gain stability from the ground.

This dry-stone wall is being built layer by layer with natural rocks of various sizes; small rocks are used to fill the cracks between the larger ones.

How to Place Rock

We've already discussed the placement of rocks when building stone walls, paths, and patios. The trick with walls is to plan ahead, excavate for a base, and use the largest rocks there. As you build up, make sure that each rock you place feels secure and stable as it sits on the rocks below it. If it wobbles or shakes, adjust it, wedge a smaller rock into an opening to stabilize it, or remove it in favor of another rock.

Construct your walls so the vertical joints are staggered. Avoid long runs from top to bottom so that the wall knits together and to reduce the likelihood that soil will leak out from behind.

A walled raised bed is nothing more then a dry-stone wall build in a configuration that brings it together. The middle can be filled with soil and planted, and plants can also be put in the cracks of the wall at any point.

The Right Stuff

Another use for the dry-stone wall is to create a closed, raised bed. You can make it any size and shape you want. Start with a trench in the shape and size of your feature, and then put in a base of firmed gravel or sand as discussed in Chapter 5. The wall-building technique is the same as for a retaining wall. Smaller rocks are useful for making curves in the wall. Soil is packed behind the wall and can be used between the rocks to create planting pockets. When the wall is done, fill the bed with the appropriate soil for the plants you'd like to grow.

If you are building a rock wall with the expressed purpose of planting it, you should do it a little differently. Here's how:

1. As with a retaining wall, you build up one layer at a time, but you still need a solid foundation.

2. Create the foundation by digging a trench deep enough to give you a 4- to 6-inch gravel base, and bury your first row of rocks to half their height. If you're building a high and heavy wall, consider pouring a concrete foundation.

3. Next build the first layer of rock into the trench and then pack good-quality soil behind the rock.

4. Being sure to leave pockets in which to plant, add the next layer of rock. Remember to use a batter, or slight backward lean, so the wall takes advantage of the soil behind it for support. (Remember the use of the angle board in Chapter 5.)

5. Pack soil behind the second layer.

6. Add additional layers, always leaving the planting pockets and being careful to retain the batter. Pack soil into the pockets from both the front and the rear.

Notice how this very old dry-stone wall is planted. There are plants at the base, in the middle, and at the top. Yet it isn't overplanted, and the grand character of the rock is still well in evidence.

7. You can plant the pockets as you build or when you finish building the wall. The growing roots of the plants help hold the soil in place.

Planted Wall Quick Tip

Another way to increase stability of your wall is to use long, narrow stones that extend into the soil behind the wall like a plug put into an electrical socket. Stagger such "tie" stones at intervals throughout the layers in your wall.

Remember these additional tips: Keep this kind of wall a manageable height. Walls, like other rock features, should be kept in scale with their surroundings. Use relatively flat stones with the largest ones at the base. Use the largest stones that you can handle safely. A few large stones are more stable than a grouping of smaller ones. The backward pitch of the wall should be at least 1 inch for each foot of height.

Placement Quick Tip

If you have some unusually shaped rocks, don't automatically discard them. They can be used as a focal point for the wall. Watch for an artistic place to use these unique stones, and build around them using the techniques we've been discussing.

Placing Rock for the Natural Look

Rule number one is to always look to Mother Nature for the best in natural rock placement. We'd like to think we can approach the grandeur we see in natural settings when we place rock in the garden. Go for a drive in the country, and look at natural rock formations and old rock features and walls. See how the rocks sit together. Notice the use of space, the amount of rock that's exposed, and the overall look of the rock.

This completely natural-looking rock garden makes a beautiful feature. The shaded area at the right is planted mainly with ferns and, as usual, the rocks stand out on their own.

We've made many suggestions about the placement of rocks. Although we have suggested that you bury rocks to half their height, you can leave a few rocks on the surface, a mixture looking best. Make sure any surface rock is placed so that it doesn't roll or tip. Use rocks of different sizes and place them in a planned, but random fashion, not in rows or symmetrical groupings.

Here are some additional tips for placing rocks in the garden:

- Set each rock with its most attractive side exposed for viewing.
- Slope the top of the rock slightly backward so rain or water from a sprinkler runs back into the soil and goes to plants' roots.
- Use the rock's natural angle of repose by setting each with its broadest side as its base to ensure stability.
- Run major rock faces in the same general direction throughout the garden.
- Put any lines of stratification on the rocks at the same angle in the entire garden.

"Planting" Each Rock

If you are going to bury a good part of an individual rock, you want to get it right the first time. Use this sound method to "plant" each rock when you are setting up a rock garden or placing rocks in another type of rock feature.

The functional purpose of "planting" is to ensure that the rock stays in place through alternating periods of freezing and thawing in colder winter climates. It also holds the stone in place during periods of heavy rains that soften soil. Here's how to "plant" a stone:

- Measure the size of the rock you are going to plant. If you are going to plant half of it, dig out a hole in the shape of a bowl with enough room to move the rock around.
- Set the rock in the hole with the best face forward. Now study it from all angles to make sure you've set it to its best advantage.
- Adjust it if necessary.
- Fill in the remainder of the hole around the rock.

- At this stage it's not a bad idea to water your rock in as you would a newly planted perennial. The soil you just back-filled with will settle, and you can top it off as necessary.
- The final step is to plant around the edges of your rock. In the wild, plants tend to grow there because of the moisture that is trapped in the soil under the rock and the cool root-run provided as a result.

Study carefully the sum of all the parts and each individual rock before it is placed. Be prepared to make any adjustments before you fill in with soil. With good planning and a little luck, the decisions you make will be on the money the first time. It's hard enough to place a good-size rock. The last thing you want to do is move it again.

When you build a rock feature, every step is important to the end result. Each stage builds upon the last, and the final result is an artistic feature that will attract attention, enhance the value of your yard and the time spent there, and stand the test of time.

The Least You Need to Know

- How you choose and use rock can make or break the feature you are constructing.
- Different types of rocks have different characteristics when used for rock features and gardens.
- Fake rocks and homemade rocks are an option when natural specimens are not available.
- Moving rock can be an arduous and sometimes dangerous task when not done correctly.
- "Planting" rocks is as much a skill as the other kinds of planting you do in your yard.

In This Chapter

- ◆ Decisions about planting
- ◆ Being aware of the overall design
- ◆ Plants and your rock features
- ◆ Special needs of rock gardens
- ◆ Choices for your rock garden

A tastefully done mixture of color and greenery highlights this natural
rock garden that is almost planted to perfection. Note there are still
bare spaces to help set off everything.

Planting Your Rock Features

All rock features have the potential to house a variety of plants to enhance and beautify both the feature and your yard. Just as you choose the size, shape, and style of your rock features, you will choose the plants that will adorn them. Flower color, foliage, texture, and size are important, as are the kinds of plants you put together. Planting your features should enhance them, not detract from the work you've done or hide the beauty of the rock.

In this chapter, we will talk about the decisions you must make before planting—the design you choose, the types of plants you can choose for your rock features and rock gardens, as well as deciding how to plant them for the best results. Because you will often be dealing with small plants in small places, this is a different and specialized kind of gardening. The more you know about it before you begin, the better your results will be.

Deciding Which Plants to Use

Deciding which plants to use can seem like an impossible task when you consider the thousands of species, hybrids, and cultivars that are available in garden centers, nurseries, and by mail. However, there are lots of ways to make the process easier.

First, do some homework. Dozens of books about gardening "on the rocks" have detailed information on plants for rock gardens and features. Magazines and nursery catalogues are additional sources of pictures, cultural information, and advice.

The Internet is also a gold mine of information for the avid gardener. Many nurseries have their own websites, often with more information than the catalogues contain. A search on the name of nearly any plant will yield data on its origins, the way it grows, and best of all, places where you can get it. Many groups of plants have their own websites with even more detailed information.

A rock garden setup like this one at a nursery gives customers an idea of what is available and how they should plant. Note the tiny plants in flats at the front waiting for a new home.

Some people keep things simple by learning what works best in their area. These "bulletproof" plants are the best bets for success in a garden. They've already proven their worth and should do well for you even if you're new to gardening and don't know your phlox from your socks.

Narcissus asturiensis, a mini-daffodil, grows from bulbs and blooms early in the season for immediate color.

Artistic types may prefer to choose plants based on a color scheme. They might choose to plan their color scheme to coordinate with the colors of their home or just the hues of the main room inside the house from which they will view their creation. It may be as simple as choosing a favorite color. With an unlimited color palette at their disposal, anyone can accomplish any design with a little research and planning.

Still others may try to recreate a scene from a favorite natural part of the world, grouping plants from a particular area or habitat. With the whole world to choose from, they are bound to hit on a combination that brings back memories of a special time in another land. Finally, there are the collector types who just have to grow everything. They keep experimenting with plants, always stretching the envelope to include the new and exotic.

Cyclamen hederifolium, also grown from bulbs, is a late-season bloomer that will keep color in the garden until late fall.

Regardless of the category you fit into, planting a rock feature is exciting and should be done with an eye toward color and diversity.

Planting Quick Tip

Don't make planting your feature a job. There is no formula, so use plants you like. It's a good idea to use plants with different forms. Plants that grow in mats and drape over rocks or stepping-stones can be mixed with "bun" plants that form little cushions, with miniature trees and shrubs thrown in for good measure. Vary your planting and your plants.

A great beginner's plant is this *Sempervivum arachnoideum*. These grow in clumps between the rocks and are very easy to cultivate.

As in the preparation for building the feature you are now about to plant, it pays to look at what others have done before making decisions of your own. Visit other gardens. Look at pictures in books and magazines, and make notes about the plants you like the looks of. Visit local garden centers and nurseries. At first, leave your checkbook at home and go just to look at the diversity of plants available to you. Talk to the experts about what plants they'd recommend for your feature. Then start a list of what you'd like to try. Look up their names in a plant book to see if you can provide the conditions they need to survive.

If all this seems like a lot of work, don't fret. It's all part of the learning process. It'll make you a better gardener and can be as fun as the actual process of making the garden. It only increases the enjoyment you'll get from the finished product.

Environmental Limitations

It's important to find out if the plants you like will live in your yard. One of the most exciting things about rock garden plants is that many of them are just as they are in the wild. But because they come from all over the world, not all of them will like your climate.

Lewisia rediviva is a colorful flower but also a plant that can't take too much water when dormant and needs a dry climate to thrive.

Nearly every area of North America, as well as some of the other continents, is mapped for what are called "hardiness zones." While these maps are generally limited in scope and usefulness, they do provide a rough guide of comparative climate conditions. Determine what your "zone" is by looking at a map that covers your locality. Your geographic area will be assigned a number or a combination of a number and a letter.

Many plant books and encyclopedias will list ranges of hardiness zones for each plant entry. This is an indication of whether a plant will or won't grow well for you. While these designations aren't surefire keys to success, they will point you in the right direction.

Don't be confused by the maps and if a particular plant isn't listed for your zone. Just be aware of what extra help you will need to provide to give it the best chance to thrive.

Planting Quick Tip

The United States National Arboretum publishes the USDA (United States Department of Agriculture) Plant Hardiness Zone Map, which divides North America into 11 hardiness zones. Zones are based on the average minimum temperature for each location. You can find the USDA zone map on the Internet.

This colorful *Draba* with its yellow flowers and dark green leaves will only thrive when it receives full sunlight for most of the day.

Then there is the question of sun or shade. Along with hardiness, the degree of light your plants get is likely to be the most important factor determining plant selection. There are plants for every light situation except the deepest shade, where only moss will survive.

Most rock features are constructed where they will get plenty of sun. This affords gardeners the opportunity to grow the widest variety of rock garden plants. This is a logical choice when you consider that alpine plants, the ones most often associated with rock, grow above the tree line where there is little or no shade. These plants have adapted to a life in the sun and must be given the same conditions in the garden. Don't despair, however, if your garden is in the shade. There are plenty of plants that would fry in the sun and will only survive in the conditions that you can provide.

Last but not the least of the three big environmental limitations is whether your garden is moist or dry, how much rainfall your area receives, and how it receives it. The amount of moisture in your soil and how well it drains will play a big part in determining what plants will do well. Growing the wrong plants in the wrong spot is and always has been a recipe for failure.

Unless you plan to irrigate your new feature, you'll have to be more or less content with the amount of water rainfall provides. You can supplement that water with your own, but many areas have restrictions on the use of water, and watering adds another chore to the gardening day. Even if the climatological records for your area show sufficient annual rainfall, the way you receive it can make a difference. In many areas, seasonal rainy seasons can result in short wet periods separated by long dry ones. While there are plants adapted to such a moisture regime, the broader range of garden varieties generally require a more regular schedule of watering.

Human Limitations

This consideration is about you and what you are willing to do to make your plantings successful. Every garden requires work. The kinds of plants you choose can increase or decrease the amount of effort you will expend. How much do you enjoy puttering in the yard? Do you enjoy being out in your garden or just like to have a beautiful view? How much time will you devote to taking care of your features and your plants?

Choosing the right plants from the start is important if you're trying to minimize work. Choosing your plants based on the conditions that exist in your yard will result in less aftercare. If your yard is dry, choosing plants that will tolerate drought is a natural choice and will eliminate or drastically reduce the need to water. Growing moisture-loving plants in wet areas of the yard will eliminate the work it takes to drain that spot for other plants. Use low-growing, mat-forming plants around stepping-stones and in the cracks of your paths, being sure to use plants that will withstand some foot traffic. This kind of planting takes up room that would otherwise be occupied by weeds and reduces the labor associated with the chore of weeding.

For the gardener who may not have quite as much time, these *Sempervivum* with colorful maroon centers in the rosettes are easy to grow and need little attention.

If you take the time to evaluate environmental limitations as well as your own approach to gardening, you'll be in a stronger position to make the right planting choices.

Design Considerations

Design considerations, which have played a major part in this process since the very beginning, now take on even greater importance. Planting is the last step in the process, the last chance you'll have to make an impact. Consider your proposed planting from multiple viewpoints. Nearly every situation has one or two major perspectives, spots from which the majority of the viewing will occur. Always plant with these views in mind for maximum effect.

Walk through the feature, particularly if steps or paths are involved. Think about creating a series of vignettes, small pictures within the larger composition. Places where you change direction or round a corner are particular opportunities for such a treatment.

Vistas are also important. Plant with a view toward what is beyond the garden as well as what is in it. Is there a view worth incorporating? If so, don't obscure it by planting a backdrop of evergreens. On the other hand, if you are faced with an obstruction to the view, plant to eliminate or minimize its intrusion into your yard.

Don't Be Afraid to Change or Experiment

Despite its obvious importance, planting is also the most forgiving element of your new feature. The aesthetic choices you make are not permanent. Your choice of plants is the most flexible part of the entire project. If something doesn't feel right, change it. If you happen upon a new favorite and there's no room to plant it, move something. Dead plants are to be expected and are not so much a problem as an opportunity to try something new.

Everything starts with the overall style of the garden. Your planting design will be different if you've chosen the natural look over a more formal appearance. If you've gone wild, your planting should complement, but not overwhelm, the rock. Remember that your stone is an equal partner, the backbone and frame of the garden. Work toward a harmonious balance, showcasing both the plants and rock with neither overpowering the other.

Planting Quick Tip

Diversity is king in the natural garden. More than in any other style, the wild garden is where you can indulge your desire for variety.

This variety of succulents not only needs little water but also provides a variety of color and texture when planted together among the rocks.

Color, form, and texture should be varied to create contrast and interest. You'll learn about classic plant combinations as you study garden design. You can recreate these for yourself or make your own inspired pairings. Repeating your color, form, and texture elements at staggered intervals throughout the garden will unify the composition.

Don't forget foliage. Perhaps the most overlooked element in gardening, leaves are around long after your plants' flowers have faded. Leaf form, color, and texture are the great hidden keys of good garden design.

Think in three layers. Use small trees, dwarf shrubs, and herbaceous perennials to create canopy, understory, and ground layers. An added benefit of this arrangement is that the taller plants create shade, allowing a wider variety of plants to be used.

Natural plantings look best when plants are grouped in odd numbers planted asymmetrically. Instead of buying two of your favorite plants, pick up three, or better yet five or seven. A grouping with an odd number is more pleasing to the mind's eye. Plant in twos and fours and the mind gets mathematical, dividing the arrangement in halves.

Dicentra, or bleeding hearts, grow in small cracks within the rocks, the interplay highlighting both rock and plant alike.

The interplay between rock and plant is important. Rock is hard and unyielding; plants, in general, represent the opposite. This sort of natural yin-yang is one of the great pleasures of designing a rock garden. Softening the great solid bulk of rock with plants and giving the soft, living tissue of plants a bulwark of structure and stability is one of the great challenges of making a successful garden.

Some rock garden plants even resemble the rocks, such as this *Gypsophila aretioides,* which grows in a tight, thick clump.

Formal Settings

Design considerations are just as important in a formal setting. However, the symmetrical arrangement and mathematical precision that you will use call for a different approach. Color, form, and texture are just as important as before, but in a formal garden the plant palette is generally limited. Where the natural gardener may use many species and cultivars of plants, the formal trowel-wielder will use fewer varieties, but greater numbers of each.

Planting Quick Tip

Instead of planting in an asymmetrical, random way, the formal gardener will plant in rows and patterns. Straight lines are important, as the garden is more a means to an end than an end in itself.

Formal plantings are often done with even-numbered groupings of plants. This makes it easier to achieve the symmetrical, mathematical, precise look that is so sought after by practitioners of this form of gardening.

A diverse group of alpines planted among smaller rocks in a trough is another rock garden in miniature that will always catch the eye.

You can do container plantings in any style. Too often, however, people overlook the opportunity to use stone. This oversight is unfortunate, since stone can provide a central focal point around which to place your plants. Troughs and other larger-than-pot containers can actually be landscaped to create natural scenes in miniature. Tufa or other porous rock is often used because it weighs less than stone.

Planting Rock Features

Major botanical gardens often group plants by creating associations of plants from around the world that come from similar habitats. Everyone is familiar with desert displays full of cacti and succulent plants. Rain-forest habitats feature exotic orchids, creeping vines, and unusual flowering trees. Woodland areas contain ferns and wildflowers that thrive in the shady undergrowth.

These *Sempervivum* hybrids are an example of a perfect planting for dry-stone walls.

On a different level, you'll make similar planting decisions in your yard. Some plants are more compatible with certain features. Walls, with their near-perfect drainage, are great places for alpine plants and others that prefer not to be in moist soil, while raised beds can be used for plants that love moisture or prefer to be dry, depending on the soil mix used. Sandy, *free-draining* areas behind short retaining walls are ideal for hardy cacti and succulents. You can make rock gardens accommodate nearly any kind of plant if you choose the right construction and materials.

> **Backyard Lingo**
>
> Nearly all rock garden plants require soil that is **free draining,** soil that water will run right through, wetting the individual particles, but not holding large amounts of water around the roots. This kind of soil is typically made by incorporating sand or grit into the soil to open it up.

The Right Way to Plant

When you build the stone structure of your rock garden, you should fill the area between the rocks with a free-draining soil mixture and allow it to settle before planting. Watering it in will help speed the settling process and identify areas where additional soil is needed.

> **Planting Quick Tip**
>
> It is always helpful to see planted features similar to those you will be building. It is well worth the trip to visit a botanical garden, nursery, or garden center. Take notes on the kinds of plants used and how they are situated in the display. Ask questions. Then use your newfound knowledge to your advantage.

The best time to plant your rock garden is on a cool, overcast day, one having a slight breeze, a little drizzle, and the prospect of a steady two-day soaker on the horizon. The soil should be damp, not soaking wet or dusty dry. The other 364 days a year we have to handle what nature throws at us.

While ideal conditions most often elude us, it pays to be smart. Most plants experience what is called "transplant shock." They're being ripped from pots (where they aren't all that happy to begin with), root pruned, and slammed into foreign soil by a well-meaning, but results-oriented gardener. If this happens on a dry, hot, windy day, the plants will wilt, gasping for their lives, before you have a chance to wash your hands after a job well done.

If the job is truly done right, the plants will settle in and take off without missing a beat. Follow these suggestions so you can make your plants happy that you were the one who took them home:

◆ Check the weather report. If that ideal day is coming in the near future, *wait*.

◆ Rock features are generally planted with small plants. Small plants call for smallish planting holes. Small holes call for small tools. Leave the spade in the shed and use a variety of trowels.

Small Tools for Small Places

Planting between rocks also requires thinking on a different plane. Large shovels and spades are of little use when you're planting in a 1-inch crack or a small pocket 3 feet off the ground. These tools may be a bit more useful.

◆ About the biggest thing you'll need is a rabbitting spade. This is a narrow-blade spade with a half-size handle, originally used for digging rabbits and other ground-dwelling varmints out of their burrows in England. It's also useful in the perennial garden.

◆ Stainless-steel trowels in a variety of sizes are the workhorses of the planted rock feature. Have a selection handy.

◆ Don't let your old silverware languish in a drawer—put it to work in the garden! Unused spoons, forks, knives, and believe it or not, chopsticks (except for the wooden ones) are favorite tools of rock gardeners and are ideal for the tight spaces you'll encounter.

◆ For those who can't psychologically handle the transition of tableware to garden implement, the British have invented the stainless steel "widger," hard to describe but even harder not to love. With one end wider than the other, this tool functions like its name sounds, squeezing into the spots between a rock and a hard place. Buy this little gadget by the dozen. Your friends will all want one, and, like all the best things in life, they're all too easy to lose.

The Pecking Order for Planting

There is also a pecking order to follow when you plant, a right way to do it. Just follow these basic rules:

◆ Plant your woodies first. Just as your rocks form the framework of the feature, small trees and shrubs form the living bones of your garden. Site them in the garden in their pots and step back. Make sure they work in the locations you've chosen. Then think about it again. Woody plants will be the most difficult to move if you change your mind, so try to get it right the first time.

◆ Next set your herbaceous plants. It's easiest to start at the top of the feature and work your way down.

◆ Take care when clambering about on the rocks. You are not a mountain goat. Footing can be treacherous even if the rocks are as secure as they are supposed to be.

These dwarf conifers are a natural for a rock garden and, as "woodies," should be planted first.

◆ Rock garden plants grow most naturally right next to rocks. They take advantage of the long cool root-runs created by the stone partners, sunk into the ground. They often look their best lining the crevices between the rocks. Some will grow no other way.

Some plants, like the *Asarina proeumbens,* can thrive when planted in the smallest cracks in the rock and appear as if they are growing out of the rock itself.

◆ Be sure to take advantage of the mat-forming characteristic of many rock plants by draping them over rocks to cascade downward. This helps soften the hardness of the rock structure.

◆ Many rock garden plants have evolved long roots to cope with conditions in their mountain homes where water may not be available close to the surface. Always dig deep enough holes to accommodate the roots of your plants.

A Word of Warning

Most nurseries that deal with rock garden plants are selling young plants from seed or vegetative propagations. At this age, the root systems aren't as developed and are easier to handle. Don't be disappointed if the plants you see or order through the mail are smaller than you expect. This is actually a good thing. Rock garden plants operate on a different scale than most perennials to begin with, and getting young plants for your feature is actually an advantage. Besides, they'll quickly catch up.

◆ Unpot plants grown in containers. Shake or rinse off most of the potting mix and loosen up the roots. If the roots are coiling around the bottom of the pot, slice off ¼ to ⅓ of the root ball before loosening the roots and planting. When planting, make sure the crown of the plant is set slightly higher than the surface of the ground to accommodate a collar of gravel mulch.

◆ Fill in around the roots with your soil mix, making sure to tamp it down to eliminate any air pockets, but don't pack the soil too tightly around the roots of your plants.

◆ When you've done a section of the garden, stop and water in the plants you have placed. Run the water slowly so that it doesn't float the plant right out of the hole or wash the soil down the feature. When the ground around each plant has been thoroughly watered, place a collar of gravel around the crown of each plant. Then mulch the area between the plants with the same gravel.

Rock Quick Tip

Rock features and their plants benefit from a 1-inch mulch of gravel. When you buy your stone, ask if "fines" are available. These are the leftover smallest pieces of gravel-making operations. Try to match the color of the gravel to that of the stone you are using. In the event that you can't find gravel made from the same stone, pea gravel will do.

Here is a proper rock garden planting with *Erigeron,* a North American alpine, growing through a layer of gravel mulch.

A Word of Warning

Do not mulch rock gardens with wood chips. It's not natural looking and will retain too much moisture around the crown of the plant, rotting it to death.

Now that you have planted and mulched your garden, all that remains is for you to place accent stones—generally stones smaller than your structural stones but larger than the gravel mulch—to add to the realism of the feature and to make any final adjustments. The final touch is to give the entire project a light watering to rinse the dirt and dust off the plants and mulch.

For the first few weeks after planting, take special care to make sure that the feature and its plants don't dry out. Although the plants you use may be drought tolerant, they'll appreciate this special attention while they're settling into their new homes.

 Planting Quick Tip

Don't be a "crowder." Remember that open, gravel-covered ground is a respite from the busyness of the plantings. Bare spots are good. Resist the temptation to jam in another spot of color.

Never overcrowd a rock garden. Here two flowers of the *Aquilegia* species stand out because there is sufficient bare space around them.

Marrying cold, hard rock and living, breathing plants to create a beautiful garden is one of the most exciting things you can do in your yard. Like any garden, a rock garden is a fluid thing, constantly changing and always ready to be improved. Take the lessons you've learned as a beginning, but don't stop here. Entire books have been written on many of the subjects covered in this chapter alone. Graduate to them and continue your education.

The Least You Need to Know

- There are many things to consider when deciding on plants for your rock feature or garden.
- Both environmental limitations and human limitations must be part of the planting mix.
- Choose a particular design scheme for your plantings and stick with it.
- View as many plants as you can in person and in planted features before you make a final decision.
- You'll need specialized tools for planting in rock features and gardens because of the small spaces in which you'll be working.

In This Chapter

◆ Keeping the plants healthy

◆ Don't forget all the little things

◆ Allowing for changing seasons

◆ Surprise!—rocks need maintenance, too

◆ Replacing and changing rock

This beautiful, terraced rock garden has a variety of color and striking plants—all of which require a degree of maintenance.

Care and Maintenance of Your Rock Features

Planting your rock feature or garden is the first step in what could be a lifelong avocation. For many it becomes an addiction. Thankfully, it's one addiction that can be easily satisfied. Once you've built your feature, you'll be able to spend as much time on it as you like, maintaining it, enlarging it, and just plain tinkering in it. Like all gardens, your job is never done. On this painting, the paint's always wet. All planted rock features and the rock itself require maintenance.

Keeping plants healthy and happy is an obvious maintenance goal. Weeding, feeding, primping, pruning, mulching, yanking, and dealing with a host of potentially destructive pests and the changing seasons are ongoing chores. Maintenance of the stone itself, however, is not something many people think of when they construct a rock feature. Rocks—and the gravel mulch between them—sink. Stones can break and may loosen themselves from their moorings. They can be undermined by chipmunks and other burrowers, tip and tilt out of place, or just not look right any more and have to be replaced. In this chapter, you will learn what you must do to maintain both plants and the rocks that anchor them.

Keeping Plants Healthy

There is no such thing as a "black thumb." If you've been married, raised a child, cooked a meal, or planned a trip, you can keep plants healthy. All of these activities and many other everyday events are more complicated than the care necessary to see plants thrive. Anyone who resorts to the "black thumb" excuse is giving himself a head-trip.

The care necessary to take plants through their growing season successfully is called "maintenance." Throughout the season regular chores need to be done to make the grade. Those with hard winters get a little time off but have more work to do in the fall to put the garden to bed and then to wake it up in the spring.

This healthy lupine is alive, thriving, and looking beautiful. But that doesn't mean you don't have to watch out for problems.

All this talk about work may put some people off, but maintenance can be fun and relaxing. Just the same, there are two major things you can do to minimize the amount of aftercare you'll have to do when you build a new garden. First, build it the right way. This starts with choosing the appropriate spot. Most rock gardens are given sunny exposures, but too much of a good thing and your plants will be begging for extra water. A well-constructed garden will have less go wrong with the hardscape as well. Choosing the right plants for the right spot is the second huge help. If you're working with a moist location, why fight nature? Select plants that love constant moisture. Are you in a location that doesn't get regular rain? Use xeric, or drought-tolerant plants. These dry-land natives will thrive even without the extra waterings that would be required to care for other plants.

Water and Drainage

Every plant needs water. It is essential to their survival. If you don't receive regular rains throughout the growing season, watering will be a part of your maintenance regime. Despite their need for water, most plants, especially those that prefer rock garden conditions, must have soil that drains well.

Most plants that grow among rocks are adapted to a "well-drained" environment. The water they receive runs around the rocks and through gritty soil, wetting the particle's surfaces. Providing this environment for your plants will help you succeed.

Many rock features provide their drainage, almost by definition. Water runs between the rocks, and if the soil is well drained, through it and away from the feature. In planted features, heavy rains can wash soil out from between rocks, creating problems for your flowers. Ironically, planting between the rocks helps hold the soil in place. Soil and mulch are easily replaced but add to maintenance concerns.

Watering Quick Tip

You need to water planted dry-stone walls more frequently than a rock garden. The pockets of soil tucked between the rocks are generally small and are more exposed than planting areas in traditional rock gardens. They dry out more quickly. Water newly planted walls daily until the plants begin to grow and then water frequently, especially when rainfall is scarce.

You must pay extra attention to watering when alpine plants are sitting in small crevices with limited soil.

Satisfying the twin requirements of sufficient water and well-drained soil is a delicate dance. Provide drainage that is too good, and you'll need to water more often. Not enough drainage can make even nature's rain a killer. A balance needs to be reached. Rainfall varies from place to place, so good soil in one area may be different than that in another.

Experimentation in your own yard is the best way to figure out how much drainage is necessary. Most homes call for soil that is better drained than what exists on site. Increase drainage by adding sand and gravel to existing soil. It's not always easy to do this *in* the ground, but it's no problem at all if you're building *up*. Your new soil mix and rock can be set on top of the ground. This means a little more work is necessary up front, but it actually makes construction of the rock garden easier and reduces back-end maintenance.

You can't control rainfall, but you can manage irrigation. Almost everywhere you live, gardens will need extra water at some point throughout the growing season. Water only when the garden needs it. Every garden has a few "miner's canary"–type plants that will warn you things are getting too dry by beginning to wilt. This is your sign that water should be given soon.

Water needs to reach the roots of your plants. It's better to water fewer times but longer, ensuring a good, deep soak, than it is to water frequently, but only so the top of the soil gets wet. The nicest time to water is early in the day when it is still cool outside for you and the plants. This has the added benefit of allowing foliage to dry before nightfall. If you can't water in the morning, anytime is fine but try to avoid the hottest part of the day.

Weeding

It's always been said that in the event of absolute nuclear disaster, cockroaches will be the only things to survive. That's only if they can find enough space to live among the weeds. Weeding is probably the most hated of all maintenance activities. Weeds must have been the model for the mythical Hydra, who grew two heads back for every one that got cut off by the champion, Hercules. Pull them and two more grow back in the place. Their seeds have almost mystical abilities to lie dormant for long periods of time and then spring to life with the briefest of showers.

To get rid of a single weed around a healthy plant, grab it near the crown with thumb and forefinger and pull it slowly but firmly out of the ground. This is called fingertip weeding.

What is a weed? A weed is a plant that is in a place you don't want it to be. Reread this definition.

In most cases, it's obvious what the weeds are. Dandelions, oxalis, crabgrass, and purslane are fairly recognizable bad guys. They're always in the wrong place, taking up valuable real estate that belongs to your "ornamental" plants.

But it's important to consider that there are plants you'd like to have in your garden that, finding the conditions to their liking, spread like wildfire. At first it's flattering; a sign of success. You may even brag to your friends about your prowess with the rare jewel you've acquired for your garden. Then reality hits. Your little gem begins swallowing its neighbors. It begins to move over your rock feature obliterating everything in its path. Then is the time to get ruthless.

Weeding a rock garden is not like weeding a regular flower garden. For starters, the rock garden is rarely flat and it's full of rocks. The footing, in other words, is less stable than in your perennial border. Many rock gardeners like to encourage the reproduction of their plants. This self-sowing, as long as it doesn't get out of hand, is a great way to increase your stock of desirable plants—and make the garden look more natural. But the little seedlings may be hard to distinguish from weed seedlings.

The general rule is "When in doubt, don't take it out." But "When you can name it, claim it." In other words, once you identify it as a weed, yank it.

When weeds get out of hand and begin to take over the garden, you often have to pull them out by the fistful.

Weeding must be done conscientiously. Don't wait, because two things will happen. One, the weed will grow. The top growth isn't much of a concern, but the roots keep going and can be a real bear to get out if they aren't removed early in life. Two, "Any weed that goes to seed does a nasty deed." If you let your weeds flower and seed, a single plant can create hundreds more. Rock gardens and their gritty soil are germination hotbeds. Many desirable plants will self-sow, but weeds have cornered the reproduction market in the garden.

When you weed, be sure to pull out the entire root system. Besides their fantastic ability to self-seed, many undesirable plants have the capacity to restart growth from a small bit of root left in the ground. To help get the whole thing, weed when the ground is soft, after a rain or watering. Grasp the weed right at ground level, between thumb and forefinger, and pull straight up.

The Right Stuff

Many chemical herbicides on the market promise quick and amazing results if you spray them on your garden. Most do a fine job killing plants. Some will kill the plants you want to keep. Even more will kill seedlings of the plants you want to keep. Most rock features are near dwellings. Why use chemicals around the house, kids, and pets, when you can take a cool drink outside and commune with nature as you weed? Besides, if you do spray, you're not going to leave little weed corpses in your rock features, are you? Of course not. Then how are you going to get rid of them? Pull them, of course. Knowing this, you may as well do it without the chemicals.

There's another benefit to weeding that may outweigh all the rest: It could very well be the most meditative act you'll do in the garden. It's relaxing, contemplative, mind-clearing, and stress-reducing. Weeding frees the creative mind and may actually result in increased productivity in your workaday world.

With thickly matted plants, you often have to gently pick up the edge of the mat and look underneath for any hidden weeds. If you find them, remove them by the roots.

In addition, you'll see things you've never seen before. You'll hear the fluttering of a butterfly's wings. Sitting among your plants, you'll experience the natural world from a completely different perspective and on a much different scale. There's a whole other world out there. Weed it.

Feeding

Most rock garden plants don't require much in the way of fertilizer. They've evolved to live in nutrient-poor environments. They don't like rich soil or constant feeding. If you overfertilize, the plants will become too lush, lose their natural form, and experience increased susceptibility to pests and disease. A light feeding with a water-soluble fertilizer in early spring is all you should need.

The Right Stuff

Fertilizers come with three numbers on the side of the bag, box, or other container, the "N-P-K" ratio. These numbers give you the ratio of nitrogen, phosphorous, and potassium contained in the product you are using. A "balanced" fertilizer has numbers that are the same, or nearly so, for each element. 10-10-10 is an example of a balanced fertilizer. These fertilizers are good for a wide variety of plants. Rock garden plants are not gross feeders. A light application of fertilizer low in nitrogen and higher in phosphorous is best. A dilute feeding of balanced fertilizer is acceptable as well. Organic, slow release fertilizers provide a light continuous feeding until they are used up. Apply in early spring and you won't need to worry about your rock plants the rest of the season. A word of warning: Pelletized fertilizers are often colored to show that you are getting good coverage when you apply them. The little blue or green pellets don't look so good on your gravel mulch and will distract visitors to your garden. To eliminate this problem, use fertilizers that are mixed with water and sprayed.

Many people who build plantable rock features quickly succumb to the lure of collecting choice plants. As a result, new additions are constantly being integrated into the garden, some needing special care. If you have plants with special feeding requirements, treat them individually. For example, some plants appreciate a more acidic soil. If you don't have a specialized area for these acid lovers, feed with a fertilizer specially made for plants like rhododendrons and azaleas. Plants that benefit from alkaline conditions can be satisfied with an occasional dusting of crushed limestone or agricultural lime. Bonemeal is a good fertilizer for plants that need additional nutrients, especially bulbs, while old rotted or dried commercial cow manure will profit plants that crave richer diets.

Plants such as this beautiful, flowering rhododendron need an acidic soil, so always feed with a fertilizer made especially for them.

Planting Quick Tip

Before starting your rock garden, have the composition of your soil tested to learn if it's naturally acidic or alkaline. It's not easy to change the acidity of your soil, and it's generally a temporary fix, since the soil will gradually go back to its natural condition. For the most maintenance-free garden, choose plants that prefer the conditions you have.

Constant feeding of the rock garden is never needed. Just be sure to know what your plants need and feed accordingly. In the event nutritional deficiencies manifest themselves (watch for discolored leaves and other problem areas;

if the cause isn't apparent, contact your local extension office to have a sample examined), you may have to adjust your feeding efforts.

Mulching

Mulching is another important technique for the health and beauty of your rock garden and can also make maintenance an easier task. There are several reasons to use mulch. From a physical standpoint, mulching helps to control weeds and keeps the soil cooler. Mulching also reduces the amount of water and mud that splash on plants during periods of heavy rain and can help reduce fungal problems. Perhaps most important, a collar of mulch helps keep excess moisture away from the crown of the plant, reducing the number of deaths by rotting. Aesthetically, mulch just looks good. It ties together and unifies your feature and its plantings, provides an attractive background for the plants, and sets off your stone elegantly.

There really aren't many decisions to make about mulching a rock feature. The only mulch that makes sense from an ecological and aesthetic standpoint is—surprise—stone. Gravel mulch accomplishes all the benefits of an organic mulch in the perennial garden. It wouldn't be wise to use a shredded bark or other organic mulch around rock because, first, it doesn't look natural; and second, it would hold too much moisture.

The gravel mulch in front of these plantings has washed away and should be replaced.

Here, washed-away mulch has been replenished with a generous supply of gravel, which looks better and is good for the plants.

Your initial mulching happened back when you built and planted your feature. It was among the finishing touches to the initial project.

You might think an advantage to using gravel as a mulch is because it doesn't break down as bark does. Don't be fooled. Although gravel doesn't break down, it disappears. Ground swallows gravel, and you will periodically have to top up the garden. This can be done at any time of year.

Pruning and Deadheading

Pruning your plants serves three purposes. First, it is the accepted method for ridding your dwarf trees and shrubs of dead or diseased branches. In addition, it enables you to shape your miniature trees and shrubs. Sometimes a little judicious nipping of a wayward branch makes all the difference in the world. Finally, pruning allows some control over the size or speed of growth of woody plants.

In formal gardens, plants are often heavily pruned to maintain geometric or fanciful topiary shapes. This is one of the most high-maintenance jobs in the garden. In a natural setting, pruning is more a matter of preventing plants from spreading into others or keeping them in scale with the rest of the garden.

Pruning for size control and rejuvenation is also helpful for perennial plantings. Some successful inhabitants of your feature may begin to cover all the rock or each other. You can bring these overachievers back into line by cutting them back. Uncontrolled growth of some specimens will make them thin and stringy. Pruning encourages the plant to branch and thicken, further beautifying your feature.

Mat formers and groundcovers occasionally need pruning to keep them from spreading, but generally rock garden plants are small to begin with, not usually much of a problem on the pruning front.

Some plants finish flowering and drop their old flowers cleanly, leaving the plant in a reasonably good-looking condition. Others are the ugly ducklings of the rock feature. They hang on for dear life to their old, decrepit flower, a tattered, pathetic reminder of their glory days. *Deadheading* encourages a second bloom. Keep in mind that if you deadhead, you will eliminate the opportunity to get seed from the plant or have it self-sow.

Backyard Lingo

Deadheading is the act of taking off the old flowers to clean off the plants and sometimes encourage a second boom.

The bloom in the foreground of this 'Melon Ball' is perfect; the bud to the left will soon be in flower, but the bloom in the background his withered. It should be removed immediately by deadheading, pinching it off just below the flower line.

Pests

Rock garden plants have a pretty good track record when it comes to pests. Fewer pests seem to invade this specialized garden. The healthier you maintain your plants, the less susceptible they will be to pests and disease. Most pest and disease problems can be reduced or eliminated with good cultural practices.

Although the record is good, most plants for the rock garden are small and don't require the level of infestation a large plant would before showing symptoms of a problem and being negatively affected. One of the most annoying pests to invade the garden is the slug. Slugs are homeless snails, slimy mollusks with no shell. They normally emerge at night and love to chew tender stems and foliage. They have an unerring eye for choice, expensive plants. These destructive pests are especially bothersome in wet, humid weather. Slugs are somewhat controlled by mulching with a gravel mix and keeping the ground free of dead leaves and debris, places where they like to hide.

There are commercial baits and pesticides and a whole raft of homemade remedies that may seem strange at first glance. But they work. Gardeners have found they can trap slugs by using lettuce leaves or slices of raw potatoes as bait. The slugs will gather on the bait overnight and in the morning can be disposed of easily. Just pick up the bait and the slugs and drop them in water or kerosene.

Pesticide Quick Tip

This one will sound strange to those who haven't heard it before. Another trick to rid your garden of slugs is to put out small containers of stale beer. Slugs are attracted to the beverage and will crawl into the saucers and drown. For those teetotalers among you, saucers of grape juice will give you the same result.

Aphids are plant-sucking insects of the highest order. They don't need to have sex to reproduce, so one is all you need as evidence of a problem. The easiest means of controlling them is to blast them off your plants with a hose. On little plants this may be a problem. A few drops of dish soap in a quart of water can be put into a sprayer. Spray this on any soft-bodied insect to mess up its waxy coating.

Aphids have invaded this quince big time. Look at them on the upper portion of the stem and leaves. You must always watch for and rid your plants of this pest.

These and many other pests are in the garden all the time. They are a part of nature. You will never eliminate them from your yard. Controlling their numbers is the name of the game.

Seasonal Care

Seasonal care is most important in climates that have cold winters. This is easier for rock features than for perennial gardens. At the end of the growing season, when the leaves are off the trees, it's a good idea to clean up your rock features. Leaves left on them will trap moisture near the plants creating problems. Carefully sweep the garden off or blow with a power blower.

However, the main enemy in winter is the wind. Plants that remain green for the winter season are exposed to cold, drying winds at a time when roots are not doing what they normally do, providing water to the rest of the plant. As a result, these plants can be windburned. Snow can be a great insulator. Many rock garden plants have evolved to take advantage of the usually reliable snow cover of their mountain homes. When grown in areas without reliable snow cover, they lose the insulating value of this blanket.

The buds of this *Pieris japonica* are set in the fall and can withstand a winter of heavy snow.

To handle both of these problems, you can cover plants in your rock features in the winter. The simplest way to do this is with pine boughs. Scattering the boughs over your plants cuts the winter wind, and the needles trap whatever snow is available, keeping it in place longer. This is a great use for Christmas trees that wind up at the curb after the holiday—which is about the right time to do the job in most places.

In spring, you have some restoration work to do. These steps will help get your garden ready for another season:

1. In early to mid-March, remove the coverings you put in the garden for winter protection. Yes, there is winter weather yet to come, but many rock garden plants are early bloomers, and you'll miss them if they're flowering away under your pine branches.

2. Next remove any debris that may have gathered from winter storms such as leaves, twigs, and small branches.

3. Once the garden is clear, check the lay of the land and restore any spots that have eroded or lost their gravel mulch from heavy rain or melting snow.

A Word of Warning

More plants are killed by the freeze-thaw cycles of spring than by the winter cold. Cold, wet springs are part of life in temperate climates, and there's not a lot that can be done about it. Your winter coverings won't help, and the only way to give your plants any assistance at all through this time is to make sure that they get their collar of gravel to lift their mats, buns, etc. off the ground when they are planted.

4. Check your plants for winter damage. Prune any dead stems or tips of branches.

5. Reset any plants that have been disturbed by the winter heaving. Do this by pressing them back into the ground and replacing their gravel mulch.

6. Then start the maintenance cycle all over again.

Maintenance Quick Tip

Maintenance of plants in rock features and rock gardens is not difficult. Spend a little time each week, and the job is done. It takes less time than most people spend cutting and caring for their lawn. It's important to be consistent in your basic maintenance routine. If you neglect your chores even a few weeks, you'll find your garden inundated by weeds.

Rocks Need Care, Too

Rocks obviously aren't as fragile as plants. By now you know the effort it takes to gather, move, and place rocks. You may have vowed never to do it again—at least until you got some rest. During that rest, however, it's important to keep an eye on your rock features to watch for changes that may signal potential problems.

If you've done the job right, your stones will set snug and solid for a long time. Even the best-laid stone, however, can be affected by shifting and settling. Most often rocks move because of improper placement, but movement of the ground, undermining, and frost heaving can also be culprits. Movement or shifting of rock can change the look of your feature but can also be a safety hazard. When you're out looking at the flowers in your feature, be sure to look past them for a second to see if the stone is in good shape. Changes will most often be visible after major rains or in spring after the ravages of winter. Make a practice of including a closer look in your spring maintenance, because any change will be more noticeable when the plants are still dormant.

Shifting and Settling

Shifting and settling of your rocks needs to be addressed with an adjustment of the affected stones. This is especially critical with walls where movement of the rocks has the potential to cause a collapse.

Regardless of the feature, remedial action is called for if the rocks shift. In most cases you can manually lift the out-of-whack rock (without completely removing it). You can wedge small stones underneath to support the rock at the proper angle or put extra soil underneath to restore it to its original position and reset the rock.

Shifting rock in a rock garden doesn't pose the same kind of safety problem as in compromised functional features like walls, steps, and paths, but loose rock anywhere is not good. Shifting and settling in the rock garden will impact your plantings and the overall integrity of the feature.

Be just as careful adjusting and moving rock as you were when you first built with it. It poses no less danger now than it did before, and oftentimes, particularly when working in your feature, your footing will be tricky. On rare occasions, rock will move so much that it is advisable to dismantle all or a portion of your feature and rebuild. Think of it as an opportunity, not a chore. You've got a chance to do something special.

This large rock has shifted during the winter and is being reset in the spring with the help of a pry-bar. This is something that must be done in many rock gardens from time to time.

Bad Rock

We've already mentioned that a tippy rock is a bad rock, but it's not the only kind you should avoid. Rock that cracks and breaks easily may not be appropriate for certain features. Stones that crack, chip easily, or break can be a hazard on paths and steps.

And then there are aesthetic problems. Sometimes you'll stand back, look at your rock garden or stone wall, and one rock will catch your eye. It just doesn't seem to fit and stands out like the proverbial sore thumb. It may be its color, shape, or size, but it has to go. Every rock should match well, complement each other, and give the garden a natural look. Each should be placed in relation to the others. All of us, to one extent or another, have an instinctive eye for what looks right.

Maintenance Quick Tip

Concrete-created rocks can crack even more easily than slabs in your driveway or sidewalk. If a faux-stone falls apart, whether it's in a rock garden or used to make a path or stairway, don't fool around. Replace it immediately.

This dry-stone wall is full of bad rock. The wall is unstable, the color and type rock doesn't mesh, and the stones are not set in the proper proportion. It's a classic example of a badly constructed wall.

Most stone will stand the test of time and remain in place for hundreds of years. On occasion you will find a bad one. You'll know it when you see it, and when you do, it's time for a change.

Replacing Rock in Difficult Places

Most rock replacement is relatively easy. A single stepping-stone, one or two rocks in a border configuration, or rocks in the garden present no real problems. Sometimes, however, you'll be caught between a rock and a hard place. Broken or unstable rock in the middle of a 4-foot wall may require taking out far more than the offending stone.

This wall is all wrong and should be rebuilt. The crevices are too wide and in line, and the stone is unstable. Besides, it just doesn't look good.

When the job is too big, you may have to call in a professional, someone with a machine to lift the rock out and replace it. Don't try to remove any rock that's in a place where your footing or the lifting involved will be dangerous. Safety always comes first—don't take any chances.

Well-constructed rock features and gardens will last your lifetime and beyond with a minimum of maintenance. But if a problem does occur, you will now be ready to deal with it.

The Least You Need to Know

- Keeping your plants healthy doesn't take a whole lot of work and is worth the effort.
- Always know the soil and water requirements for the different plants you put in your rock garden.
- Weeding a rock garden must be done often and consistently, while mulching and feeding take far less time.
- Pests are not a major problem in the rock garden, but those who arrive must be made to leave.
- Rock features also need maintenance, especially when rocks shift, heave, crack, or break.

In This Part

Building and Maintaining Water Features

Although many of the same rules for planning and installing water features mirror those for rock features, there are also some significant differences. Artificial ponds, waterfalls, and streams require careful construction and, in most cases, the use of an artificial liner to keep the water from draining out.

In most cases, water features also require an electrical source to run the pumps and filters that will help keep the water clean and healthy, as well as giving it movement. The use of plants, in and around a pond or waterfall, help bring it to life while making it look as if it was carved by nature. Water features need more seasonal maintenance than rock features. There are certain procedures that need to be done before winter and in the spring, but a healthy, well-constructed feature should be with you for many years.

In This Chapter

- ◆ Choosing a feature and deciding where to put it
- ◆ Considering size and movement
- ◆ Making it look good
- ◆ Thinking about plants and fish
- ◆ Deciding if you need a pro

This breathtaking waterfall appears to have been completely carved out by nature. On the contrary, it is manmade and shows the exquisite work of a professional designer.

Chapter 9

Planning and Preparation for Water Features

In Chapter 3, we introduced you briefly to the joys of having a water feature in your yard. Now we begin the journey that will make the dream a reality. You have many choices. Depending on the size of your yard—and also your pocketbook—you can have anything from a small container water garden or burbler to a fish-filled water garden or a complex and beautiful backyard waterfall.

The sound of water running over rocks has been described as one of nature's most enchanting and soothing symphonies. Even the smallest yard can experience this sensation. Simply decide what type of feature you want and where you want to put it so that it fits your yard and overall landscaping theme. This chapter will tell you how to begin the process.

Things to Consider If You Want a Water Feature

Every size and type of yard can house a water feature. Even if your yard is just a flat mat of grass, you can change its dynamic with the addition of water. If you already have a garden— no matter what kind it is—water becomes an even more attractive addition to the landscape.

First you need to make an evaluation similar to the one for rock features.

◆ Examine the overall look of your house and yard.
◆ Consider the size and topography of your property.

This large, tranquil pond is a great feature, but you need a very large yard to make it work. Always be mindful of your scale.

◆ Be aware of how your yard is used regularly.

◆ Know the amount of money you are willing to spend.

◆ Think about the time you want to put into the construction and maintenance if you plan to do it yourself.

All these things will make a difference as to what you should and shouldn't do, so consider each point very carefully.

Which Feature Best Fits Your Landscape?

Water features and water gardens have become increasingly popular in recent years, prompting more people than ever to consider adding them to their yards. No matter how you do it, the addition of water to your yard creates a focal point and will dominate the overall design scheme. More important, it is something you can enjoy every day.

Water Feature Quick Tip

People have always used their backyards as a place to relax, and the addition of a water feature adds an extra dimension. Whether it's the soothing sound of a small burbler on the patio, the spray from a fountain in the backyard pond, or the constant sound of water flowing over the rocks of a backyard waterfall, water features provide a way to escape the stresses of the workaday world, furnishing you with a refreshing oasis that is never more than a few feet away.

When thinking about the best type of water feature to fit your landscape, start by asking the following questions:

◆ Are you a gardener? Do you already have one or more gardens in your yard?

◆ Do you enjoy having various forms of wildlife coming into your yard?

◆ Do you normally spend a lot of free time relaxing in your yard?

◆ Is the bulk of your yard used for recreational activities by you or your children?

◆ Is your idea of a water feature a swimming pool?

Let's take the last question first. If you want to put a family swimming pool in your yard, you may not have the inclination to add a second major water feature. The swimming pool will be your focal point, and a high maintenance one at that.

Gardens are another matter. If you already have one, the addition of a water feature is a natural enhancement to the existing ambiance. Whether it's a small stream running through the rock garden, a reflecting pool surrounded by formal flower gardens, a trickle of water spouting into a trough of Water Lilies, or a simple bowl-style birdbath, your garden will suddenly take on new significance. Adding water brings a garden alive in new and exciting ways.

Use your imagination for your water feature. This gardener set pre-formed liners on top of the ground, surrounded them with rocks, then added plants to the water.

How do you feel about wildlife? There's no escaping the fact that most water features will attract wildlife. The sound, movement, and thirst-quenching attributes of water are irresistible to our animal neighbors. Not long after it's installed, your water feature will draw a wide variety of amphibians, birds, mammals, and insects to its surroundings. You'll see critters where you saw none before. If you find this exciting and interesting, then a feature such as a pond or waterfall is for you. If you view this kind of wildlife as something you would rather avoid, then you may want to reconsider your decision to incorporate water in the garden, or opt for a feature with less appeal, such as a small recirculating burbler.

Water features can be simple and safe. This natural rock has been drilled out to house a very basic birdbath, yet it still has character.

You should also consider young children and family pets. If your yard is often populated with them, you might avoid the larger, deeper features in favor of those that will not create more problems than enjoyment. Finally, if you just don't do the backyard thing and prefer a quick mow and a cold drink in front of the TV, then stick to a birdbath.

Water Feature Quick Tip

As suggested in the section on rock features, consider the style of your house and yard when adding any new feature. If you have a formal home with formal gardens and rock features, then a formal pool makes a better addition than one with a natural look.

In the end, be sure to take careful stock of your existing yard and your situation before you decide to add a water feature. Once you decide to proceed, be sure to add the kind of feature that will best suit your needs and your lifestyle. Don't bite off more than you can chew or more than you really want to deal with.

Location, Location, Location

Plan the location of any water feature very carefully before you dig the first shovelful of earth to begin construction. Although a well-constructed pond, stream, or waterfall can be a beautiful focal point, if it's placed in the wrong spot, your yard will lose much of its intended character and appeal.

This huge aerator in a large pond provides not only oxygen for the fish but also an impressive visual and constant sound for one to watch and enjoy.

A huge part of the pleasure of a pond or a waterfall is the sights and sounds of the fluid environment you've created. It's always a good idea to locate a good-size water feature close enough to comfortable viewing areas like a terrace or patio, so that the water's surface, reflections, and sound are accessible. Your efforts may be wasted if it's tucked away in the corner of a yard and difficult to see.

Water Feature Quick Tip

Reflections are not the most obvious of benefits to consider when installing a water feature. However, water is like a mirror and reflects the sky and the clouds, flowers and trees, and people. Who can forget the story of Narcissus peering at his reflection in the water and the punishment the gods meted out for his vanity? He was turned into a flower—hence, *Narcissus,* our daffodil.

Believe it or not, the plants and trees depicted here are all reflections. The photo is of the water. Any water feature becomes more special because of the many reflections it can produce.

If you must build away from your preferred viewing area because of other restraints, consider constructing a small sitting area nearby the new feature so that you can enjoy it. Small features in out-of-the-way locations can function as an element of surprise and delight.

Location is also important if you plan to grow water plants in and around your pond. Most water plants grow more robustly and only bloom profusely if they receive the required amount of sunlight. Water Lilies, one of the most popular of pond plants, need at least 4 hours of direct sunlight per day. Some flowering water plants need even more. If you put the pond in a location where it is shaded by trees or your home, it may be difficult to keep such plants happy.

Small features, such as the container water gardens, can be placed close to your home on a deck or patio. However, in many ways they are similar to larger features. If you plant them and locate them near the house, be sure the plants will receive enough light.

A Word of Warning

If you decide to add fish to your pond, you should not only check the location for sunlight but also for the presence of deciduous trees. Leaves and other debris can fall into the pond, sink to the bottom, and rot. Thus, water quality becomes even more important if you're putting animals into the mix.

To test a location for sunlight, pick your spot and outline the proposed feature with a rope or garden hose. Leave the outline in place for a few days and watch the area so that you can determine how many hours of sunlight the location receives. Doing this as a preliminary stage will also give you time to reconsider the size and shape before you start the actual work. While you're at it, note the amount of traffic around your outline and whether the place you've chosen is easily seen from popular locations around the home and yard. If it's not the perfect spot, moving it only a matter of a few feet in one direction or another could make all the difference.

Do You Have Time for Maintenance?

Be forewarned, you cannot install water features and leave them to their own devices. If your interest is solely in having a low-maintenance yard, think twice about water. Many people underestimate the amount of aftercare needed for a water feature. The right location and proper installation can certainly reduce the amount of work keeping a water feature clean, handling the change of seasons, and providing a healthy environment for plants and fish.

Water runs over the top of this clay pot and back into a formal pool in another example of a simple but effective water feature.

The amount of work required varies. Small features like container gardens and barrel waterfalls don't require much time once they're set up. Ponds are another story, especially if they are planted and include fish. To keep a live stock of fish in your pond, you must maintain a balanced ecosystem for both plants and fish to thrive. Water needs to be kept fresh and clean, liners checked, filters and skimmers cleaned regularly. None of the work is difficult, but you just need to do it.

If you live in a climate where the seasons change, there are chores you must do in the fall and then again in the spring. These will be discussed in detail in Chapter 13.

The more complex the feature is (plants and fish), the more you have to learn about its care. If you don't feel you have this kind of time, then stick to the small stuff. But if you enjoy working in the yard and are willing to maintain a pond or waterfall, your efforts will be rewarded.

Water Feature Quick Tip

Have a goal in mind before you start. A wildlife pond is a very different thing than a formal reflecting pool. A waterfall is different than a birdbath. This seems very obvious, but the preparation, equipment, materials, and construction of these features vary widely depending on your final goal.

What Will It Cost?

The cost of water features, like the expenses of any hobby, can vary greatly. If someone gives you an old wooden barrel, you can set up a basic water garden for almost nothing. You might want a small pump to make a burbler or a small recirculating fountain. As the features become larger and more complex, the cost rises, and the sky's the limit. Professionally installed ponds and waterfalls can cost many thousands of dollars. Where space and budget allow the expenditure, however, the results can be fantastic.

There's a whole gradation in between, so you must decide on how much you want to spend. If you do the work yourself where you can, you'll save one third to half the cost and maybe more. Also, do not forget the value of your time. If you do a project carefully once, investing the necessary time to do it right, it

will pay off. Do it fast and not only may there be mistakes, but your expense in time and money will take a big jump as well.

Building Quick Tip

If you want to build your own water feature from scratch, look at similar features, read about the ways to construct them, and get all your materials ahead of time. Just as with building rock features, this extra knowledge will pay big dividends. Get the help you need to make the job easier, ensuring that you will do it right the first time.

Small or Large, Standing or Moving

The size of your feature, as with the rock constructions discussed earlier, is relative to the size of your yard. A huge pond or waterfall in a small yard won't work. It will overpower the yard and likely be in the way of other activities. Conversely, a tiny pond or fountain in a large yard will look like the proverbial drop in the bucket.

Existing features in your yard may also play a part in your deliberations. Make a careful note of what is already established, keep the scale of the existing features consistent with the new, and don't overcrowd your yard.

Keeping It Simple

The simplest water features are containers that do no more than hold water. Rocks with depressions that held rainwater were the first water features and are still useful today. Incorporating these "depressed" stones in your rock features will bring birds and other animals into the garden and provide an interesting addition to your plants.

Birdbaths are probably the most familiar simple water features. Build one and they will come. Large glazed pots, bowls, and tubs also function as holders of water. These can be planted as water gardens and can hold a few goldfish, whose habit of breathing at the top of the water helps them survive in conditions where there is not a lot of oxygen in the water. (They help keep the mosquito population in check, too.)

This carved stone water feature even houses a couple fish. Again, it's simple but effective.

Movement in water creates a number of dramatic effects and contributes something for nearly all the senses. The sound of water moving over the rocks or splashing into a pool is magical and has restorative properties. The continuous cascade of a waterfall, the ripples created by an aerator or burbler, and the spray of a fountain delight the eye. Dipping a hand into a rushing stream or feeling the mist of a fountain cools the skin and eases the mind.

Ponds and Containers

Many people want a completely natural pond, without all the pumps, filters, and electricity that others employ. The challenge in this situation is to create a balanced ecosystem, one that maintains itself. In this kind of pond the water will not "move" in the sense of being pumped or recirculated. To keep the nonmoving pond "alive" there must be a delicate balance of plants and wildlife. This balance needs to be geared to oxygenate the water, prevent overgrowth of algae, and keep the pond relatively clean. We will give you additional details on how to do this later. It takes knowledge and constant monitoring to keep the pond from becoming stagnant and polluted, a place where virtually nothing can survive.

A Word of Warning

Natural ponds are generally not pristine expanses of water surrounded by beautiful plants. They are the water equivalent of a wild-flower meadow, as compared to a manicured lawn. They will not look crystal clear. There's just too much going on, yet this is one of the attractions of such a feature. Crystal-clear water, at least some of the time, is achievable, but getting it requires continuous filtration.

Container features are usually small enough to work, with or without movement. Water can be easily changed if it becomes dirty. Keep in mind that any standing water can be a breeding ground for mosquitoes, which can become pests and carry a number of diseases, like West Nile virus. Even the smallest containers, however, with the attachment of a small recirculating pump, can keep the water moving, heightening the sensory experience of your feature and eliminating the problems of stagnant water at the same time.

Ponds stocked with fish, particularly koi, almost always require the use of a filtering system, if only to see them. Nothing's more frustrating than committing to a koi pond, investing in the fish, and then not being able to follow their graceful movements and observe their activities. A good system keeps the pond clean and the fish healthy.

In a healthy, balanced pond, a school of goldfish swim happily amid the proper selection of plants.

Fountains, Streams, and Waterfalls

If you mention moving water, most people think of fountains, waterfalls, and streams. These projects are usually larger than the small ones we've just discussed and feature moving water. The enjoyment and relaxation derived from the sight, sound, and movement these features provide is the main reason for their growing popularity.

This small, formal fountain is all ready to find a home in someone's yard. Once hooked up, water will spray out the center and run over the carved stone back into the pool.

The larger the feature, the more costly it will be to construct and maintain. Consider your plans carefully. Mistakes are not as easy to fix as with the other features we've talked about. Plan carefully and with the knowledge that whatever you can create on a large scale can be created on a smaller one. Small features may not be as dynamic as larger ones, but you'll still derive the same benefits, both sensory and psychological.

Waterfall Quick Tip

There are a number of ways to achieve variation in the sound of moving water. If the water spills over a single overhanging rock and falls several feet into a pool, it makes a different sound than if it tumbles slowly over a series of rocks. If sound is important to you, consider it in your planning to ensure that every sense is involved.

Small water features can be made with almost anything. Enterprising people with limited funds have created features from old stone urns, wooden washtubs, shallow metal bowls, the cut-off ends of barrels, and discarded boiler tanks. In-ground pools can even be fashioned from old bathtubs. Just think before you sink.

Plants and Fish—More to Think About

Water and plants go together in much the same way as rocks and plants. The two elements complement each other beautifully, bringing out the best in each other. Adding koi or goldfish to a planted water garden completes the picture, giving you a small ecosystem in your own backyard. But the addition of both plants and fish takes—you guessed it— a little planning and forethought. All three (water, plants, and fish) must be considered in relation to one another.

Many kinds of plants thrive in a watery situation. While they are different from those you'd use in a rock feature, they are equally beautiful and can be as dramatic. Water plants fit into a few general categories, each with its own characteristics.

- ◆ **Below-surface plants.** These plants are known as oxygenators. Providing oxygen to the water is their prime function. They may not be the most attractive of the bunch, but they perform a necessary service for the other plants and animals in your feature. Oxygenators can be rapid growers, easy to propagate. Sometimes they grow so fast you'll need to thin them out to keep them in check.

- ◆ **Floating plants.** This class of plants floats on the surface of the water with their roots dangling beneath the surface but not attaching to the bottom. Some floaters are extremely attractive, but be careful not to allow them to cover too much of the water's surface because they may keep light from reaching those plants below.

- ◆ **Deep-water plants.** These plants have their roots in the bottom of the pond and their leaves and flowers floating on the surface. Many of these plants have large round or oval leaves and very attractive, aromatic flowers.

This hardy Water Lily features a beautifully patterned leaf, which adds even more character to a pond or pool.

- ◆ **Marginal and bog plants.** Marginal plants are located around the edges in shallow water. Because of their location, they are easily viewed. They have many different-shape leaves and flowers of many forms and colors. Bog plants grow in moist soil and are often planted near ponds and pools, or in specially created bog gardens.

By mixing the classes of plants discussed here, you can have a beautiful garden in and around your pond, a colorful extravaganza that carries your garden into the water.

Goldfish, koi, Golden Orfe, and Rudd are four types of popular pond fish. If you decide to add any of them, be sure to learn as much about their lifestyles as you can before you go ahead. It's even more important to maintain balanced, healthy conditions in the pond when you in-clude fish. That usually means adding a pump and a filter to help keep the water clean, so your design will be a little different and the cost a little higher.

The Right Stuff

Water gardens, like all others, are complex living habitats. Like the others, each can be compromised if one organism exploits the setting at the expense of the others. For example, if one type of plant crowds the others or blocks out too much light, the pond will become unbalanced. The same thing happens if algae get out of hand. It's important to keep a balance between the number of plants on the surface of the pond and the amount of open water. This is necessary for both keeping a visual balance and allowing enough light to penetrate the surface of the water for the plants and animals below. Too many plants on the surface result in other plants dying from lack of light and nutrients. The ensuing rot of dead plants pollutes the water and knocks the pond out of balance. In most ponds, planting should not take up more than a third of the open water, or the pond will begin to have an overcrowded appearance.

Two beautiful koi frolic among the water lilies in another ecologically balanced backyard pond. Notice the bloom coming out of one of the lilies.

Before making a decision, you must know the characteristics of each kind of fish, their needs and habits. You must know how and when to feed them, whether they nibble on your plants, how to maintain their home, what to do for the change of seasons and over winter in colder climates. Know the growth habits of your fish and the carrying capacity of your feature so you don't overcrowd your animals.

A Word of Warning

Make a note of the mature size of the fish you want to include. As a rule of thumb, give them the largest home that you can. Goldfish can grow to 6 to 10 inches. Koi can grow to 18 inches, and some specimens have been known to grow to 5 feet. That won't happen in your pond, but you can still have some large and beautiful fish and should not overcrowd them.

As with plants, fish beautify your pond and make it a more interesting place. They are the final challenge after building your pond and adding plants.

Should I Call for a Pro?

Any time you feel uncomfortable about the planning or construction of your feature, call a pro. Large, complex features on large pieces of property should be professionally installed. These exotic water features can be extremely beautiful, eye-catching, and quite costly. If you work with a professional to design and install them, the worries are his, not yours. There is sure to be a reputable company specializing in these features somewhere near you. The basic design and layout is still for you to decide, but always listen to the suggestions of the professional. He has done this before and knows what will look best in your yard.

Smaller features are easier to do yourself. Doing it with your own sweat and toil gives you the satisfaction that you have accomplished something for yourself, your family, and your friends to enjoy for many years. If you are certain you can build it, go for it!

If you begin a job and find that it is beyond your capabilities, don't be afraid to call the pros for help. They will either show you what you are doing wrong and how to fix it or take over and finish the job for you. If you're stuck, don't hesitate. You'll be glad you made the call.

The Least You Need to Know

◆ Before deciding to install a water feature, consider your home, yard, and lifestyle.

◆ Water features stocked with plants and fish require constant maintenance for a balanced, living ecosystem.

◆ Almost any kind of water feature can be built in miniature.

◆ A wide variety of water plants is available to enhance and balance a water garden.

◆ The addition of fish represents another level of commitment and should not be taken lightly.

In This Chapter

- ◆ Working with electricity in your yard
- ◆ Safety and building codes
- ◆ The right equipment for the job
- ◆ The workings of pumps and filters
- ◆ Basic installations

This above-ground tub garden is fully planted and requires electricity
to run a small pump and fountain.

Chapter **10**

Pumps, Filters, and Electricity

We often put rock and water features in our yards to look timeless and natural, but our enjoyment of them sometimes requires that the modern world intrude. Electricity, a natural force to be sure but one that we have tamed and bent to our own purposes, is often employed to power pumps and filters for features with running water. In addition, our hectic lifestyles often leave us little time during the daylight hours to enjoy our surroundings. Artificial lighting stretches the day, allowing us additional hours to relax with family and friends in the welcoming environment of the yard.

This chapter explores these finishing-touch additions. As you decide upon the rock or water features you want, consider the use of electricity, pumps, and filters. You'll need to know about the safe use of electricity and how to make decisions about the right size and types of equipment. Finally, the chapter will discuss several basic installations to give you an idea about how these additions can enhance your rock and water features.

Electricity in the Yard

Electricity can be added to existing features, but it's a good idea to include it at the beginning, when you are planning the additions to your yard. Like surgery, the addition of an underground line and its connections is an invasive procedure and one that must be done correctly, conforming to all local building and safety codes in your area.

Unless you are lucky enough to have a natural stream, any feature with moving water will require electricity. Streams, fountains, waterfalls, even small recirculating features need to have pumps to move water, and electricity is the power source of choice.

Ponds, especially those with fish, may also require electricity. Far from being bodies of standing water, ponds need to be balanced to remain healthy and for the fish to survive. Often this is achieved using pumps, filters, skimmers, and aerators, all of which are powered by electricity.

Lighting is always an option in the yard as well. Adding well-spaced lights along paths or to highlight features is not only attractive, but also helps make the yard safer for after-dark activities.

Electricity Quick Tip

Rock and water features should be lit subtly. Hide fixtures among rocks and plants, and be sure they are of a color that blends into the surroundings so that they don't stick out and divert attention from the feature. You can light ponds from within with special underwater fixtures.

This small stone water feature has a submerged light, which does a subtle job of further beautifying the feature.

Safety First

Electricity can be dangerous. If not handled appropriately, it can become an unruly monster, biting you hard when you least expect it. Always be sure to turn off the power at its source before doing any electrical work in your yard.

Electricity Quick Tip

Never get cheap or lazy with electricity. Running an inexpensive extension cord over the ground to your appliances is not a smart move—and probably violates your local code. It's dangerous to do any kind of garden maintenance around such a setup—as it's all too easy to slice through the line. Don't cut costs or labor. Do it right.

There is much more to adding electricity to your rock or water feature than running an extension cord from the house or garage. Extension cords running along the top of the ground are a recipe for disaster. Electricity in the yard means a trenched cable, installed in accordance with local building and/or electrical codes.

In addition to burying your cable, make sure that your power source contains a ground fault interrupter. This is especially important around water features. If any kind of fault or surge occurs, the interrupter cuts the power instantly, preventing damage to your equipment and reducing the possibility of serious electrical shock.

Here is a general list of safety measures to take when working with electricity in the backyard. Pay close attention to each of the following:

◆ **Call before you dig!** Always call Digger's Hotline before you do any new digging. This free service will come out and mark any existing underground power lines. Ask if cable television and gas lines are marked. If not, contact these utilities. They all provide this service, and the last thing they want is for you to interrupt service or injure yourself.

◆ Don't use electrical appliances or extension cords around water features. Electrical equipment for use in water features is specially constructed for this wet environment; other tools are not.

◆ If you must use an extension cord outdoors, be sure the cord is designed for outdoor use. Never use a lightweight cord that is intended for indoor use only.

◆ Don't work with electrical tools or appliances when the lawn is damp or wet.

◆ Always exercise caution when using cutting tools, lawn mowers, or any other tools or machinery around your power source or outlet.

◆ If you bring in a contractor to work in your yard, make sure that he contacts all appropriate utilities to have cables, pipes, etc. marked before the project commences.

Handling Electricity

The basic rule of thumb for working with electricity in the backyard is: If you aren't totally sure how to do it, call a qualified electrician! If you're confident of your ability to work with electric power safely and according to code, wiring your own feature is possible.

The Right Stuff

A new electrical line for power in the yard must start at a junction or breaker box, usually located in the basement or garage. At some point, the cable must leave the house and run in a deep trench to the spot where the outlet will be set. Try to plan the shortest route to the spot where you want the power outlet. This isn't always possible because of immovable obstructions, but keep it as simple and straightforward as you can. Find a logical place for the cable to pass from an opening in the house to the outside, before going underground. You may have to drill a hole in a wall or near the foundation. Be sure there are no other wires or pipes in the area. Try to make the exit hole in a place where the cable has a straight run to its destination and bring your trench right up to the house. Any portion of cable that is exposed must be enclosed in metal conduit. This prevents accidental cutting or puncturing of the electric line. There should never be exposed cable outside the house.

If you are moving power outside for the first time, add a separate circuit to your main junction box. First, make sure there is space for this new circuit. If you are not sure that this is possible or don't know how to wire it, call in a licensed electrician. Even if you complete the installation yourself, consider having an electrician test it before putting it into service.

A Word of Warning

Whenever you work with electricity in any capacity, be sure to turn off the power. This is especially true when installing a new circuit or running cable. Never work with live wires under any circumstance. If the power is turned off, you are protected from accidental shock.

Local Building Codes

Never begin a project involving electricity without knowing all the laws and regulations that apply to your particular installation. Follow them carefully and never take shortcuts. Local building codes may require a permit and/or inspection(s) before completing an installation.

If you run an underground cable, you must be sure to obtain wire that is made specifically for underground use. You need to know the required depth for the cable. Make sure your trench is dug to specification. If you are not sure about your local building codes, call your town hall or building inspector. A licensed electrician may be able to expedite matters.

A Word of Warning

Follow the codes. One of the most dangerous things you can do when installing an underground electrical cable is to dig a shallow trench. Putting cable just under the grass creates potential danger. Accidentally severing the cable could result in severe electrical shock. Dig deep enough to satisfy the inspectors. There's always a good reason to follow building codes.

The End Result

Once you have installed electricity in the yard and have made sure the installation is up to code and has been inspected, you can add light or movement to your rock and water features.

We introduced you to some of the options available for lighting in Chapter 4. They enable you to light paths, gardens, patios, and water and rock features for safety and viewing enjoyment. Now you can also run the pumps that will help keep your pond clean, your waterfall flowing, and your fountain spouting.

Electricity Quick Tip

Electricity is one area of backyard construction that clearly benefits from the know-how of an expert. Unless you are absolutely certain that your installation has been done correctly, call a licensed electrician and have the work inspected by a professional after you complete it. Better yet, have him do the work and eliminate all questions.

The Right Filter

A purist may seek to avoid mechanical additions to his pond, trusting in nature to keep it clean. This may be a noble ambition, but it's not easy to keep a pond healthy without the help of pumps, filters, and skimmers, unless you can create a balanced ecosystem. In most cases, if you're putting a water feature in your backyard— a pond, a waterfall, even a small stream—you should consider the use of a filter. If you add fish, the filter is even more necessary.

A filter can serve several purposes. It traps floating matter on the surface of the water, including fish waste and leftover food, floating algae and decaying organic matter, such as grass and leaves. Some filters remove ammonia and other toxic chemicals from the water. If the water quality in your pond is good, it will go a long way to making the entire experience a positive one.

There are two basic types of filters. Learn the characteristics of each type to help you make the right decision.

Mechanical Filters

Mechanical filters are very basic. They remove particles from the water by trapping them in filter pads or a similar medium. Most small ponds use an in-pond, cartridge-type mechanical filter. The effectiveness of the mechanical filter depends on its size and your water's flow rate.

Filtering Quick Tip _____

To maximize the effectiveness of a mechanical filter, make sure your pump can circulate the entire water volume of your pond through the filter once every 2 hours.

Biological Filters

Biological filters are more complex systems. They are especially recommended if you keep fish in your pond. Living systems, biological filters utilize beneficial bacteria that feed on impurities in the water. These organisms in the filter play a critical role in regulating the nitrogen cycle of the water.

This is what one type of biological filter looks like. Notice the attached ledge to help create a waterfall as the water returns to the pond. (Photo courtesy of Aquascape Designs, Inc.)

Biological filters contain layers of medium that harbor large concentrations of these naturally occurring bacteria. When water flows through the medium, the bacteria break down fish wastes and other organic matter. As this process takes place, toxic ammonia—a by-product of fish waste—is changed into harmless nitrates that return to the pond and nourish the plant life. Biological filters don't require the same high flow rate of mechanical versions to operate efficiently.

It is not difficult to run a biological filter, but here are a few simple rules:

◆ Run the filter 24 hours a day, because the organisms in the filter need a constant supply of oxygenated water to survive.

◆ Follow the manufacturer's recommendations regarding the rate of water flow. Too high or low a flow rate will reduce the efficiency of the filter.

◆ Maintain the filter by cleaning the pre-filter and settlement area whenever waste builds up.

Pumps

Pumps move water. They make your pond, waterfall, fountain, or stream go. In addition, they keep your filter supplied with a steady stream of water and oxygen to clean the water. There are a variety of pumps. They are usually classified by the amount of water they move in a measured period of time.

This submersible pump will push enough water to run a filter and skimmer to help keep a pond clean. (Photo courtesy of Aquascape Designs, Inc.)

Pump Quick Tip

There are many different kinds of water pumps serving a variety of purposes. When choosing a pump to use in a water feature, be sure you obtain one made specifically for that purpose. Pumps for water features are designed to run 24 hours a day, 7 days a week. Opt for a heavy-duty pump for increased life. All pumps eventually fail, but spending a little extra on a heavy-duty model will pay off in the long run.

Step one in choosing a pump is to determine its use and the amount of water you have to move. Calculate the volume of water in your water feature. Then choose a pump that can move half the total volume in one hour. For example, if you have a pond that holds 500 gallons of water, the pump should move at least 250 gallons an hour. If your water feature includes a waterfall or stream, then you'll need an even more powerful pump to circulate the water your display needs. When in doubt, buy a more powerful pump.

A Word of Warning

Though it is wise to choose a more powerful pump if you are in doubt about size, you can overdo it. Never select a pump that moves more water per hour than the total volume of the pond. If you have a 500-gallon pond and your pump moves 1,000 gallons per hour, it's too big.

There are two basic types of pumps—the submersible pump that sits on the bottom of the pond underwater and the inline pump that sits outside the water feature and is inserted into the waterline. Inline pumps are usually larger and are often used to power waterfalls and run large filtration systems.

This submersible pump is heavy-duty and able to drive the filtration system in a very large water feature.
(Photo courtesy of Aquascape Designs, Inc.)

Special needs may determine the type of pump you choose:

◆ If you build a stream or waterfall, your choice of a pump will depend on how wide you plan the streambed or the waterfall. For every 1 inch of width of the water flow of the stream/waterfall, you need a flow of 150 gallons per hour (gph). If your waterfall is 18 inches wide, you need to move at least 2,700 gph. Again, when in doubt, opt for a larger pump.

◆ If you have a reflecting pond or a "still" water garden, you might still consider using a pump to unobtrusively circulate the water. This helps keep the water from becoming stagnant. In this situation, the pump need only move 30 percent of the water in the feature every hour.

◆ For fountains, the pump must be powerful enough to push the water into the air to the height you desire. There are special pump heads designed to fit over the outlet of the pump for special spraying effects, and some pumps are specifically designed for fountain use.

Setting Up Your Pump and Filter

Your design is unique in one way or another, as is every installation. Ask questions and do your homework. Get recommendations from someone who knows ponds and their associated equipment. If possible, look at installations similar to what you're planning. You're local pond equipment supplier will help you locate one. The Internet is a fertile source of ideas and pictures.

To make life easier, you can buy pump and filter kits that supply everything you need to set up a complete filtration system in your pond. (Photo courtesy of Aquascape Designs, Inc.)

When you make your final decision, learn all you can about the installation you've chosen. Learning from the experts in your area is the best way to avoid mistakes. After doing this, you should know just what kind of pump and filter is best for you. From there, you simply have to follow the manufacturer's instructions in setting it up.

Ponds and Waterfalls

Here are some sample installations for ponds and waterfalls.

The simplest installation is the small pond, one that may have a few plants but no fish. The purpose of the pump in this feature is to keep the water moving, but not necessarily visibly. A submersible pump that circulates 30 percent of the water each hour is recommended. Installation is a two-step process:

1. Place the pump at one end of the pond. Follow the instructions about anchoring it. Some pumps just sit on the bottom.
2. Attach a hose to the outlet and run it across the bottom to the other end of the pond. You can put a layer of gravel over the hose to hold it in place. With the intake on one side of the pond and the outlet at the other, you will achieve the constant movement of water that will keep the pond from stagnating.

Pump Quick Tip

A flexible, ribbed-style hose is the easiest to work with in a pump and filter installation. This kind of hose does not restrict pump-flow when bent to form curves.

In another common pond setup, the outlet hose runs outside the water and returns water to the pond over a small bed of rocks. Although not quite a stream or a waterfall, it hints at both. It uses the same submersible pump.

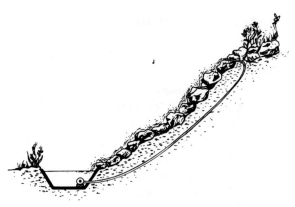

No matter how big your waterfall, the setup is the same. The submersible pump is in the pond, pushing the water through a hose where it is returned to the top of the falls and runs back down over the rocks.

1. Sink the submersible pump at the end of the pond.

2. Run the outlet hose to the other end of the pond, hidden either in or alongside the pond. If alongside the pond, it's better to bury the hose in a trench.

3. At the other end of the pond make a pile of rocks that emerges from the surface of the pond.

4. Run the hose in between the rocks near the top, but keep it from sticking out. This way the water will run out over the rocks and back into the pond.

5. Just be sure your rocks are in the pond. If not, you'll pump your pond dry. Running the water over rocks that are outside the pond requires extra work as detailed later. Water running over rocks is a very natural-looking special effect and provides the circulation your pond needs.

Adding a Filter

The simplest kind of biological filter is an all-in-one unit that also houses a submersible pump. This filter includes a microbe-filled fiber media that simulates biological activity in a streambed. This type of filter should be placed in the lowest point of the pond to ensure that it will operate at maximum efficiency.

Pump Quick Tip

Ponds that contain fish must always have enough oxygen in the water for the fish to breathe. This is achieved by aerating the water. In an indoor aquarium, air pumps and submerged air-stones create bubbles in the water. Small ponds can also use this method. A more natural way is the creation of a waterfall, a fountain, or having the return water break the surface of the pond to stir things up.

Installation of an external biological filter is different. An attractive way of handling a filter of this kind is to create a waterfall at the point of filtration. Here's how it's usually done:

1. Place the filter box at one end of the pond. It needs to be above the surface of the pond. It can sit on the ground so it is higher than the pond or can be partially or fully dug into the ground, depending on how far you want the water to travel.

2. You can make the box look natural by building up around it with soil and rock.

3. If you have a submersible pump, place it at the opposite end of the pond with the hose running under the pond or around in a trench to its connection with the fitting on the lower part of the filter box.

4. The water is pumped up through the biological filter, then returned to the pond over the rocks, which helps aerate the water.

5. If you have a large pond, you can install a skimmer at the opposite end to trap floating debris and to keep the pump from clogging. The water is drawn through the skimmer by the pump, then moved along to the filter before being returned to the pond.

6. Set the skimmer at the water's edge and recess it into the ground so that the water flows into the top.

7. If you are using an inline pump, set it outside the pond following the manufacturer's instructions. The external pump will pull the water into the skimmer, then push it to the filter box before it is returned to the pond.

This basic setup can be used with a variety of water features and will keep water quality high and aerate your feature so it can support a variety of plant and animal life.

🐦 Pump Quick Tip

Because there is a wide variety of pumps and filters on the market, no two installations will be exactly alike. The basic installations described here may vary. Always follow the manufacturer's step-by-step instructions. They know best.

Fountains

Fountains are among the most dramatic additions to a backyard pond or water feature. The sight and sound of water being pumped into the air is always a showstopper.

Installation is simple. You will need a specially designed pump, to be installed in the pond at the point of the desired fountain. This pump is in addition to the one that operates your filtration system. You will turn on the fountain pump only when you want the effect. The filter pump should remain on continuously.

Fountains add movement and beauty to water features. This one has a main stream of water in the center and also sprays water outward on all sides.

The Least You Need to Know

◆ Electricity in the backyard can help enhance rock features and is necessary for moving water features.

◆ Contact your local authorities to learn about permit requirements and building codes, and call the Digger's Hotline and utilities before you dig.

◆ When installing electricity outdoors, it's best to have a professional do it or at least have your work inspected by a licensed electrician.

◆ There are a wide variety of pumps and filters for water features from which to choose.

◆ Be sure you select the right-size pump and correct type of filter for your needs.

◆ Always follow the manufacturer's instructions when installing pumps and filters.

In This Chapter

- ◆ Having the right equipment
- ◆ Setting a backyard pond
- ◆ Planning and creating a waterfall
- ◆ Adding fountains and small streams

This beautiful pond installation features a double waterfall, a stone sculpture, a variety of interesting rocks, and a perfect complement of plants. It's a great example of a professionally designed water feature.
(Photo courtesy of Aquascape Designs, Inc.)

Chapter 11

Installing Water Features

Now it's time for the nuts and bolts of installing water features. By this time, you should have a good idea about how feasible it is for you to try it yourself. Once you make that decision, you have to prepare carefully. Take your time and don't rush the project. Part of the work is physical, like digging the hole for a pond or building a waterfall. Some is more technical, like laying the liner correctly and setting pumps and filters. A good installation coupled with proper maintenance will last for years.

Basic Equipment You'll Need

Water, rock, or a combination of both, the same basic rules apply. Rule number one is to have all the equipment and materials you'll need on hand before you begin. Nothing is more frustrating than not having the right tool there when you need it.

To build a small project on your own, you'll probably need the following:

◆ Pick and shovel
◆ Wheelbarrow
◆ Length of rope or garden hose
◆ One or two straight boards
◆ A carpenter's level
◆ Stakes to mark the excavation
◆ A supply of builder's sand to line the excavation
◆ Spades and a pry-bar or pick ax for removing soil and rock when you excavate

For the installation of a basic pond, you'll also need the following items:

♦ Your liner, either preformed or flexible.

♦ Rock, soil, and other hardscaping material for borders, waterfalls, streambeds, and accents.

♦ Pumps, filters, and associated hoses and equipment.

♦ If you are going to use a pump and filter, be sure your electrical source is also in place in accordance with local building codes.

Pond Quick Tip

The only things you need not have on hand when you begin constructing a backyard pond are plants and fish. Once you have completed the installation and are sure of your water quality, you can purchase and add both plants and fish.

Gathering the correct materials takes planning. Know the size of the feature you are going to install. Decide if and how you want the water to move and whether you will use filters and skimmers. If movement is in the works, choose your pump(s). If you plan carefully, everything will be on hand when you begin, eliminating those annoying last-minute trips to the hardware store or pond supply dealer.

Installing a Backyard Pond

The backyard pond is one of the most basic and beautiful water features you can build. As mentioned early, it will enhance your yard, becoming a focal point, a place where you can relax and enjoy a bit of nature. Once you have decided where you want the pond, what its size will be, if the water will be moving, and whether you want plants and/or fish, you're ready to proceed.

Before taking that first shovelful of soil, you should consider style. If a formal pond fits better with your overall décor, choose a prescribed geometric shape, such as a rectangle, square, or circle. If the natural look is more appealing, select an abstract or irregular shape, which may contain a small stream or waterfall.

The style and shape of your pond may also be impacted by where you are going to put it. If it is to be installed within or alongside a formal garden, you'll want a formal pond. If you decide to build your pond at the base of a natural-looking rock garden, then the natural look will be a better fit.

Decide on Size and Depth

Size and depth are a matter of design and function. Size depends on the space you have available and how it relates to the rest of the yard. Budget and maintenance are also factors influencing how big you build. Depth is primarily a matter of function. Your pond must be deep enough to satisfy plants that need to be submerged. In northern reaches with cold winters, ponds should be at least 2 feet deep to allow fish to overwinter outside.

The size and depth of your pond will have a major impact on the amount of work necessary to maintain it. It should be a manageable size for you. Preformed liners eliminate many questions. Size and depth are decided ahead of time, and all you have to do is pick the size that's right for you.

Several companies offer pond "kits," all-in-one solutions for the do-it-yourselfer. The kits come with everything you need (including instructions!) and eliminate much of the guesswork involved in building a water feature. The kits generally come in set sizes, for instance: 4×6 feet, 6×8 feet, 8×11 feet, and 11×16 feet. Most now use flexible liners, so the only decision really left to make is to choose one of the sizes. That doesn't restrict you. You can purchase components separately and build any size you want in a larger configuration. Commercial installations are often much larger.

No matter what size you choose, you'll still be able to have plants and fish and can include a small waterfall, fountain, or aerator to provide movement and oxygen. When deciding on the size that is best for you, think about the location of the pond, the purpose it is going to serve, the amount of work you are willing to do, and the cost.

Planning Quick Tip

Nature doesn't do straight lines, 90-degree corners, or perfect circles. If you want a natural-looking pond, it's best to make its outline irregular. Many people prefer an easy-on-the-eye kidney shape, but don't restrict yourself to what everyone else does. Get creative. Vary your dimensions and outline to fit your design and taste.

Size does matter. If you can't decide between two sizes for your pond, always err on the larger side. Many people build ponds, only to regret later that they didn't build them bigger. Besides creating the potential for a showier feature, a larger pond doesn't heat up as quickly as one with a small volume of water. Eliminating quick temperature changes will keep your plants and fish healthier.

Most ponds range in depth from 18 to 30 inches. If you plan to include fish, there should be deeper areas so that the fish have a cooler place to go in summer and can survive the winter in colder climates. Large koi will benefit from even deeper water. Some koi enthusiasts recommend the deepest area of the pond approach 5 feet. They feel that this larger vertical swimming area allows the fish to increase muscular development and results in a healthier lifestyle.

Plants aren't as fussy about depth, but those that need to be submerged want their rootballs underwater. Most water gardeners include "shelves" in their excavations. These shelves are raised areas around the rim of the pond that don't go as deep as the center. In other words, while your pond may be 24 or 30 inches deep in the center, you can plan for a 6- to 10-inch-deep shelf around the outer edge of the pool for plants. A secondary shelf roughly 10 inches deeper can be used for water lilies, plants that send their floating leaves to the surface but need to have their bases well below water. Include some variation in the depth of your pond to increase the choices of plant and animal life available to you.

Measure Before You Dig

Before you begin, you must know the size of the pond you are going to build. It's the only way you'll be sure to have enough of the right materials on hand. If you are building a 4×6 or a 6×8 pond, measure it out and stake the dimensions on the spot you've chosen for it. Next, decide upon the shape you want by using a piece of rope or garden hose. You can manipulate the hose or rope until you are satisfied that the shape is just the way you want it.

Design Quick Tip

When you're ready to dig, borrow a sod cutter. This tool, with a long shovel-like handle and a sharp, bean-shape blade, allows you to slide under the sod and separate it from the ground below. Using it, you can remove the grass in sections that may be useful for patches in other areas of your yard. Remember: Waste not, want not.

Once you've measured and marked the area, you are ready to do the most physically demanding part of pond construction—the digging. Depending on the quality of your soil, digging can go smoothly or be very difficult. Rocky soil and hard clay will require chopping with a pick ax. Remember that favor your neighbor owes you? Two backs are better than one.

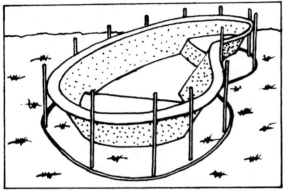

Before you begin digging out for a preformed shell, mark the shape by driving a series of stakes from the lip of the liner straight into the ground.

When you dig for the preformed shell, be sure to make the hole the same shape as the shell, allowing for the shelves.

The Right Stuff

If you've purchased a preformed shell, the shape of your pool has been chosen for you. Many shells are shaped asymmetrically, to look like natural pools. Look for rigid fiberglas that can last up to 50 years. The hole you dig should accommodate the exact shape of the preformed shell. Begin by setting the shell on the ground and mark the edges by driving in a series of stakes or pegs from the edge of the liner in a number of places vertically into the ground. Then remove the shell and begin digging. Start by digging the entire shape to the level of the first ledge. Then put the shell back in place and mark the edges of the second ledge, if you have one. Dig to the second ledge; then dig the area that goes to full depth. You may have to set the shell in several times to make sure all the digging is to the right level. This kind of digging has to be more precise than with the flexible liner, which will conform to the shape of the hole. You should also level the preformed shell by placing a board across it at several points and checking with a carpenter's level.

It's best to dig your hole in layers. In this way the shelves for plants are left in place, solid and ready to go. Excavating in this fashion also minimizes the need for backfilling. Doing it step by step will help eliminate excess work and effort. Keep in mind that if you're installing pumps, filters, or skimmers, your excavation should reflect their use. Do all the digging and trenching at once if possible.

A Word of Warning

Once you have finished digging, make a careful check of the entire bottom area of the hole. Try to remove any jagged rocks or protruding roots that might damage the liner. There are ways to cushion the ground to protect the liner, but the more potential damage-causers you remove as you dig, the better the installation will be.

Setting the Liner, Preformed and Flexible

Once you've dug the hole for your pond, the most taxing work is over. Though you may not sweat as much doing the rest of the installation, the work's not over yet. Installing your liner correctly is the most important part of the construction process.

A Word of Warning

Whether you're on level or sloping ground, the edges of your liner need to come to the same level. If the edges of your pond aren't in the same plane, water will leak out the lowest point until the level of the pond is reduced to that spot. This could result in your liner showing.

To level the hole, lay a straight 2×4 across the hole at various places and put a carpenter's level on top of the board. If the edging is not level, scrape away enough dirt from one side or the other to correct it. Check the entire perimeter of the pond.

To install the preformed shell liner once the hole has been completed, follow these simple steps:

◆ With a helper, lower the shell into the hole. The rim of the shell should be about 1 inch above the surrounding ground to prevent runoff from entering the pond. If you have to adjust the height, do it now by adding sand to the bottom of the hole until you're where you want to be.

Once the preformed shell is in the ground, make sure it's level. If it isn't level, the water won't sit level in the shell, which is a look you don't want.

◆ Next place your 2×4 and level over the shell in several places and make sure it's level. If it isn't level, pull it out of the hole and re-level it either by digging or by adding sand. This is very important, so don't become impatient.

◆ Using dry sand, slowly dribble in backfill around the entire perimeter of the shell. Then wiggle the shell to settle the sand and eliminate any air spaces. Refill any area of backfill that sinks.

◆ Slowly fill the shell with water. As you do, water the dry sand backfill thoroughly so that the water takes the sand down to fill in any leftover air space underneath or alongside the shell. Refill any open spaces around the perimeter of the shell. Make sure the shell is stable all around and in full contact with the sand underneath.

A wide variety of preformed shells are available for use in the backyard. Take your pick.

Flexible liners come in rolls of various lengths. Measure what you need and a serviceman will cut you just the right length.

A Word of Warning

While you're engaged in the backfilling process around your preformed shell, don't fill the pond with water too quickly. The two should be done at the same time to prevent the shell from bulging outward. Try to equalize the pressure on both sides of the shell as you backfill.

◆ When the shell is filled with water, conceal the rim with stone and overhanging plants. If you use flagstones or pavers, allow them to overhang the pond edge by 1 or 2 inches. Make sure they are adequately supported so they don't damage the edge of the shell. Try to avoid the artificial-looking "necklace" effect that happens when you simply ring the pond with rock.

With a flexible liner the procedure is a little different. Flexible liners come in sheets and conform to the size and depth of the hole. Larger ponds almost always use this type of liner. A thick, high-quality flexible liner can easily last 20 years or more. The size of the liner you buy should take into account the size of the pond and its depth with enough excess to run well out of the hole you've dug. Once the pond is filled and settled, you can trim away this excess and hide it.

You'll still use a layer of sand or cushion over the ground in the hole before installing the liner. Once the hole for your flexible liner is dug and inspected for jagged rocks and pointed roots, you should add a layer of at least 2 to 3 inches of builder's sand or a commercial, carpetlike cushion sold by pond supply centers. Cushion the shelves and pack damp sand into any holes in the side walls of the hole where large rocks have been removed.

Building Quick Tip

A good liner is heavy and awkward—definitely a job where an extra pair of hands (or two or three …) helps. Try to install your flexible pool liner on a warm, sunny day. You can set the liner out in the sun, preferably on warm pavement, for 15 to 20 minutes, and soften it up, giving it more flexibility. This makes it much easier to handle.

Stone used in a functional and aesthetic way can move you from one part of the garden to another.

Water and stone work together in the garden to create magic.

Stone steps between two garden levels.

Create beautiful vignettes with rock and water—even in small places.

In this simple waterfall, water drops from a flat rock into a small pool.

A small pump converts these half-barrels into an attractive water feature.

Moss, a gift of nature, adds just the right touch to your work.

Decorative water features bring the sight and sound of moving water to even the smallest gardens.

Aubrieta provides sheets of color in spring.

Saxifraga means "stone breaker." These plants are naturals for the rock garden.

Mazus reptans is a mat-forming perennial. It also comes in a white-flowered version.

A relative of the African violet, *Haberlea rhodopensis* is hardy in many cold-winter areas.

This *Dianthus* is one of the "pinks." The shorter-growing varieties are perfect for a spot among the rocks.

Phlox subulata 'Tamaongalei' is often found in nurseries as 'Candy Stripe.'

Nymphaea (Water Lilies) come in many colors and both hardy and tropical varieties.

Carnivorous plants like *Sarracenia leucophylla,* the white-topped pitcher plant, are at home in the bog garden.

Sacred in some cultures, *Nelumbo* (Lotus) can be grown in your backyard water feature.

Nymphoides geminata is a delicate fringed beauty, perfect for a small pool.

Beautify your water's edge with *Iris pseudocorus.*

Koi add an indefinable quality to the water feature.

A stone bench provides a restful place for contemplation.

A garden with stone terraces is a more formal alternative to the natural-looking rock garden but provides the same planting opportunities for fantastic rock garden plants.

It's easiest to use stone from local sources, but for a specific look, it can be shipped in. The stone in this New York wall is from Maine.

For a more traditional style, make the look and feel of your garden classic.

This small pond made with a rigid preformed liner is a simple yet charming addition to any backyard.

Hide the edges of your liner with plants or rock.

Use small containers to create special places.

In larger settings, spectacular fountains provide visual excitement and aerate the pond.

Combine water, rock, and plants to create a fantasy world in your backyard.

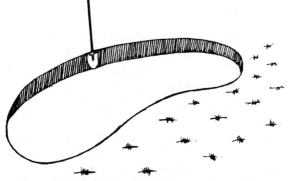

When digging for the flexible liner, always dig in layers. Start by digging the entire shape you want, but only to the depth of the spade.

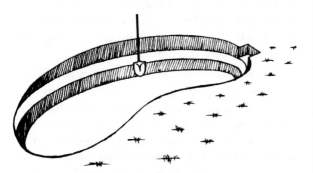

Once you complete the first layer, begin digging your shallow shelves, one at the time. The cutout at the right is for the skimmer.

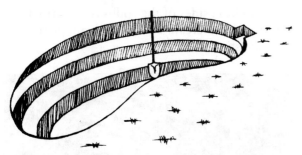

The final part to dig is the deepest section of the pond. Remember, no two natural ponds are exactly the same shape.

Now follow these simple steps:

◆ With someone to help you, drape the liner loosely into the hole with an even overlap on all sides.

◆ Get into the hole and push the liner to the sides to get it to form to the hole as much as possible. Make sure the overlap is still relatively even all the way around.

◆ Weigh down the edges with a few smooth, flat stones or bricks.

◆ Once the liner is in place, begin filling the pond with water.

◆ As the pond fills, adjust the liner to conform to the sides of the pond and try to smooth out as many creases and wrinkles as you can.

◆ Begin removing the stone weights as the pond fills so the liner doesn't overstretch.

◆ When the pond is full, trim off the excess liner with scissors or a utility knife, leaving enough liner around the pond rim to extend at least 6 inches underneath the stone, sod, or plants that you will use for edging.

This completes the installation of the liner. We talked about pumps and filters in the previous chapter, but to add a skimmer to your pond you need to build it in from the beginning.

As mentioned earlier, you must dig the skimmer hole at the end of the pond opposite where the water enters. Dig this hole to the specifications of the skimmer, allowing the water to enter at just the right place.

In most cases, the biological filter sits on or above the ground at the end of the pond where the water enters and gives you the perfect opportunity to return water to your pond via a small waterfall. The water can either run over a series of rocks into the pond or fall over a single rock, depending on the effect and sound you want. Either way, it's a good idea to have enough extra liner to put under the rock so the water doesn't leave the system.

The Right Stuff

The water level in a self-contained, lined pond may rise and overflow during periods of heavy rain or snow. If your yard has a slope or good natural drainage, the overflow will simply drain away. In other situations, you may have to build an outlet for overflow from your pond. You should locate the outlet at the edge of the pond in the best place to divert the water. Make that section of the pond's edge lower than the rest of the pond so as to ensure that rising water exits at that point. You can fill the overflow with rock and plant along its edge so that it isn't conspicuous.

Creating a Waterfall

To many people, waterfalls are the most beautiful and interesting of all the backyard water features. The sight and sound of water cascading over rocks is tranquil, soothing, and beckoning. Waterfalls come in all shapes and sizes, from one half-barrel spilling into another to large, professionally installed structures that almost boggle the mind.

Basic waterfalls you can build and install yourself or with a little help from your friends are the easiest to work on. As you will see, there are several styles of small waterfalls you can design and install in your own backyard. In fact, some of the work is very similar to the basics described for installing a pond. With a little more ingenuity, you can have a waterfall.

Electricity Quick Tip

Unless you have a natural stream and plenty of contour in your yard, you're going to need power to pump water to the top of your feature. You will need electricity available to your pump, and it should be in place before actual construction of the waterfall begins. You can find help with installing electricity in Chapter 10.

Consider Your Options

All waterfalls make use of gravity to carry water downhill. You will either need to make use of existing slopes or hills, or you'll need to build a slope to facilitate your falls. Often you can do this with soil excavated for the pond. Most of the time, water is pumped to the top of the falls and cascades down into the pond. Sometimes an upper pool is used, into which the water is pumped. An overflow directs water from the upper pool to the falls, from which it drops into the lower pool to begin the cycle again.

You should excavate the "fall" area between two ponds as a "half-pipe" and line it with a piece of flexible liner so the water doesn't leave the system. Then carefully set rocks to hide the liner and create the falls.

Constructing rock waterfalls is an art. If stone isn't properly placed, water will simply run beneath them, out of sight. Since the idea is to create a pleasing visual scene, you should continuously test your rock placement as you put things together to make sure the sight and sound of your feature matches your expectations. Make sure your pump is powerful enough to accomplish your goals.

You should also plant the upper and lower pools and the sides of the spillway to further the attempt to create a scene and complete your artistic vision.

With waterfalls, you can vary the sight and sound of the cascading water. This stone slab allows for a single stream of water to fall several feet into the pond.

┌─────────────────────────────────────┐
Waterfall Quick Tip

Rock placement and the distance between drops and spills will change the look and sound of your feature. Experiment until you have the combination you want. Use your imagination to create the perfect feature. The possibilities are endless.
└─────────────────────────────────────┘

The Pondless Waterfall

One of the newest innovations in backyard waterfalls is the "pondless waterfall." Some people prefer the look and the mystery of the disappearing water. Others may have small children in the house or neighborhood and simply don't like the idea of any kind of pool in their yard.

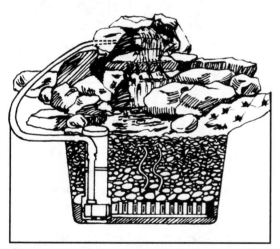

This cutaway of the innovative pondless waterfall shows how the cascading water disappears through a bed of gravel and rock before being pumped back up to the top of the falls.

The pondless waterfall is built just like those with pools but the water recirculates without accumulating in a pond or pool. The lower pool is replaced by a deeper hole filled with rock and gravel. The pump sits like a sump-pump at the bottom of a large tube attached to a special module that allows the water to enter at the bottom of the gravel-filled hole.

Maintenance is reduced to adding some water every few weeks to replace that lost to natural evaporation. Some companies are now selling kits with everything needed to build the pondless waterfall. You just dig the hole and create the spillway as outlined previously.

Liners or large containers must be used in the hole and the spillway should be underlaid with a flexible liner.

If you want to build a pondless waterfall, you can buy a kit that will give you all the accessories you need to complete the job. (Photo courtesy of Aquascape Designs, Inc.)

Pondless waterfalls can be put in relatively small areas near the house or in small rock gardens. A basic kit calls for a 4×6-foot structure, a beautiful waterfall in miniature. They can be turned off whenever the homeowner desires, perhaps at night or if the family goes on vacation. Because there is no standing water, nothing will become stagnant, filled with algae, or serve as a mosquito hotel. Because it is small and self-contained, this kind of feature is easy to drain and clean.

Fountains

Fountains are usually used in conjunction with other water features. They can be used to dress up a pond, or, in their smallest incarnations, as part of a small feature, often as a decorative figure spouting water into a container. The common element in all fountains is water being moved or pushed into the air. Many effects can now be achieved by creating special spray patterns with fountain heads sold for just this purpose. Fountains create the sight and sound of moving water without taking up much space. They are particularly spectacular if illuminated at night.

A Word of Warning

Some plants may not like to have water pounding on them continuously. If you decide to put a decorative fountain in your pond, leave clear water around the spray pattern.

The height and size of the fountain spray should take into consideration the size of the pond and prevailing wind patterns. For example, if you live in a windy area, a tall, fine spray can be blown a great distance from its starting point, taking water outside the pond. This constant water loss will be a problem, and your neighbors may not appreciate being constantly wet.

Sculptural fountains are generally the central feature in a formal garden. Many classic designs can be purchased and set up in a garden or pond. Some are self-contained and need not be installed as part of another water feature. The urn-type fountain, for example, can consist of a single bowl or a series of different-size bowls. It can be self-contained or part of a pond/pool setting.

Another type of fountain is the wall spout, which can be placed on a wall overlooking a pond or pool, or more often recirculates from a container. The pipe is set in the wall, and the spout emits one or more trickles of water. Again, these are used in more formal situations and may require a professional to install the plumbing.

Decorative figurines, like animals, small boys with bladder-control problems, and abstract art pieces have spouts and can be set up to flow into barrels, containers, or small pools, and can be delightful features where space is at a premium. They usually come complete with pump for installation in minutes.

Finally, there are small, safe fountain features such as the millstone bubble or burbler fountain. This is a simple construction that almost anyone can do. Here's how it's done:

To make a simple millstone burbler you begin by setting a waterproof bucket into the ground.

◆ Dig a hole in the ground where you want to place the feature. Next place a wide, round, waterproof container, such as a large round pail or bucket, into the hole and backfill as for the preformed pond liner.

Once the bucket is set, place the pump on the bottom or on one or two bricks so it is in the right position.

◆ Place a pump in the bottom of the container, setting it just off the floor on one or more bricks, and adjust the flow rate so that the pump produces only a bubbling of water.

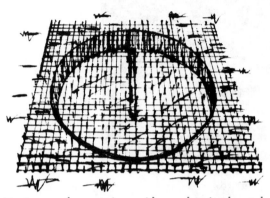

Next cover the container with a galvanized metal grid. Be sure it's strong enough to support a layer of stones.

◆ Then cover the container with a galvanized metal grid strong enough to support a layer of rock to hide it. This grid can usually be purchased at home and garden centers.

Next add a small millstone on the grid that is smaller than your container. You can purchase millstones at a garden or home center.

◆ Place a small millstone, or drilled boulder, on the grid and insert a piece of tubing from the pump through the middle. You can purchase these millstones and/or boulders at most garden centers. Make sure the millstone is smaller in diameter than the buried container so the water continues to circulate.

Always cover the grid with a layer of small stones to hide the grid. This is strictly for aesthetic purposes. Now you're ready to fill and turn on the water.

◆ Finally, place large pebbles or cobbles around the millstone to conceal the grid. You can vary the size and color of the pebbles to suit your décor and to add visual interest. When you turn on the water, it will bubble up and run off the millstone and back into the bucket.

The Small Stream

Nothing is quite as soothing as a small mountain stream with water running slowly over rocks and colorful plants growing along the banks. If you've ever come across one of these streams while hiking, chances are you've stopped to rest, enjoying the tranquility and sounds of nature.

This stream is beautifully set with a variety of rocks and appears to have been carved by nature.

There's no reason the same experience can't be had in your own backyard. You can construct a stream on a small scale and still have many of the benefits of that natural stream in the mountains. The construction is not that different from the waterfall and is most easily done if the stream has a slight downhill slope.

Like the waterfall that connects two pools, a stream can run between two small bodies of water. Pool construction is done the same way described earlier in the chapter, with a flexible or preformed liner. The pools do not have to be large, but should be in scale with the overall length and position of the stream. The distance between the two pools depends on your topography and where you plan to put the stream. Dig a shallow half-pipe trough for the length of the stream and line it with a flexible pool liner. If you don't want to dig a half-pipe shape, you can dig the bottom flat but with outwardly sloping sides. It's easier to fill this style with rocks for a natural look.

This cutaway shows one way to add gravel and rocks to your new streambed. The larger rocks can be set in different positions along the bed for a more natural look.

Once again, use a pump to move the water and place it at the low end of the water flow buried or camouflaged by rock and plants. Its job is to push the water up to its starting point. The size of the pump determines the kind of water flow your stream will have. There's no need for Niagara Falls. A stream is to waterfalls what burblers are to fountains.

Curve the stream as it runs downhill, giving the stream a more natural look. You can place a few rocks, plants, and small stones in the stream as well as along the bank.

A Word of Warning

Every water feature is an "attractive nuisance." Children are instinctively pulled to moving water and can't resist dipping hands (sometimes entire bodies) in and playing around water. Never leave an unguarded pond in a place where young children play. If young children are present, fence off any water feature in which they can unintentionally get into trouble.

The Least You Need to Know

◆ Always have all your materials on hand before beginning any water feature installation.

◆ The pond is the cornerstone of most water features. If you can install a pond, you can also build your own waterfall or stream.

◆ You can build a wide variety of ponds and waterfalls.

◆ The pondless waterfall is another innovation to consider.

◆ You can make small, man-made streams look as if they were created by nature.

In This Chapter

◆ Beautifying your water feature with plants

◆ Combining groups of water-friendly plants

◆ Recognizing the importance of an ecological balance

◆ Doing it all in miniature

The foliage and blooms of this grouping of pickerel
rush help to accent the natural pond.

Planting Your Water Features

Installing a water feature successfully is, in most cases, just half the battle. Unless you construct a formal stone fountain with the sole purpose of spraying water into the air, chances are you are going to want to add plants both in and around your new pond, stream, or waterfall. Plants play a major role in any natural-looking feature, giving it color and life. Use plants along the damp banks, in a nearby bog garden, among the rocks, and even in the water. With plants, you have the potential to turn your water feature into a beautiful, natural-looking restive oasis.

Plants are also important helpers in conditioning your water and keeping an ecological balance in your pond. This is especially important if you plan to keep fish. If you've decided to pass on fish, plants will still provide the final piece to the package, the texture and color that make the picture complete. In this chapter, we will discuss ways to plant water features, as well as the best types of plants to mix and match in order to give you a good-looking, healthy feature.

These Water Lilies planted alongside pickerel rush show the kinds of contrasts the different water plants can create.

Enhancing Your Water Feature

After you've completed the basic installation of a water feature—whether it's a pond, waterfall, or small stream—stand back and look at your creation. The hardest work is done, but like a fine meal, presentation is everything. The crowning touch, the garnish on your plate, is plant material. Rock and water alone look cold and barren. A mantle of green and sprinkling of flowers will warm the feature, making it come alive.

Gardening in or near the water may be new to you, but there are many plants to choose from. Besides looking great, plants serve to both cleanse and purify the water. In this way they help balance the garden environment, not just to the eye, but ecologically.

Backyard Lingo

Planting your new water feature isn't "planting" in the traditional sense. Because backyard ponds have a liner, planting in water does not involve burying plants in soil. You'll learn a new way to grow, using pots and gravel.

Before you begin adding plants to your pond, you've got to "plant" something else first. It's important to add rocks and gravel to your pond, but it's not just an aesthetic choice. This act will pay dividends, reducing the amount of maintenance you will have to do.

Some of the advantages of adding rocks and pebbles include the following:

◆ Gravel provides surface area for healthy bacteria to colonize in the pond.

◆ The bacteria that gather on the rocks help break down fish waste and other organic matter.

◆ Covering the liner with rocks and a layer of gravel protects it from potentially harmful ultraviolet rays of the sun, as well as from damage by animals or sharp objects.

◆ Rocks and gravel also help hold the liner down during bad weather and high ground-water conditions.

Gravel and large rocks should be part of every pond built to have a natural look. As you can see, these additions help bring the pond to life.

◆ The gravel and rocks give small fish a place to hide from potential predators.

◆ Gravel is safer to walk on than an exposed liner, which can be quite slippery.

◆ It provides a more natural-looking bottom.

Once your pond is built, the water is in place, and there is a rock and gravel bed over your liner, you're ready for plants.

Planting in the Water

There are four main categories of water plants, each adapted to particular environmental conditions. They add color and beauty to the pond and improve water quality at the same time. For attractive and well-balanced ponds, it's highly recommended that you use all four types.

Here's what they are and what they do:

◆ **Marginals.** These plants grow in shallow water or saturated soil at the edges of ponds or along the wet banks of streams. They soften the transition between land and water while providing an attractive frame around the body of water they surround. Because of their attractive nature, marginal plants are primarily ornamental, but they grow in an environment too moist for many other garden plants.

Lobelia cardinalis is a moisture-loving marginal plant that can beautify the edge of a pond or wet banks of a stream.

◆ **Submerged oxygenators.** These unique plants grow with most or all of their foliage underwater. Their category name describes their function as they release oxygen into the water. In addition, they perform a valuable environmental service by removing excess nutrients from the water, which reduces the growth of algae. They also provide fish a protective cover and spawning areas. Most of them are grassy and sold in tied bunches.

This emerging leaf of a Water Lily is close to taking its position floating on top of the pond. Notice the fish swimming beneath.

◆ **Floaters.** These plants float freely on the surface of the water and also help to reduce algae by competing for nutrients, shading and cooling the water. Floaters are usually rapid multipliers, and some have strong, trailing root systems. Because floating plants have a natural filtering ability, they are even used for water purification at treatment plants.

◆ **Submerged floating-leaf plants.** These are great plants for providing surface shade on the water and are among the most beautiful of all water plants. They tend to root on the bottom of the pond, then send floating leaves to the surface. The water lily, which may be the most popular of all pond plants, is part of this group.

These beautiful Water Lilies and their blooms are spreading across this pond. You just can't let them get too thick.

How to Plant Them

Planting your feature is the most artistic step of the process. It adds color, texture, and nuance to the framework you have created with rock and water. The shelves you created in the construction process, the edges, rockwork, and the water itself will all provide you with room for plants.

If your water feature is new and you're using water from a chlorinated source, wait several days to a week after filling before adding plants or fish. This will give any chlorine in the water a chance to dissipate.

Because your pond has a liner and no soil, you need to either plant in pots or anchor your nonfloaters in gravel. For ease of planting and maintenance, many people plant in pots.

Growing water plants in pots is a little different than what you might be used to.

The Right Stuff

Floaters are, by nature, the easiest water plants to situate in their new home. Simply move them from one container to your feature. They float with their roots dangling in the water, so they will drift along the surface. This and their amazing reproductive capacity create maintenance concerns that other water plants don't have. From time to time, you may have to "harvest" floaters to keep them from completely covering the surface of your pond. To keep your pond looking its best, try not to have more than one third of the surface covered with plants. Your submerged oxygenators and aquatic animals all need for a little sunlight to make it through the water. Share the excess with friends or compost surplus plants to benefit the rest of your garden.

This cutaway shows potted plants in a container garden. The lattice-type pots are also used when planting pots in a pond, allowing the water to flow through them.

- The pots used are generally lattice-type or net pots, plastic containers with holes or openings on all sides to allow circulation of the water. You can find these anywhere water plants are sold.

- If you're concerned about potting medium leaking out, line the pot with a burlap type material.

- Fill the pot with heavy garden soil and water it in so it settles. Top it off if necessary.

- Next place the plant into the soil with its crown at the surface and firm it in. Obviously this is a messy job. Don't worry if the soil temporarily clouds the water when you lower your pots into the pond. The water will clear on its own as the particles settle out.

Planting Quick Tip _____

Whenever you bring in a new plant, it's a good idea to rinse it well to remove any algae that may be present. It's impossible to completely eradicate algae in planted ponds because it's everywhere you find sun, water, and nutrients in the same place. However, checking each new introduction helps control it.

- Cover the compost around the plant with a layer of gravel or small stones. This will keep the lighter bits of the compost from floating away and will help keep the plant in place.

- Once the plant is prepared, set the pot in the water on the shelf that is at the appropriate level for that particular species. Use the rock and gravel at the bottom of your pond to help hold the pot in place.

Planting Quick Tip _____

When planting your new pond, it's best to start with the plants that will be put at the deepest level. This eliminates tromping through all the beauties you've planted at the edge of the pond. The planting process is a little messy to begin with, so there is no need to complicate things.

While planting in pots is the easiest alternative for water gardens, some gardeners prefer not having pots sitting in their ponds. You can plant without pots in two ways.

This cutaway shows one way plants can be set in a pond. The plant at the left is in the gravel; the one at the right, in a planting pocket. You can also plant directly in pots.

The first involves planning well in advance. If you know ahead of time where you'd like to locate your plants, you can excavate "planting pockets" when you dig for your feature. Planting pockets are bowl-like depressions dug at various points on the shelves. When the liner is pulled over the installation and allowed to settle, these areas provide a ready-made planting location. The pockets should be 6 to 8 inches deep and 10 to 16 inches in diameter. Fill them with the same heavy garden soil used for water plants in pots and cover them with gravel. Plant roots will spread naturally and eventually find their way into the surrounding gravel. This way of planting prevents the plants from becoming root-bound in pots and needing special maintenance.

The second method is easier and allows for changes later on. If you're not sure where your plants will be going before you build, you can anchor them in mounds of gravel on the shelves. You'll achieve the same potless effect with less trouble.

Creating an Ecological Balance

Fill up a tub with water, let it sit out in the sun, and watch what happens. Soon the water will be green with algae, bugs and scum will accumulate on the surface, and the stagnant pool will become a breeding ground for mosquitoes. Pop a couple of plants into the tub, such as Water Lilies, and it's likely the same thing will happen. The reason is simple. There is no ecological *balance* in this tub of standing water and, therefore, no way for the water to cleanse itself.

Backyard Lingo

For your planted water feature, the simplest definition of a *balanced* pond is one in which the nutrients in the pond are at the appropriate level for the plants and animals that are present. Too little in the way of nutrients and your plants will not thrive. Too much and, in combination with light, algae grow explosively. The proper use of plants, biological filtration, and the inclusion of scavengers such as snails will help keep nutrients at appropriate levels.

Natural bodies of water are extremely complex systems, an orchestra of different players all playing their own part to give us a symphony. If one player is out of tune, well, you get the idea. The best we can do when we build water features is to emulate natural systems. You'll never be able to reproduce nature's design, but the better you are at putting the right ingredients together, the more successful your feature will be.

Regardless of the type or size of your water feature, you must strive to maintain healthy conditions and a favorable bacteria balance if plants and animals, and the pond itself, is to survive. Surprisingly, it is easier to keep the ecological balance in a larger pond than a smaller one. The addition of fish, however, will make the balance equation more complicated.

Besides looking good, these flowering Water Lilies provide shade to the pond bed and hiding places for fish.

With a good-size pond, it is possible to create a balanced ecosystem by the careful use of plants, animals, a gravel-lined pond bed, and a pump/filter to move the water. It's possible to get by without filtration, if crystal-clear water isn't a major goal.

Plants provide many ecosystem services. They add oxygen to the water while removing carbon dioxide, remove excess nutrients from the water, provide cooling shade from the sun, and make food for your animals.

Ecological Quick Tip

Even if you decide against adding fish to your pond, it's a good idea to add some scavengers, such as aquatic snails and tadpoles. These animals will help to control the growth of algae in the pond and aid in creating the ecological balance.

New ponds take some time to reach a balanced situation. Algae grow quickly, and after just a few days the water may suddenly appear green. Don't dismay. Be patient. Once your plants and animals begin to work together, things will stabilize and the algae should remain at respectable levels.

Filters and skimmers can help. As detailed in Chapter 10, mechanical filters trap floating matter, such as algae and leftover fish food, as well as decaying organic matter, while biological filters contain beneficial bacteria that feed on impurities in the water. These favorable bacteria contribute to your pond's balance by breaking down fish wastes and other organic matter that would otherwise create problems.

The Right Stuff

It seems you can't talk about water in your yard these days without talking about the mosquito-borne West Nile virus, which originated in parts of Africa. Mosquito control is the key to avoiding this problem. Moving water is not as attractive to them, and if you have fish, mosquito larvae are like hors d'oeuvres, eagerly snapped up by your finny friends in anticipation of the main course. If you don't have fish and are concerned, you can buy treatments for your water feature. These come as little doughnuts treated with Bt (*Bacillus thuringiensis*), a bacteria that kills mosquito larvae. This organic compound is safe to use with both fish and plants. Each doughnut treats 100 square feet for 30 days of water, and they can be broken into pieces for small fountains, ponds, or container gardens. Use them anywhere stagnant water collects: rain barrels, watering troughs, or unused swimming pools. Even though mosquitoes don't like moving water, your circulating features, such as waterfalls, may create moist areas under rocks or small backwaters where water can stand. Just hose down these areas periodically. With good design and construction and a few simple precautions, there's little need to be concerned.

Creating a balanced ecosystem reduces daily maintenance by keeping the negative aspects of pond life in check. In a sense, Mother Nature takes care of her own business.

The Container Water Garden

Almost any rock or water feature can be created in miniature. The water garden is no exception. If you don't have the right yard, the time to do a lot of work, or the budget to create a bigger pond, think about a container water garden. You can create these water gardens in miniature in a tub, a barrel, or a trough—nearly any container will do. They can hold a variety of water plants as well as a goldfish or two.

This large bowl contains water, gravel, and plants, making it a full-fledged container water garden.

Container water gardens have a charm and elegance all their own. They need little maintenance and can serve as a centerpiece for a group of container plantings either on a patio or terrace or in a flower garden or small rock garden. You can quickly set up a container garden without having to do the digging and work that goes into the conventional pond. If you want a small water feature, this can be the right choice for you.

Making a Basic Container Garden

Choose a watertight container that will have enough water surface area to accommodate the plants you'd like to grow. You can use wooden containers with liners to prevent water loss. Make sure that any container you use is washed well before you set it up. A 10 percent bleach solution will clean and disinfect it. Rinse well before filling.

The smaller the container, the fewer plants you'll be able to use and the faster the water will heat up. Dark-colored containers will absorb heat. While many water plants thrive in water that feels comfortably warm to the touch, too high a temperature creates problems. You can moderate this by occasionally adding water from your garden hose. Don't add too much at once but keep the temperature change gradual.

Planting and Maintaining

Containers are planted the same way as ponds. Pots are the easiest, but direct planting in gravel is an alternative. Depending on the size of the barrel, only use three to five different plants. It's a good idea to include an oxygenator, and apply the rule about not covering all the container's surface. In a container situation you can cover more surface than in the pond. Consider using a floater and a marginal plant to provide design interest at multiple levels.

This series of 50-gallon barrels are bulging with water plants. Add the surrounding plants on the ground, and you have a unique look that will attract lots of attention.

A Word of Warning

Mosquitoes, for the most part, are not a problem in container water gardens. Even though the water is sitting, the living plants keep the water from becoming stagnant. A goldfish or two—or even a few guppies from your aquarium, will eliminate any larvae. In the absence of fish, simply overflow your container and the mosquito larvae will float out to meet an untimely demise.

Your container garden should have about 6 hours of sun each day for optimum health of the plants and to encourage bloom. This will lead to some evaporation of the water, which can be easily remedied by simply adding water every few days to keep the level near the top of the container.

The Least You Need to Know

◆ The use of plants is the best way to enhance an otherwise barren water feature.

◆ Always line ponds with rocks and gravel instead of leaving them with a bare liner.

◆ Strive for a "balanced" system to avoid problems while minimizing maintenance.

◆ To help create a balanced ecosystem in a pond, use several different types of water plants.

◆ The use of filters will help to keep a water feature healthy and balanced, especially if fish are a part of the equation.

◆ Container water gardens provide a great touch to your yard or garden without the work and expense needed to create a full pond.

In This Chapter

- Providing general maintenance
- Checking and repairing your liner
- Making sure your water stays clean
- Performing seasonal cleanups in winter and spring
- Dealing with algae and animal and plant pests

This natural stream features a graveled bottom, large rocks, and select plantings. But it is man-made and requires maintenance.

Care and Maintenance of Your Water Features

Properly constructed water features don't need as much maintenance as people think, but that doesn't mean they are maintenance free. Some things must be watched and others must be done on a regular basis. And if you live in an area with freezing winter weather, special care may be needed in winter and spring.

Occasionally, as in the rest of gardening, you will have to deal with unexpected situations, like invading plant and animal pests. In most cases, if caught early enough, these pests can be easily controlled. Watching for problems doesn't mean you're going to have them, but the sooner you see them, the sooner you can correct them.

If you follow some routine maintenance procedures outlined in this chapter, your feature will stay vibrant and healthy for many years.

General Maintenance

For the most part, a good balanced water feature will take care of itself. Some things always need to be done, but they shouldn't take up any more time than any other gardening chore. The easiest and most important water feature chore is basic cleanup. Keeping the feature free of debris and excess plants nips many problems in the bud. Remove fallen leaves and twigs. Scoop out any dead or decaying organic matter. Cut back or divide plants that are growing too quickly or encroaching on others.

Keep an eye on the water level in your feature. Assuming you've properly constructed it, you won't lose water into the ground, but evaporation will gradually catch up with you. Top your feature up on a regular basis. Your filter, skimmer, and pump also need regular inspections to keep water clean and flowing. Liners and the tubing used to circulate the water need to be watched for leaks.

Routine maintenance of your plants is pretty much the same as with your other gardens. Pests and disease don't take days off and don't care much whether their hosts grow in water or on land. Establish a routine. Check your feature regularly, and you'll stay on top of any problem that arises.

Here's a maintenance checklist to help establish a routine for checking your plants:

- ☐ Check the water level for evaporation and top it off. If the rate of water loss seems excessive, check the liner for leaks.

- ☐ Check ponds with preformed shells instead of flexible liners periodically for cracks or punctures.

- ☐ If you have a pump and filter, check to make sure there are no clogs in the line and that the water is flowing freely. If there are screens to catch debris, make sure they are regularly cleared.

- ☐ Keep an eye on the amount of algae in the pond.

- ☐ Check all plants for signs of disease or rot. Make sure healthy ones aren't over-growing their allotted space.

- ☐ Lift potted plants early in the season to make sure the root system is healthy and they aren't root-bound.

- ☐ Remove any dead or floating plant material from the surface of the water. Scoop any dead or decaying organic matter from below the water's surface.

Now let's take a look at some of the specifics and how you can address any problems.

Checking and Repairing the Liner

Whether you have a flexible or preformed liner, it is essential to find and correct problems as soon as possible. Leaks are most often the result of damage during installation or improper preparation. Once the feature is up and running, leaks are unlikely to occur unless there is an accident.

Leaks create problems maintaining water level and can lead to permanent damage to the liner. If you've properly cushioned the line and included a layer of gravel on top of it prior to filling it with water, you'll achieve some protection from punctures.

Though this planted shell is sitting on the ground, exposed pieces of liner at ground level should periodically be checked for leaks often caused by settling rocks.

Professionals find that the great majority of all leaks in flexible liners occur along the perimeter of waterfalls and streams. Ground settling often causes small leaks, which in turn causes the water to trickle over the edge of the liner. They aren't always easy to find, but you'll know there is a leak if you have to add water more frequently than usual. You can repair these kinds of leaks in this way:

1. Check the perimeter of the pond for areas that are wet. Damp soil where there shouldn't be moisture is a good sign water is seeping over the liner.

2. Next, check to see that the overflow isn't being created by obstructions in your water flow caused by leaves, plants, or other debris.

3. If you find a leak caused by settling soil, you need to pull any plants or rock in the area, lift the liner edge back to its original position, and pack soil and/or gravel underneath to hold the edge above the water level. Then replant the vegetation and stone to hide the exposed liner.

If a puncture or cut in the liner is what's causing your water loss, the process of finding and repairing the leak may require you to drain the feature and clean out the bottom down to the liner. After locating the leak, you need to thoroughly dry and clean the area, then patch it with an appropriate material. Your liner supplier will have patch kits available.

Liner Quick Tip _____

Always fill your feature and let it sit for a while before finishing. If there's a hole or small cut in a liner, it's infinitely better to discover it beforehand so that repairs can be made before the rock and gravel go in to finish the bottom.

Correct installation of the liner and care in building the feature will minimize the possibility of any leak. With a minimum of care, your liner should last for many years.

Keeping the Water Clean

The number-one question of everyone considering the installation of a water feature is "How do I keep the water clean?" The good news is that if you establish a good balance of plants and animals in your pond, the water should stay clear on its own. Most often, cloudy water and algal blooms are caused by some disruption in the balance.

Keeping the water clean is an absolute necessity for the health of pond fish, such as this school all swimming together.

If you're regularly removing spent organic matter from the pond and have floating aquatic plants on top of the water to provide shade and oxygenators beneath the surface to soak up excess nutrients, the algae will have neither the light nor the nutrients to flourish.

Manually keeping the water clean in a pond is primarily a matter of removing debris. You can use a pool skimmer to dip under and lift out flotsam and jetsam like leaves and twigs. It is a little more difficult to remove dead organic matter from the bottom, especially if your pond is heavily planted. Use a small net to maneuver between plantings, stirring up the sediment and scooping the bigger pieces. Your water will cloud for a time, but gradually clear again as things settle.

Although the plants on the bank of this pond reflect beautifully in the water, their proximity on the banks will result in plant debris falling into the water that will have to be removed.

Adding a filter and skimmer to the mix will ensure even clearer water. Debris and floating matter will be removed for you, easing the maintenance. Including these mechanical aids means you now have to maintain them. Be sure to check the filter, skimmer, and any screens regularly so they don't clog. They won't work if they can't.

The nonmoving water near this bridge is full of floating debris. This pond needs the benefit of a full-time skimmer, or the debris will have to be removed with a net.

Many skimmers have a net that traps larger debris that floats in. You need to clean this net periodically. Take it out and flip it inside out to shake the gunk out. Then re-install it. Skimmers also have a secondary screen to trap fine debris that passes through the net. This secondary screen, called a mat, does not have to be cleaned as often as the primary net, but should be regularly rinsed. To do this, shut down the pump, remove the mat, clean it by forcing water through it from the back side, and replace it. You'll know it's time to clean the filter mat when the water flow coming from the filter goes down.

Maintenance Quick Tip

Pumps can also become clogged. If you clean your skimmer and filter, and the water flow is still diminished, take a look at the pump intake. Follow the manufacturer's directions found in the pump documentation. This is a process that usually takes no more than 5 minutes.

Cleaning mechanical filters is fairly straight-forward. Biological filters are slightly more complicated because they harbor favorable bacteria that help keep your water healthy. They shouldn't be cleaned more than once a year. Because there are many different filters on the market, follow the manufacturer's suggestions for the best time to clean and directions on completing this chore properly.

Preparing for Winter

In climates where the winter includes the possibility of a deep freeze, you should take special precautions to insure your water feature isn't damaged and you don't lose valued plants or fish. Standing water expands when it freezes and exerts pressure on the sides of ponds. It takes a heck of a freeze to solidify moving water, so if your pump moves at least 2,000 gallons of water per hour, you can run the waterfall throughout the winter in all but the coldest areas, but only as long as the pump runs continuously.

With a powerful enough pump you can keep a waterfall running all winter without damaging the feature.
(Photo courtesy of Aquascape Designs, Inc.)

The moving water will keep the area around the waterfall and skimmer open and provide oxygen to the feature. Without this opening, gases dangerous to your underwater life can accumulate under the ice and damage your plants and animals.

A Word of Warning

Ponds that are part of long or slow-moving streams can present a problem in winter. If you leave the feature running, ice dams can form and divert water over the liner. If you're running during the winter, watch your feature carefully. If jams occur, clear them or shut down for the season.

Features that continue to run during the winter still lose water to evaporation. Always check your water level, and if it drops, be sure to add water to keep the level where it should be.

If you are nervous about allowing your feature to run all winter, drain it and shut it down. Remove your pump and store it where it will not freeze. It's best to keep the pump in a bucket of water. This will prevent the seal on the pump housing from drying out, which can lead to cracking.

If you have a biological filter, you should also remove the biological media bags and the filter mats. Wash and store them. By doing this at the beginning of winter, you will save some work during the spring cleanout.

Maintenance Quick Tip

You should drain small ponds with preformed liners in the winter months. If you have a pump, take it inside and store it in a bucket of water. Some people also like to remove the entire shell and flip it over so it doesn't become a winter trap for small wildlife. Spring brings a new season and you can start again.

Winters in cold climates can be harsh, but they can be beautiful. If you are careful and have the kind of water feature described earlier, you can leave it running to make your feature a four-season wonder. Smaller features and those you decide to close down for the winter just take a vacation like the rest of the garden.

The Spring Cleanup

In the spring, Mother Nature takes care of her own. Snow melts, and spring rains flush out lakes, streams, and ponds; raise water levels; and flush away the remnants of the old season, all resulting in renewed purity of the water. Because your backyard features are generally smaller and self-contained, you have to lend Mother Nature a helping hand to get your features ready for the new season.

Performing a yearly cleanout every spring will get your pond, waterfall, or stream rolling in grand fashion. Even if you achieved the mystical "balanced system" the year before, spring cleanout is a good idea for the long-term health of your pond.

This beautiful pond will need a complete spring cleanout to ensure another summer of vibrant, healthy water and plants.

Early spring is the recommended time for this maintenance task because your pond still hasn't awakened from its winter dormancy. If the temperature is below 55°F, favorable bacteria aren't going to be growing in your filter or on the gravel, so the pond is dormant. Once the bacteria are cranking away, a cleanout of this nature will reduce their numbers and interfere with the good work they're doing to keep your water clean.

While a cleanout is more than routine maintenance, you can usually do it in a day. You'll need some equipment and, as with other projects, you should have everything ready before you begin. Gather up the following items before you start:

◆ One or two 5-gallon buckets or a wheelbarrow to collect leaves and debris.

◆ Waders, hip boots, or wading boots and old clothes. You will get wet.

◆ The pond pump or a sump pump with a homemade screen of chicken wire or similar material.

◆ A high-pressure nozzle for your garden hose, or a power washer.

◆ If you have fish and frogs, a net to catch them and a container to put them in.

◆ Pruning shears to trim any plants that need it.

Begin by using the pump to drain most of the water from the pond. It's not necessary to get every gallon. Then hose down the rocks and gravel with a strong spray from the garden hose or power washer. This will flush debris caught between the rocks and wash away excess algae. Don't try to scrub all the algae away, because some algae left on the rocks will help restore the balance of the feature when you refill the system.

Maintenance Quick Tip ⎯⎯⎯⎯⎯

Collect the water you drain, and use it to water your awakening garden plants or houseplants. The nutrients in pond water are a natural, dilute fertilizer and are a great way to give your plants a spring boost.

After spraying off the rocks, remove the nozzle and wash out the loosened debris between the rocks and gravel. The runoff will go to the deepest part of the pool. Drain this again so that more of the dirty water is removed. Clean from the top down. You'll know you're done when the water being drained from the pond is nearly free of sediment and debris.

The next part of spring cleanout is to follow the manufacturer's instructions for cleaning your filter and skimmer. After that, you can begin refilling your pond. If you have fish and plants to be re-introduced, don't begin this phase until the pond is half full.

Maintenance Quick Tip ⎯⎯⎯⎯⎯

If you are refilling your pond with city tap water, it may contain chlorine. Remember to let the newly filled pond sit for a day or two before putting in plants and fish. This will allow the chlorine to dissipate naturally.

Spring cleanup is probably the single biggest chore you'll do once your feature is built. Despite the work, it's worth the effort. It is part of the cycle of the seasons, and it will get your water feature ready to enjoy for another year.

Maintenance of Your Water Feature Plants

Plants are not only the perfect visual accompaniment to water but are also essential for maintaining it in good condition. Maintenance of your plants helps them do their jobs efficiently. Neglect them at your peril and at the risk of throwing your feature's balance out of whack.

Maintenance is no more difficult than in any other area of your yard. Routine maintenance is similar, and vigilance, as always, is key.

You can do routine tasks in your regular walk-arounds:

◆ Remove dead vegetation as soon as it appears on the surface or bottom of the pond.

◆ Remove dead or dying plants immediately.

◆ Carefully cut off spent flowers to promote continued blooming and help keep the feature clean.

◆ Remove *excess* floating plants by raking them out or lifting them from the water and trimming away unwanted parts.

Routine maintenance involves thinning and removing excess plants. These lilies are so crowded they are pushing each other out of the water.

◆ If your potted plants aren't doing well, check if they are root-bound. If this happens, remove the pot from the water, then the plant from the pot. Either repot in a larger pot, trimming off dead roots, or trim about one third of the roots away, repot them in wet soil in the same pot, and top off with gravel. Then reset the pot in the pond.

Maintenance Quick Tip

Excess means "more than is required." Removing it is important because more than is required upsets the balance you're working so hard to achieve. It's important to thin and remove plants that are growing too quickly. Don't hesitate to remove the excess to keep your feature balanced.

Winter and Spring Care

If you live in an area with harsh winters, consider these additional end-of-season plant-care matters.

◆ If you have plants classified as hardy, you can leave them in an undrained pond. Hardy water lilies deeper than 12 inches can winter in the pond with no difficulty once the dead leaves and stalks are removed to within 2 to 3 inches of the base of the plant. If you drain your feature, treat these plants as tropicals (see the next bullet).

◆ You can bring tropical lilies and floating plants inside for the winter or treat them as annuals and discard them. If brought inside, remove the lily leaves and keep only the tubers, which you can store in a greenhouse or cool basement in buckets of water, then replant in the pond in the spring.

◆ Remove the dead leaves of hardy bog and marginal plants. Trim to just above the water level.

◆ Hardy plants wintering in the pond should always be placed at least 18 inches beneath the freeze line. They will nearly always survive when in water 3 feet deep.

◆ Remove and check potted plants. If they are overgrown, plan to divide and replant them in the spring.

Hardy perennial water plants require a cool dormant period. In the spring, they'll be back in all their glory.

Springtime reawakens interest in water features and the plants that live in them. Here's what to do with the plants you removed and stored for the winter:

◆ Examine your plants for signs of new growth. If none shows, check to see if the roots are alive. Also check for evidence of disease or insects.

◆ Trim off any dead plant material left from the previous growing season.

◆ Divide and/or repot plants as needed.

◆ You can also add a time-release aquatic plant food tablet to each pot. Be sure to push these tablets well into the soil.

Planting Quick Tip

When returning potted plants to the pond in the spring, always be sure to allow them to sink slowly to prevent soil from escaping into the water. Even with a gravel topping, the air in a submerging pot quickly floats soil out. Wait for final placement until the pots are completely submerged.

Watch for Disease

Don't always expect a perfect experience with your plants. They all die sometime, and like us they have encounters with disease and pestilence. Some of the common problems associated with water feature plants are:

◆ **Root rot.** This is a fungal disease which can come in with new plants or be caused by having too little oxygen in the system, plants not being right for a particular climate, introducing plants too early in the season, or plants being set at the wrong depth.

Symptoms: Look for root rot if:

◆ The plant is not thriving or appears to be dying.

◆ Leaves are wilting and yellowing.

◆ Roots have a brown or black appearance with few or no white roots or root tips visible.

◆ Roots are not crisp and brittle. Instead they are mushy and limp.

◆ The outer layer of cells easily strips off the roots.

Remedy: Remove the suspected plant from the water and discard. Then watch the other plants closely for similar signs. Make sure there is sufficient oxygen in the water and that plants are set at appropriate depths.

◆ **Scorch.** This occurs more often during periods of hot, dry weather and is caused by the inability of roots to take up enough water to replace what passes into the air from the leaves through transpiration. Scorch can also occur when there is insufficient water available or when the roots are not functioning well and can't absorb it.

Symptoms: Leaf edges appear burnt or dying with no signs of insects or disease.

Remedy: Always be aware of the conditions each of your plants must have and be sure those conditions are present in your pond. Then move any plants that might not be at the right depth or location to a better physical setting. You do not have to remove the scorched plant.

◆ **Helminthosporium leaf spot.** This is a stress-related fungal plant disease that can be caused by overcrowding, having poor air circulation, setting plants out too early, putting plants in containers that are too small, and setting plants in water that is too deep.

Symptoms: This disease becomes a possibility when you see reddish spots on leaves and stems, a yellowing of the leaves, and some dieback of the plant.

Remedy: You can do a number of things to reverse leaf spot:

◆ Improve air circulation. Move the plants farther apart.

◆ If the plant is root-bound, either trim the roots or repot in a larger container.

◆ Remove and discard affected leaves and stems.

The common thread between these conditions is how you care for your plants. If you observe proper cultural conditions, you will never see most of these problems. If you encounter a problem, the sooner you take steps to correct it, the better off your plants will be.

Additional Maintenance Issues

Here's a quick look at two more potential water feature problems—algae and animal pests.

Algae

Algae have already been mentioned a number of times. This green plant is part of nearly every water feature that is exposed to the sun. There are two basic types of algae found in backyard ponds—suspended algae and filamentous (string) algae.

Too much algae can spoil the look of a pond. This green plant can be controlled by a balanced pond with plants, filters, and fish. Otherwise, you have to take other measures.

Suspended or planktonic algae consist of millions of microscopic algae floating in the water. This is what causes water to turn green—the "pea soup" syndrome. Filamentous or string algae forms hairlike strands that attach to rocks, gravel, plants, or any other surface it can find. You can manage both forms of this green plant by maintaining proper balance in the pond.

You can control algae artificially by using chemical additives or ultraviolet light sterilization. Most backyard water gardeners try the natural way, keeping their systems in balance. The following are natural ways to control the spread of algae:

◆ Circulating the water by use of a filter and skimmer isn't totally natural, but it does simulate moving water in nature. A continually moving surface is naturally being swept clean of all debris, including floating algae.

◆ Algae require nutrients just like other plants. The combination of aquatic plants that you introduce to your garden will compete with algae for nutrition. By minimizing the amount of nutrition available to the algae, you can control its growth.

◆ If you have fish in your pond, they will graze on algae, helping to keep it in check.

◆ Favorable bacteria in the pond will compete with the algae for nutrients, limiting its growth.

◆ Gravel used to line the pond provides a home for favorable bacteria, allowing it to help with algae control and break down waste and debris.

By creating all these favorable conditions in your water feature, algae will not overtake the system, and you won't have any problems with "pea soup."

Animal Pests

A healthy pond attracts a wide variety of wildlife to your yard and the water. Most wildlife add pleasure to the experience of your water feature, but a few can be annoying and potentially dangerous to you and your water plants.

Mosquitoes are the biggest potential threat and annoyance. We talked earlier about ways to control them. Larvae are rarely found on moving water. Standing water raises the risk of infestation. The easiest way to control them is to overflow the feature when you refill, allowing the water to carry all the floating larvae away.

All the insects that trouble you in your garden will also make the water feature plants their homes. Aphids, mealy bugs, and scale suck sap from leaves and cause damage. They are everywhere, but are usually controlled by "good" bugs. No control measures are necessary unless they are out of hand.

The simplest way to control aphids is to hose off the leaves with water. If you have fish, they might snack on an aphid or two. Remove any yellowing or dead leaves from your plants, because aphids are attracted to them.

If all that doesn't do the trick or you're dealing with mealy bugs or scale, remove infested plants to a separate bucket or tub and use an insecticide soap to spray the pests. Make sure that the product is not harmful to fish, even though you've removed the plants from the pond for treatment. Allow the spray to dry, then return them to the garden.

One additional insect pest is the aquatic leaf beetle. It can be introduced with new plants or simply attracted to the water garden. These pests will chew holes in the leaves of your plants and leave speckled areas on them.

To control these beetles, you must keep dead foliage cleaned up, especially at the end of the growing season, because the beetle will overwinter in dead foliage at the pond's edge. Check the undersides of leaves and wipe off any eggs that are found there. The larvae, which look like small grubs, can be handpicked off the foliage. To control severe infestations, take the plant out of the pond and use an appropriate insecticide.

No water garden will ever be pest and maintenance free. With regular checkups, it's easy to stay ahead of the game and keep your garden healthy, balanced, and beautiful.

The Least You Need to Know

- Maintenance of water features is a lot less difficult than most people think.
- Daily observation will enable you to spot problems early and stop them in their tracks.
- If you live in an area with changing climates, you must prepare your feature for winter and give it a good cleanout in spring.
- Plants must be observed carefully for signs of disease and overgrowth to maintain the ecological balance.
- Algae and pests can be a problem if unchecked but can be controlled by a balanced ecosystem and a helping hand.

In This Part

Adding, Combining, and Planting Features

Adding goldfish, koi, or other fish to a backyard pond is not an easy decision. Keeping fish in an outdoor pond can be a delightful and rewarding experience, but you've got to create a healthful, balanced environment for the fish to survive and thrive. And you can never over-stock.

Whether you have fish or not, water and rock features placed together can often bring your backyard to yet another level. A small waterfall running through a rock garden or well-placed rocks around a pond and in a moving stream once again replicates the look found in nature. Rocks not only help accentuate a water feature but also increase the possibility for a variety of different plants to adorn the area, giving it color and a look that will make the homeowner proud.

In This Chapter

- ◆ Choosing fish for your pond
- ◆ Creating a healthy environment
- ◆ Caring for your fish
- ◆ Protecting fish in colder climates

Playful koi break the surface of the water alongside
a water lily in a healthy, clean pond.

Chapter 14

The Question of Fish

Legions of backyard water gardeners don't consider their features complete without fish. These sleek, graceful, colorful animals make water gardens come alive. They provide movement and beauty under the water to complement that occurring above and give hours of enjoyment to those observing them. Many achieve the status of true "pets" and will begin to come to you when you feed them. Some can even be hand-fed like a dog or cat.

Fish play an important role in the ecological balance of your feature. Learn to care for them, and their presence will be a positive experience in many ways. This chapter will discuss the commitment and care needed to successfully keep fish in your backyard pond.

Fish: A New Level of Commitment

Having fish in a backyard pond creates a refuge from everyday life. It's a whole new world under the water, and you can be part of it. Come home after a tiring day and relax at the side of your own backyard pond. Tropical fish hobbyists know the stress-relieving benefits of watching their fish and you will, too, as you watch your school of goldfish or koi swimming in their watery home.

Creating and caring for their small world—keeping it healthy and vibrant—is a satisfying experience. It does complicate care of the pond, however, because now you are responsible for the life you add to the water. It's one thing to lose a plant or two, another thing entirely to lose your favorite koi. Fish have personalities, and, unlike plants, respond directly to your care in a conscious fashion.

The great blue heron is a natural predator that can grab pond fish if they have no place to hide.

Your fish will undoubtedly face natural predators in your pond habitat. Neighborhood raccoons and cats will visit, and herons and other water birds may stop for a snack. These hazards are largely beyond your control, but water chemistry, sufficient food, and physical health are in your hands.

A Word of Warning

Many of the potential problems faced by backyard fish are well within your control. However, animals such as cats, raccoons, ducks, and turtles are natural predators that may be attracted to your water feature. Provide hiding places for the fish in your pond. Besides giving them a shady, safe harbor from the sun, hiding places will protect them from the reach of hungry visitors.

If your pond is large enough, a mallard drake such as this one may land on it and become a danger to your fish.

Before making your final decision to add fish, do your homework. Read about the different species and varieties available, as well as their care and feeding. Visit other gardens to see setups and talk about fish care. Talk to fish suppliers and ask for recommendations. Ask about winter care in your area. When you've done the background work, the fun begins.

Fish to Consider

Any number of species can thrive in a healthy backyard pond. In temperate climates, any fish that can take the unheated water will survive in a pond. In warmer climes, tropical fish can be included, but must be protected or brought in if the temperature threatens to drop. Each has its own characteristics and habits, and you can add more than one species if you choose. Let's take a look at the more popular temperate choices, which can be used almost anywhere.

Comets (*Carassius auratus*)

Most people have been familiar with Comets, or common goldfish, since they were kids. Everyone's "first fish" is a goldfish. They are inexpensive and sold at all pet shops. Because they are hardy and can tolerate a wide range of conditions, they make great pond fish and will often do better outdoors than they do in the ubiquitous goldfish bowls on kitchen counters and bedroom dressers. A happy goldfish can live up to 20 years in a healthy environment.

Goldfish range from cream to nearly all black in color, but the majority are generally orange-red. Average length for a mature fish is about 6 inches, but they can grow to 10 inches or more in a pond. It will surprise those with "bowl" experience that goldfish will breed freely in a large pond. In smaller areas the adults will eat the fry before they mature if they aren't kept well fed. In addition to the everyman's goldfish, there are fancy varieties of goldfish, like Shubunkins, Orandas, and Calico Fantails. They are beautiful but less hardy than the common variety. These fancy types will need more protection over the winter months.

Goldfish are among the most popular of pond fish and can live up to 20 years in a healthy environment.

Golden Orfe (*Leicuscus idus*)

Golden Orfe are long, slender-bodied fish that look almost tubular because of their snub nose. They grow very quickly the first few years in the pond and can reach lengths up to 18 inches. As their name implies, they have golden-orange bodies sometimes marked with black. Their undersides are silver.

Golden Orfe are especially attractive pond fish because of their character traits. They are surface feeders and can often be observed darting from deep water to capture gnats, mosquitoes, and other insects on the surface. They may leap into the spray of fountains and will become tame if they are hand-fed. Another variety, the Silver Orfe, is all silver.

Rudd (*Cyprinidae Scardinus erythropthalmus*)

These fish aren't as popular with pond owners because they aren't as colorful as the other varieties. Some feel they look more natural in features than more colorful varieties. Rudd can grow to 8 inches or longer and have red fins to go with silver bodies. They are fond of ponds with lots of plant life but enjoy the sun so they appreciate open water, too. They do well in larger ponds where both conditions are present.

Rudd breed freely when happy and can be seen swimming together in large schools with fish of various sizes. In ponds with sufficient insect populations, these fish won't require much in the way of supplemental feeding. They also eat filamentous algae, which helps keep the pond clear in the most natural way.

Koi (*Cyprinus carpio*)

Koi are considered by many as water garden royalty. These beautiful fish are by far the most popular pond fish and have roots that go far back in Japanese culture. They come in a wide range of colors and markings and can grow to 18 inches or more, sometimes a lot more. Koi are a fancy variety of the common carp and are bottom feeders who love to root around in the rocks and rubble on the bottom of the pond. They have appendages, like some catfish, that resemble whiskers on each side of their mouth that help them root around.

Koi are often called the royalty of water gardens. These playful fish can become real pets and have been known to live more than 100 years.

Koi Quick Tip

As amazing as it seems, koi have the potential to live up to 100 years. They become as individual in personality as a dog or cat. In Japan, long-lived koi are often willed to the next generation. Keep your pond healthy, and koi will be with you for a long time.

Koi are extremely hardy and built to withstand the real-world extremes. While it's best to minimize dramatic changes in condition, koi can survive changes in the temperature and pH of their water and lack of commercial food. Koi are rainbows with fins and come in a bewildering array of patterns featuring white, orange, red, black, bluish, yellow, and a metallic sheen. No two individual fish are exactly alike, and buyers pay premium prices for the particular look of their fish.

Breeders raise three classes of koi—pond, ornamental, and show quality. Most backyard water gardeners will be very happy with pond-quality koi and will save money. Fish are sold by class, look, and size. Needless to say, ornamental and show-quality fish demand a substantial premium.

A Balanced Environment

A "balanced" pond is even more important when fish are added to the equation. Fish contribute positively and negatively to this balance. On the plus side, they help control insect and algae populations. On the other hand, their waste product remains in the pond, altering the chemistry of the water if the plants and filtration you've installed aren't functioning as planned.

The first rule of keeping fish is to not overstock your pond. This school of goldfish might be happy now, but as they grow they can begin to overcrowd the feature and encounter health problems.

The most common mistake new pond owners make is to overstock with fish. You can have too much of a good thing. Don't assume that if 3 fish swimming together look good, then 30 will look 10 times better. Every ounce of fish in the pond has an impact on the water and the other life in the pond. Even if the number of fish you have stays the same, their impact on the system will grow as they do.

It's the "mass" of fish that's the most important measurement for pond health. Serious ponders actually weigh their fish on a periodic basis to make sure that they don't overstock. Approximate mass is usually good enough because the main reason of determining the total fish mass in the pond is to set general rules for your pond's operation and for acceptable populations of fish. Ratios of koi length to mass have led to the creation of tables that assist in estimating your total mass.

One commonly cited rule is to have no more than 1 inch of fish for every square foot of surface area. A 4×6 pond has 24 square feet of surface area. Using the formula, you can have 4 (6-inch) fish. But remember, the fish will grow. As they grow, this rule goes out the window. Now your original choice of fish will be too much for your pond. There is another problem. When a koi doubles in length, its mass doesn't just double, it increases by more than eight times. If you start with 4 (6-inch) koi and through your good care they grow to 12 inches, the fish load is not twice as great; it is 8 times as great, or more!

A Word of Warning

There are several formulas for determining how many fish to stock in a pond. Whichever you use, the objective is to not overstock. Koi, incidentally, need more space than other fish. When in doubt, leave a few out.

Growing fish and increasing populations add to the amount of waste and toxic ammonia in the water. A pond with plants and a good filter will neutralize these contaminants and keep the water healthy. When the system can't support the waste produced, you've disrupted the balance and you've got trouble, so you must take immediate steps to restore a healthy balance.

Starting with the annual spring cleanout discussed in the maintenance chapter is helpful. It gives you a fresh start every year.

Introducing the Fish

After you've calculated the number and size of fish you want to live in your pond, it's time to find them. As with everything else, doing a little research is the key. Only deal with reputable suppliers for your livestock. Avoid places with dead or sick-looking fish in their display and sales tanks. Talk with the fish experts, and bring your fish home alive.

Fish are introduced into ponds the same way you would introduce them into a home aquarium. Purchased fish are generally transported in plastic bags filled with water. When you get home, let the bag float in your pond for a couple hours. This will allow the temperature of the water in the bag to slowly adjust to that of the pond, eliminating sudden shock to the fish.

After a while, mix some pond water into the bag as it continues to float. Every half-hour, add more pond water. This helps the fish adjust to any differences in water chemistry.

These suggestions are especially important in new ponds and ponds being reopened in spring where the water isn't "seasoned" by being lived in by other fish.

The combination of floating plants and oxygenators is necessary for a balanced pond and healthy fish.

Plants and Filters for Healthy Fish

Keeping your fish healthy requires a varied population of the types of plants discussed in Chapter 12 and the use of mechanical or biological filters. In theory, a combination of plants can do the job, adding oxygen to the water, balancing nutrients, and cultivating good bacteria and other beneficial pond life. The more plants you have, the better the benefits.

The reason for this healthy pond is obvious. The fish swim among a perfect balance of plants to help keep the water clean. (Photo courtesy of Aquascape Designs, Inc.)

Natural processes don't always work as they should in a man-made setting, so skimming and filtration are always recommended in the garden pond with fish. Removing organic matter and particles from the water is more important with fish, which produce their own waste to add to the negative side of the ledger. Anything you can do to reduce waste will help buffer the water against the contribution from the fish. Creation of ammonia is a great concern. Plants will utilize much of it, but a biological filter, with its population of bacteria, keeps the control of ammonia working. In fact, rules for keeping everything working together when you have fish are similar to those for fishless ponds:

◆ Keep the filter running 24 hours a day. Fish don't take the night off, and the organisms in the filter need a constant supply of oxygenated water to survive.

◆ Always follow the manufacturer's instructions regarding the filter's flow rate. Too high or too low a flow will reduce the efficiency of the filter.

◆ Also follow the recommendations for maintenance of the filter. You will have to clean the pre-filter or settlement area whenever waste builds up.

Water Chemistry

We need to make a couple points about water chemistry. Municipal water is treated with chlorine and other chemicals to make it safe to drink. This is good for us but not so hot for fish. Make sure you let your water sit for a while before putting fish into it. It takes at least 24 hours for the chlorine to dissipate.

The gravel and large rocks in this pond not only help keep the water clean but also give the koi living there plenty of places to seek refuge from possible predators. (Photo courtesy of Aquascape Designs, Inc.)

The *pH* of the water is the degree to which the water is acidic or alkaline. Too much of either is not good for the fish. Aim for a pH of 7.2 to 7.8, which is slightly alkaline. Your fish will be fine between 6.5 and 8.5. A test kit will provide you with instructions and a reading on your water. As with indoor aquariums, you can obtain safe chemicals that will alter the pH if it is necessary for the health of your fish.

Keeping water and pond clean is just a matter of routine maintenance. As with the water garden, the task isn't difficult. But you should keep a constant eye on both plants and fish, as well as the filtering system, to make sure everything is functioning smoothly and looking good.

Backyard Lingo

Almost everything you put in your water affects its **pH** (from the French meaning "strength of hydrogen"), the measure of acidity or alkalinity of a solution on a logarithmic scale of 0 to 14, where 7 is neutral. If you don't remove dead leaves and plant debris and allow them to collect in your pond, the water will become more acidic as they break down. If you have a pond or water feature made with concrete, cement, or mortar, then lime can leech out causing the water to become more alkaline. It's a good idea to check the pH of your pond on a regular basis, especially when fish live there.

In theory, this cutaway shows a balanced ecosystem for fish. There is a biological filter and waterfall at one end, a skimmer at the other, gravel and plants in place, and a deep section for the fish to swim.

Feeding

Feeding your fish is a relatively simple matter, with one hard-and-fast rule. Don't overfeed! Get a good commercial food for the fish you have. If you can't feed two or three small meals a day, feed once a day but give the fish no more than they can consume in 5 minutes. Remember, fish will scavenge in the pond, eating insects and plant material, so they do not need an abundance of food.

Fish also do not digest their food well in cool weather. So as the temperatures begin dropping in the fall and your water temperature becomes lower, lighten up on the feeding even more than usual. There are special foods for spring and autumn feeding when the temperatures are low. They help the fish digest better even though it's cold. Excess, uneaten food will decay and just cause problems with your water and the overall balance of the ecosystem.

Again, know your fish. Some, such as koi, prefer to feed on the bottom, while Golden Orfe are surface feeders. Small fish can't handle the pellet foods made for larger specimens. Flake foods are best until they grow larger. When fish are about 3 to 4 inches long, you can move them to stick foods, which are made in floating and sinking formulas. These soften faster than the dense pellets for the big boys so that smaller fish can break them up. Be sure you get the appropriate kind of food that is best for your fish.

A Word of Warning

Because long-lived pond fish can become pets, many people like to hand-feed them. This can be a fun experience, but it can also put your fish in danger. If they are used to being hand-fed, they may come to the surface as soon as they see movement above them. No one knows if a fish can tell whether it's you or if it simply responds to the movement. If a cat or raccoon is up there, it could be the end for the fish. If you use sinking food pellets, the fish will get used to feeding on the bottom and stay clear of danger at the surface.

Climate Considerations

In warm climates, fish can stay in the pond all year round. If you plan to do a spring cleanout to refresh your feature, net the fish, put them in a temporary tub (covered so they can't jump out), and return them to the pond when you're finished.

Winter is another matter. If you have a relatively small pond and live in an area where the pond will freeze solid from top to bottom, it's best to bring the fish inside. Put them in a large aquarium and watch your feeding. Float them, the same as when putting them in the pond. Check the water periodically to make sure it's clean. Filter to remove impurities just as in the pond.

In most cases, pond fish can winter over in the pond if certain conditions are met. The pond should be at least 2 feet deep. In fact, the deeper the better if you're going to leave them in the pond during a cold winter. There should also always be a hole in the ice to allow for a gas exchange. Otherwise, gases will accumulate beneath the ice and kill your fish.

This moving pond, which remains open in winter, is a good environment in which fish can survive sub-freezing temperatures.

You can keep that important hole in the ice in two ways. One is to place a pump that pushes at least 150 gallons of water per hour close to the surface of the water. The water from the pump should not bubble more than 1 inch above the surface. This kind of agitation will prevent freezing and allow for gas exchange. You should place the pump in a bucket with the intake surrounded by stones to prevent clogging. In the alternative, if you've got a waterfall, you can keep if running.

You can also put a floating heater on the surface of the pond to keep the ice open. These heaters can be expensive to operate, so it's your choice. If you opt for the heater, you also must use a small submersible pump to keep a steady supply of oxygen in the water.

A Word of Warning

If you winter your fish in the pond, be extra careful at spring cleanup. Fish wintering in cold climates are weak in the spring, and any undue stress can be damaging to them. When you drain the pond, don't net the fish until there is only about 6 inches of water in the deepest part. That way, they will be easier to catch. Never leave their holding bucket in direct sun for long periods of time. Make sure the new water has been properly de-chlorinated (if city water) and equalize the water temperature in the pond and holding buckets. You can do this by floating the buckets in the pond and slowly splashing pond water into them. Once the fish are back home, they should be fine and ready for another year.

On the whole, pond fish are a hardy lot. Their care and well-being, however, depends on you. With basic knowledge, the proper equipment, and an observant eye, you should have no trouble keeping your fish happy and healthy for many years.

The Least You Need to Know

- Pond fish are mostly hardy creatures that can live a long life.
- The biggest mistake most people make is overstocking their pond. When in doubt, leave a few out.
- The process for keeping a pond with fish clean is the same as keeping a planted water feature clean.
- The spring cleanout is a very important part of fish maintenance whether the fish winter over in the pond or not.
- If your fish are wintering over in an outdoor pond, keep a hole in the surface of the ice no matter how cold it gets.

In This Chapter

- ◆ Rock and water go together
- ◆ The importance of rocks to water features
- ◆ Enhancing a rock garden with water
- ◆ The backyard pond as a work of nature

Rock and water dominate this home front. A rock wall leads to a
small waterfall with a pond nestled among the rock and plants.

Chapter 15

Combining Rock and Water Features

Rock and water features can be built in isolation, but the best of each of the features includes the other. Rock is nearly essential for the creation of water features, so it's natural that the margins of the water feature be rock gardens of one sort or another. And a rock garden without a stream, waterfall, or pool is something less than it could have been.

In this chapter, we discuss the various ways rock and water work best together and how you can incorporate the two elements to make the best features for your backyard. Remember, you can have one without the other, but it's best to think about incorporating the two for the best of both worlds.

Rock and Water Together

Rock and water together is a marriage made in backyard heaven. Just because the two look good together doesn't mean you should tie the knot. Style, design, and scale still matter. Don't jumble the yard up with a hodge-podge conglomeration of brick-a-brack constructions. Make sure that what you're doing makes sense in terms of the whole of the yard and your plan for its design. When the combination works, the effect is magical. When it doesn't, it can be something decidedly less.

Oftentimes you're working with elements of rock and water from the very beginning. In almost all water features, particularly those that include a pond, waterfall, or stream, rocks play an integral part. In addition to providing a natural look, they often direct the moving water and, by extension, control its sound and speed.

Including water in a rock feature involves a little more forethought. Adding water at a later date will involve deconstruction and rebuilding, not an easy task in a finished garden.

No matter what the situation, rocks and water go together. They highlight each other and together build the character of the garden. Even a small container water garden set among rocks makes a big difference, adding sound and movement to the hard, unyielding stone. Any time you build one, you'd do well to think about including the other.

This house has a relatively barren yard, one that is just begging for a design using rock and water.
(Photo courtesy of Aquascape Designs, Inc.)

After the installation, a stone path leading to a natural pond surrounded by rocks and filled with plants has replaced the lawn. It works.
(Photo courtesy of Aquascape Designs, Inc.)

Rocks Around the Water Feature

Rocks are most often used in and around water features because of the look they create. The reason that rocks are part of the game plan is simple. We're oftentimes imitating nature. The use of rocks is often the best, most artistic way to complete construction of certain features. Without them, the feature would look artificial and barren.

Rocks are used at the pond's edge to help define the boundary of land and water. Used in this way, the rock should extend into the pond at one or two spots so that it looks like a large outcropping, rather than a cheap necklace draped around the pond. In streams and waterfalls, rocks are the material of choice for creating a natural and aesthetic path for the water to traverse as it makes its way into the pond. There's really not a better way to do it. In fact, large, flat rocks near your features can even function as seating. Just be sure the stones are placed well and secured.

In a formal feature, rock might be superfluous. But even in these cases stone is usually used, though in this situation it's often cut and shaped.

Rock Makes the Waterfall

Natural-looking waterfalls are among the most beautiful and graceful of the backyard water features. In Chapter 11, we described the basic installation procedures for several types of waterfalls, including the pondless waterfall. Professional designers and installers use the same basic methods. Much of what they do works so well because of the way they use rock.

This waterfall, surrounded by rock, is located right outside the home, an installation the homeowner obviously preferred.   (Photo courtesy of Aquascape Designs, Inc.)

This rock-ledged waterfall has been left running during the winter. The snow blends in perfectly with the rock and water to create yet another great look.
(Photo courtesy of Aquascape Designs, Inc.)

No one is going to have Niagara Falls in his or her backyard, with water taking one long fall from top to bottom. But anyone can construct a miniature waterfall with just a single cascade of water. Most people prefer several levels with the water running over each. After the appropriate digging and placement of the liner, the cascades are created by a series of flat rocks placed at different levels, almost like a stairway. Smaller rocks are then placed off to the side to flank the spillway, with more rock as a border for the streambed.

Waterfall Quick Tip

Even with a small waterfall, the creative placement of rock can help give the feature character. For example, if you have just a single stream of water cascading over a single rock ledge and then falling a foot or so into a pond below, you can place rocks at the base of the fall to deflect the water and make for a more interesting runoff into the pond.

If you have a pond with a biological filter returning water at the end of the pond, it's easy to use rock to conceal the filter and create a small waterfall at the same time. Raise the filter at the end of the pond, and set a rock ledge with smaller stone beneath to form a miniature waterfall. Build a mound of earth with larger rocks or a small wall around the filter box to conceal it and provide an additional area for planting. The entire setting will look very natural, and the waterfall will provide aeration to your pond.

The success of most waterfalls is almost entirely dependent upon the creative use of rocks. Water spills downhill. It will course over nearly anything. The precise placement of stone will determine the direction, speed, and sound of your water flow. Adjust the placement of stone during construction and run tests to see if you've got the look and sound you want. Like tuning an engine, you can "tweak" your waterfall. There are many things you can do. The more of these features you see, the more you'll realize how vital the use of rock becomes to creating an effective water feature.

A Natural Rock-Filled Stream

Backyard streams always include rock as a vital part of their construction. Rock is used alongside the stream and should be included to give something for the water to chase around, gurgling and splashing. Without rock, streams would be dull, quiet, and bland.

Most backyard streams have a width between 2 and 4 feet. The best streams vary their width to provide interest. The rock used along the edge should vary in size as well, and should, in places, spill over the bank and into the stream.

Make sure your pump and recirculation system will handle enough water to make the feature flow. Width and depth of your stream are, to some extent, dependent on the number of gallons per hour your pump can push. Talk with your pump vendor/pond supply dealer about the size you'll need to accomplish your goal.

This cutaway of a streambed shows how to alternate deep and shallow areas to create an interesting but irregular flow of water.

Though the depth of streams is usually 6 inches to 1 foot, it's advisable to vary the depth, creating pools where the water will gather and swirl, shelves where the water will skim quickly over the top, and deeper sections that may even be sufficient to house fish. Rocks of various sizes should be put around the perimeter of the stream, with some large pieces set right in it. Plan where you want to place the larger boulders and dig out for them before placing the stream liner. Digging out allows the finished placement to look more natural because the rocks sit in the bed of the stream rather than on it. Apply the same principle to rock placement in the stream as you do to placement in the garden.

Rock Quick Tip

Set your rock well, making sure the bottom side has the fullest possible contact with the liner. The idea is to have the water race around the rock, not go under it.

If your stream has shallow shelving for the water to skim over, disrupt the flow in a spot or two with smaller rocks placed on the shelf. Nature rarely sets a flat table.

Rock Quick Tip

If your pump's churning its heart out and your stream still seems a bit sluggish, you can speed things up by selectively damming the flow. Blocking the water and forcing it to flow through a narrow opening concentrates the water in the center, speeding up the flow as it squeezes through the opening.

One way to get an increased flow in spots is to narrow the stream by damming it with rocks, as this sketch illustrates. The water will pick up speed as it pushes through the narrow opening.

Rocks set in groups along the bank of the stream create a perfect planting area for rock plants and marginals, depending on the moisture available in the soil. Utilizing all the available planting spots allows you to expand the number of plants you can use and provides additional design opportunities, each of which contributes to the picture as a whole.

Putting a Water Feature in Your Rock Garden

Just as the use of rock in and around a water feature opens up a world of opportunities for design and planting, so too, the inclusion of a water feature in the rock garden has sizable impact on the look of the entire area.

A rock garden by itself can be an impressive sight. A properly constructed rock feature, even on a small scale, creates an imposing backdrop for what, with proper selection of plants, can be a veritable jewel-box of a garden. A limitless array of tiny plants with outsize flowers will provide endless interest and fascination.

Though this rock garden doesn't have a totally natural look, it's still an effective feature with the small waterfall running through the middle.   (Photo courtesy of Aquascape Designs, Inc.)

Adding water to this equation takes the garden to a whole new level. It's as if you've been looking for a missing piece for a long time and just haven't found it until now. The look of the feature and your design, your enjoyment of it, all will be enhanced.

The addition of water creates areas where you can include mountain plants that come from moist alpine meadows and craggy bog gardens. These alpines won't grow in a traditional rock garden with its exceptional drainage and relatively dry soil. Include a water feature and a whole new suite of opportunities presents itself.

If you have an existing rock garden, consider the addition of a water feature. If you're starting from scratch, mark out and build the water feature first; then construct a rock garden around it as explained in Chapter 5. Making the water portion of this project first will save you time and trouble. Imagine a small waterfall running down the center of the garden, with rock coming down to its banks along its course. Here's how you can do it:

1. To install the waterfall, begin by digging out a small pool or pond near or at the bottom of the garden. If you're adding to an existing garden, carefully remove and pot any plants you wish to save, and move existing rock to a safe area out of the way of your project.

This is a nice yard with a garden on the perimeter, but the homeowner wanted more.   (Photo courtesy of Aquascape Designs, Inc.)

2. Next, dig a trench up the hill from the pool as wide as you'd like your stream to be. Consider digging in drops and areas that are deeper than the average depth you've chosen for your feature.

3. The trench does not have to be in a straight line but can be irregular, with bends and different widths.

4. Use the same procedure described earlier to line the pond and trench with a flexible liner. This step may get more complicated if you get fancy with your streambed, but you can glue liner sections together to create nearly any arrangement.

This is the same yard as in the previous photo. Only now rock and water have been combined into another backyard pond with a small waterfall. It changes the entire ambiance of the yard.
(Photo courtesy of Aquascape Designs, Inc.)

5. Place a submersible pump in the pond with the return line running alongside the trench, either buried under the ground or camouflaged by rocks and plants.

6. Then set up several flat rocks at various levels in the runway, adding smaller rocks and gravel between them. Set stones to create falls at intervals down the watercourse.

7. Fill and test your new construction.

Now the waterfall is ready. Adding the sight and sound of running water to the solid, permanent, and stable feel of your rock garden brings it alive in a way that nothing else can. Combining rock and water is a win-win situation. Each adds to the other in immeasurable ways, and the benefits are all yours.

Giving the Pond a Natural Look with Rock

Imagine installing a backyard pond, digging out the ground, setting your liner, filling it with water, and leaving it. Such a feature looks more like an outdoor bathtub than a pond. Fortunately, these kinds of installations are rare. Even the most basic yard ponds, whether installed with the preformed shell or flexible liner, involve some use of rocks. Some people simply use a rock border around the pond to camouflage the top of the shell or cover the liner. Others employ a more formal look with flat pavers and may put a small patio alongside the pond.

This newly installed pond already has the makings of a fine feature. It has few rocks, no plants yet, and only a beginning ecosystem. (Photo courtesy of Aquascape Designs, Inc.)

Those who make the decision to truly combine rock and water at their ponds go much further. Typically, these homeowners are after the natural look. They use a lot more rock. First, they'll line the pond with gravel. This has beneficial consequences for the plants and fish that will live there as described earlier. They may construct a stream or waterfall to return filtered, circulating water to the pond. They might also construct rock features at some distance from the pond that will balance and enhance the entire composition.

Here is the same pond with additional rocks and many new plants. It not only looks better but also now has a healthier ecosystem coming into balance. (Photo courtesy of Aquascape Designs, Inc.)

There are a couple things to avoid when using rock at and in a pond. First, don't simply ring the pond with stones. This "necklace" effect is unnatural and is not a good use of stone. It's far better to leave sections rockless and build an intermittent ring, including piles of rock at selected locations to break up the shoreline. Next, too few people think to put rock into the pond. They'll happily put rock everywhere around it, but the pond bed is left looking sterile and incomplete. Build a few stone structures underwater, with rock surfaces exposed. Turtles and other wildlife will make use of these spots for sunning and be much more visible themselves. Fish will appreciate

the underwater portions of these structures and use the crevices and irregular surfaces to their advantage. You can even build some stone structures totally underwater to show through the surface but retain some mystery and intrigue.

The rocks won't exist in isolation. Use water and marginal plants to soften, colorize, and blend your hardscaping. Their presence will help tie the water to the land, providing a transitional zone that grades one environment into the other.

You can also use rock if your only concern isn't making your feature look like nature's child. Especially if your water feature is close to your house, combining rock with water may mean building a walk or patio from which to view your creation. A sitting area is a delightful addition to the garden. A small fountain or burbler near it can give the pond movement and sound for those nearby to enjoy.

The Least You Need to Know

- Rock and water are natural complements, and their sum is far more than the total of their parts.
- Rocks in and around a water feature add character, bring more creative planting possibilities, and produce an enduring framework for the entire picture.
- Waterfalls, streams, and ponds have added character when rock becomes part of the equation.
- You can add a small waterfall to your rock garden even long after you have completed the garden.
- Almost every kind of backyard pond will benefit from the use of rock, whether in a natural or formal setting.

In This Chapter

- ◆ Marginal plantings, a perfect blend
- ◆ Spreading from water to land
- ◆ Plantings around ponds, streams, waterfalls
- ◆ The bog garden, the great divide

This large pond is highlighted by three small waterfalls and all kinds of plants and comes right up to a patio from which it can be fully enjoyed. It is a great feature.   (Photo courtesy of Aquascape Designs, Inc.)

Planting Where Water Meets Land

There's a place where the usual rules don't apply, where what you know will be challenged, and where you must face and conquer new problems. It's a whole new world, the place where water meets land, and it's an indispensable opportunity. Expand your mind and the beauty of your yard with marginal plantings.

We've already talked about planting in the water and in the rocks. Now we will discover how we can use the plants of the margins, bogs, and shorelines to add to our garden and knit the entire package together. Marginal habitats include plants along the banks of ponds and streams, and for our purposes, those of a special kind of wet garden—the bog. Some people will create bog gardens along the banks of their water features and marginal areas extending from shallow water areas to those that are on shore but still moist.

Marginal Habitats

Marginal plants are often classified in three different groups. These are marsh plants, which like to keep their feet in the water; waterside plants that grow in moist areas such as bog gardens but not with their feet underwater; and moisture-loving border plants, which seek out moisture but don't have to live in wet earth.

Marginal plants are often found in nature along the perimeter of lakes, ponds, wetlands, and streams. In an aesthetic sense, they serve to soften the edges in the transition zone between water and land, and where rock is involved, will blend it into the plantings.

This sequence will show you how to plant and develop the rocky area near a water feature with marginal plants. Here the area to be planted is only inhabited by weeds.

The first *Carex conica* 'Snowline' is being positioned by placing the pot on the spot where it will ultimately be planted.

Once the position is determined, dig a hole with a small trowel.

Depending on the type of feature you have and the way you have surrounded it with rock, you can sow these marginal plantings as individual plants or in groups, whatever appears more effective. This is not bog planting. The soil surrounding a pond or stream is often as dry as that in the rest of your garden, especially if the liner has been installed correctly and water is not spilling over the banks. You will do the actual planting in the same way as with other plants on dry land. The exception to this is those marginal plants that will be planted within the margins of your liner in the shallow water areas at the edges. You will plant these plants like pond plants that root into the bottom.

The new plant has been removed from the pot, its root ball intact, and it is carefully placed into the hole.

There are some design and horticultural things to keep in mind when planning your marginal plantings. These aren't hard-and-fast rules because the habitats around water features can differ. However, it is always a good idea to think about them.

The first plant is in place. The look of the area is already changing, and many of the weeds are already gone.

Now it's time to add the gravel mulch, which will help keep weeds down and retain soil moisture, while looking good at the same time.

◆ Always think about how marginal plants will look from the other side of the pond. The use of color can be dramatic, especially when the plants and their blooms are reflected in the water.

◆ If your water feature doesn't have a rock border, marginal plants can hide any liner that shows. Many marginal plants in the wild colonize down the bank and into the water. Don't be afraid to use this very effective tactic.

Several more plantings of 'Snowline' have been added to make a grouping. Note the different type of plant that has been added behind the rock for contrast.

◆ In most cases, try to place the low-growing plants beside the bank and the taller ones farther back so they can be equally appreciated from across the water.

Plants and mulch are together at last. Now this section of the feature is complete. Note how different it looks from the beginning of the sequence.

◆ If you do any mulching of your upland marginal plants to help retain moisture, be sure the mulch isn't close to the water. Excess organic matter in the water will upset the balance of your system.

Unless you've got a formal, edged water feature, you'll probably welcome the chance to add these marginal plantings. You may also find it worthwhile to add a bog garden to the mix. (More on that later.)

Connecting Pond to Yard

The primary purpose of marginal planting is simple. You've made a wonderful pond in your yard, a healthy feature with moving water, the right ratio of plants, and fish. On its own, the pond looks a little lost. It has no connection to the rest of the yard and is an island of sorts, surrounded by a sea of lawn. That's when you decided to use rock around it to make the feature appear more natural and to add more character to the entire area. To complete the picture, you now need to tie the two together. Marginal plants or a bog garden are the perfect solution.

Planting Quick Tip

You can add bog gardens in two ways: The first is outside the liner entirely. This method usually involves excavation and the setting of a separate liner, which is filled with a planting mixture rather than water. The mixture is lined so that it stays moist. The second method is to create boggy areas within the water feature, making use of the water you've added to the garden to keep the soil moist. These are usually at the pond's edge, sometimes with the liner slightly breached to create a slow overflow.

Marginal plants, like water and rock plants, will quickly hook you. Therefore, don't overload the area around the pond with rocks. As with the rock garden, use rocks judiciously, leaving enough planting areas to create the look and color schemes you want. A spotty planting among the rocks just won't do the trick.

If you do not have a rock border around your pond, use some low-growing plants around the edge. These plants will soften the edge and also hide any liner that shows. Avoid plants that grow tall and flop over, creating an unsightly situation.

Lysichiton camtschatcense is a long name. Simply put, this is an effective and striking bog plant perfect for the water's edge.

These small plants will usually not stray too far from the edge. Leave space behind them for some of the wetland plants that are big and bold. Many of these plants have stately foliage and brightly colored flowers. They can make a dramatic statement, being reflected in the pond and drawing attention from the edge, which helps the transition from water to land.

A Word of Warning

Whenever you're planting, think of nature. Plants don't grow in a perfect circle or line. Your plantings should appear more random, with several varieties and small groupings juxtaposed against individual plants of different sizes. The more random and natural the marginal plantings appear, the more dramatic effect you'll achieve.

Be sure to include plants with leaves of different sizes and textures. Although the planting is "natural," look for patterns and repeat elements to unify the design. The color of the flowers is not the only important factor. Consider the size and shape of the flowers as well. This will accomplish the same kinds of design goals.

Time of flowering is also important. It's useful if your plants bloom at different times of the season. All these suggestions are geared to accomplishing one objective, every gardener's goal and number one concern: maintaining season-long interest.

A Word of Warning

How far back from the feature you take your marginal plantings depends on the placement of the pond in your yard and the amount of space in which you have to work. Don't crowd out the yard by overplanting. Scale, again, is an important consideration. If your marginal plantings are too wide, they will gain more prominence than the water feature they are intended to frame.

Primula and ferns planted together on the margins of a pond create a beautiful contrast of blooms and foliage.

Think before you sink. Always plan your planting before you lift a trowel. If your plants are potted, place them in position in their pots. Then step away and take a look. Adjust the pots until your placement is just right. It's easier to change things now than it will be when everything is in the ground.

Planting Quick Tip

Because your water feature is going to need regular maintenance, be sure to leave a way to get to the mechanical elements. Don't overplant the banks. Too many rocks and plants can block access to the pond or will result in a pathway that looks like a herd of wildebeest has come through. You shouldn't have to become a rock climber or trample your plants just to remove debris or check the filters in your pond.

As your plantings move farther from the pond, you should begin using plants that aren't dependant on moist conditions and actually prefer a drier, better-drained soil. It's necessary to be aware of the conditions your plants require so that you can put them in the right spot.

A Word of Warning

Your water feature with its marginal plantings may look like something you'd stumble across deep in a wilderness, but remember that it's man-made. This has implications for the soil conditions at the margin of your feature. An artificial feature doesn't have the same kind of moist bank areas found in a natural pond or stream, where the water is not stopped from penetrating the ground by a liner.

Marginal planting around a pond is the best way to tie the feature to dryer upland areas. Similar plantings will work alongside streams and waterfalls, although it's not as easy to maintain moist soil because of changes in the slope.

A small trickle of water over the edge of these rocks keeps the area moist and perfect for the sedums, mosses, and ferns that are growing in the area.

Planting the Stream or Waterfall

The same general rules apply for planting streams and waterfalls, but with some differences because of their construction. It's less likely that you'll have significant numbers of plants actually in the water, so marginal plantings gain in importance.

Natural-looking, asymmetrical planting is again the preferred way to soften the banks of your water feature. As with the pond, if the sides of the stream are linear and not bordered by rock, it's a good idea to use some plants that will billow over the edge and break up the straight line of the bank. Plant a mixture of foliage and flowering plants in various locations around the banks. Leave room for groups of plants among your rockscaping as you did with the pond.

Even more than with ponds, and because the watercourse is artificial, the banks will be relatively dry with the liner preventing water from moving into the soil. Although this appears to be a marginal habitat, it won't have sufficient moisture to grow water-loving plants. If you use marginal plants in such a location, be sure that they receive the moisture they need.

This small waterfall gives the area the makings of a great feature. What's missing are the plants, which can be carefully positioned between the rocks.

Waterfalls present a different challenge. Natural waterfalls are heavily bordered with rock and don't really have a bank area like ponds and streams. Consequently, plantings—and there should be plantings—must be done among the rocks. Make use of pockets and areas between the rocks. If they remain moist, use marginal plants to transition from the watercourse to drier areas. If the soil is dry and remains so, you may have to choose other plants to create the effect you are looking for. A mixture of foliage and flowering plants that complements the rock but doesn't overwhelm it will enhance the appearance of your waterfall.

A waterfall in your rock garden gives you a range of interesting possibilities. If the spillway flows into a small pond, the possibilities are even better. Gradually shifting from marginals near the water to rock garden plants in the drier areas and aquatic plants in the pond gives you an incredible number of species to choose from. Combining plants in this way creates an attractive and diverse garden.

This small waterfall already has moss growing on the rocks with perfect conditions for moisture-loving mosses and ferns.

Be innovative, mix your plants well, and allow them to complement the feature in which you set them. Your selection of plants is the best way to make the meeting of water and land work and puts your personal stamp on the garden.

The Bog Garden

The bog garden is a unique feature, almost a combination of a land and water garden. In essence, the bog is like a swamp, with soil that is constantly wet but not flooded. Bog gardens are often installed on the banks of a pond and look very natural there because they are sometimes found around dying bodies of water. They have their own fascinating flora, including many carnivorous plants, orchids, and other acid-loving species.

Bog gardens can also be installed as separate and interesting features in their own right. These unusual gardens should be excavated to about 18 inches deep. They can be constructed with a rigid or a flexible liner.

Bogs are easy to combine with other water features. They can be installed alongside a pond by excavating an additional shell, extending the liner from the pond and situating it so that the liner is just low enough to allow overflow from the pond to seep into the bog area. The bog should not fill with water. Puncture the liner in the bog with a pitchfork or other sharp implement in several places to allow excess water to drain off.

A Word of Warning _____

If you install a bog garden either on the banks of your pond or as a separate, stand-alone feature, you'll have an interesting place to plant. But a bog is also a magnet for weeds, which love the moist conditions. Weeds must be checked often and rigorously in a bog garden, or they can quickly take over the entire area.

This peaty bog soil is perfect for bog and marginal planting, as evidenced by the beautiful low grower that is thriving in the moisture.

Special Soil

Bog soil is typically moisture retentive, acidic, and low in nutrition. The plants that grow in bogs have adapted to these conditions, so the soil in your bog should provide that. The best soil for bogs is a mixture of peat and sand in nearly equal measure. Because peat is an environmental hot button, you should explore peat substitutes like coir, leaf mulch, and composted fir bark. Incorporate old pine needles or use them as mulch on top. Avoid anything that is rich in nitrogen, which will add unneeded, unwanted nutrients to your bog. The mix you use should retain moisture but not be saturated. Excess water should drain through.

How Do You Maintain Moisture?

During periods of regular rainfall, the bog garden by its very nature and construction will remain moist. If you live in a dry area of the country or hit a dry spell, you'll have to supplement the water nature provides. If you anticipate dry conditions, you can bury a soaker hose or perforated pipe in the bog during construction with an above-ground connection to attach a hose. As an alternative, hand-watering is a good means of providing needed water. Just be sure that a gentle soaking application of water is made so you aren't washing away the soil you've made for your plants.

Garden Quick Tip _____

If your bog garden is too large for you to reach in from the sides to weed the entire garden, you might consider installing a small stepping-stone path through the garden. Provide a firm gravel base for the stones to minimize their sinking after you install them. If you strategically locate the stones, they won't even look like a path. Bog soil tends to be spongy and compacts if you walk on it. Using stepping-stones will prevent sinking and restrict compaction to designated access areas.

The bog garden is a unique feature, unfamiliar to many gardeners. If you have a water feature, the bog is a great way to make the transition from water to land. If you don't have a water feature, a stand-alone bog garden will give you the opportunity to grow fascinating plants that you can't grow anywhere else.

The Least You Need to Know

◆ Marginal planting is an important opportunity to expand the kinds of plans you can use in your garden.

◆ The use of marginal plants helps make the transition between water and land.

◆ By using marginal plants, your water feature will take on a more natural look.

◆ Ponds, streams, and waterfalls all benefit from marginal planting along their banks.

◆ The bog garden can be part of a water feature or can stand alone as a different and unique garden.

In This Part

Part **5**

Tools, Projects, Plants, and the Future

These are the things that make it all work. You'll need tools for constructing features, as well as special tools for planting and maintaining gardens. You'll have to know which plants are available and which are the best for both your rock and water features and the climate in which you live.

Then there are the basic projects for rock and water features, step-by-step instructions showing you just what you need and how to construct a rock garden path, trough garden, tufa planting tower, waterfall, miniature pond, bog garden, and muddy ledges. Finally, from the basic projects, there are the more advanced and larger features, many of which need a professional designer, but some that the homeowner can do as well, as he comes full circle in his use of rock and water.

In This Chapter

- ◆ Tools of the trade
- ◆ The big dig
- ◆ Hand tools
- ◆ Finger tools
- ◆ Finger tools on the cheap

A basic tool bucket will allow you to carry
nearly all your basic maintenance tools out to
your feature in one shot.

Chapter **17**

Tools of the Trade

Having the right tool for the job has saved many a do-it-yourselfer. Backyard gardeners are no exception, and when you're working with rock and water, the right tool can be a lifesaver. Surprisingly, the most important tool you have is yourself. Your body is an incredibly complex machine capable of an astonishing array of tasks. Take care of it. Know your limits. Don't overdo it.

Because power tools require a certain amount of specialized knowledge and can be dangerous if used improperly, we'll leave those to the experts. But remember this: Never use a tool you're not familiar with, especially if it is powered by electricity and has the ability to cut.

This leaves us with hand tools, which are still the tools of choice for most gardening chores. Their design has been largely unchanged for generations, a testament to their enduring utility. The biggest change has been a growing selection for people with special needs. Designers have worked to make gardening accessible to people who previously would have had a hard time with even the simplest garden task.

Hand tools can be dangerous enough if not used properly or if stressed beyond their tolerances. Used properly, you'll be handing them down to the next generation. In this chapter, we will examine an array of tools that will help you do many of the tasks described in this book.

Tools You Will Need

Next to plants and books, there is nothing gardeners love better than garden tools. Most avid gardeners seem to accumulate many tools over the years, the numbers always increasing because garden gadgetry has tools and aids multiplying like rabbits.

If you can avoid the temptation to acquire every new tool designed to "make your life easier," rock and water gardening can be accomplished with a few basics. With a 5-gallon container and a bucket organizer, most of your needed tools will be an arm's length away.

Now for some conflicting advice: Buy the best tools you can afford, and scavenge for tools at the same time. There is a wide range of quality in garden tools. This is one of those times when you really get what you pay for. In general, more expensive tools are much better made. Only quality materials are used, and the actual construction method results in a tool that will last longer, frustrate you less, and be a joy to use.

Scavenging is another matter. Especially for rock gardening, where small tools are the order of the day for close work, free or low cost is a good thing.

The Big Dig

Moving rock and soil requires some leverage. Long-handled, round-point shovels are usually the digging tool of choice. Pick axes and mattocks are useful for loosening particularly tough soil and for dislodging rock. A spading fork is also useful for loosening soil, but don't use it to mess with rocks. It simply is not the right choice for that job.

Here are the handy straight-blade nursery shovel and a spadefork.

Flat-blade nursery spades are useful for slicing through compacted soil and roots.

Pry-bars and crowbars give you extra leverage when lifting and moving rock. This means you can move a rock by hand that is much heavier than you'd be able to lift.

The pry-bar (top) and crowbar (bottom) are great aids for moving and adjusting rock.

A traditional crowbar is useful for smaller pieces, but a long-handled pry-bar, which can weigh as much as 40 pounds, is the only tool that will give you enough leverage to handle the really big stones. Both are also useful in a maintenance context when adjusting and resetting rock.

Maintenance Tools

Maintenance tools can include those discussed previously, but many are smaller and more specialized.

Perennial spades are narrow and sharp edged, perfect for smaller digging jobs and dividing large perennials.

The rabbitting spade from England, basically a small perennial spade, is a workhorse. With a heavy, forged blade, it's used for all but the heaviest jobs and is particularly useful in a garden with rocks where there may not be space for a larger shovel.

The rabbitting spade is great for removing sod.

An assortment of rakes from small hand-helds to long-handled leaf and straight-head steel rakes, make cleanup a snap.

Here are an assortment of rakes, all of which you will need for one chore or another.

Use the little rakes between your plants for cleaning up debris. Leaf rakes make "sweeping" areas clean of leaves and twigs a much easier chore, and the straight-head steel rakes do a fine job of dethatching areas around your features to keep the lawn nice and are perfect for grading gravel and soil. Larger rakes make the job go faster, but in tight places, you'll need to have the little guys.

A folding pruning saw can not only be slipped into your back pocket, but it is also sturdy enough to handle all but the largest pruning jobs in the rock and water garden.

Use the folding pruning saw for cutting small branches and the hand cultivator for working in tight places.

Hand cultivators loosen surface soil, can be used for small area grading, and, like a tiny hoe, will disturb a weed's root systems, helping to control them before they get out of hand.

Hand Tools

Two classes of tools you should never buy on the cheap are trowels and shears. Strength and durability are important for both, and you won't find these qualities in a cheap tool.

With larger tools, much of the leverage you achieve comes from the length of the handle. In the hand tool arena, all the leverage comes from you. Your hand, wrist, and arm will be put to the task. Cheap trowels won't last a season; choose a well-constructed trowel, and your descendants will be using it long after you are gone.

This is a selection of valuable stainless-steel trowels.

Large, medium, and small bypass pruners have many uses.

Trowels come in a wide variety of sizes and shapes. Here you can see, from left to right: a long-handled trowel, useful in tight places between rocks and for precise digging; a digging trowel; and a specialty trowel with a pointed tip, good for breaking into compacted soil or planting bulbs. There is also a small trowel, more useful for container gardening; a weeder, which can also be used for small digging jobs and working between the rocks and in containers; and, in front, a large trowel, almost strong enough to be a small shovel. These tools feature one-piece stainless-steel construction and won't break or rust.

Shears for pruning and trimming herbaceous and shrubby plant material should also be chosen carefully. If you can, try out several varieties and manufacturers to choose a pair whose weight and fit is comfortable for your hand. Cheap shears are the most frustrating of garden tools to use, and you definitely should avoid them.

Bypass pruners, whose blades have a scissors action, are generally preferable to other models as they do less damage to the plant material when they cut. They come in different sizes. Rock gardeners appreciate the smaller shears because the plants they work with are so small and the pruning work more delicate. Perennial gardeners can usually get by with a larger pair.

Use your shears appropriately. They were built for a specific purpose and should not be used on material that is too large or on things other than plants.

Finger Tools

"Finger tools" are the exception to the rule that says you should buy the best tools you can afford. These tools are controlled by your fingers, as opposed to your hand or arm, and are used for the fine detail work in the rock garden and containers. They can usually be found around the house or purchased very inexpensively. These fall into three basic groups.

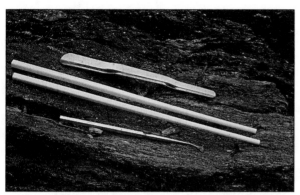

These poker-prodders are for close work in tight places.

The "poker-prodders" are little tools useful for working with seedlings and small plants. Like the other finger tools, the more you use them, the more you'll find for them. Pictured here, bottom to top, are: a probe from a high school biology class, a pair of plastic chopsticks (wood will eventually rot), and a stainless-steel "widger" a great little English tool for working in really small places.

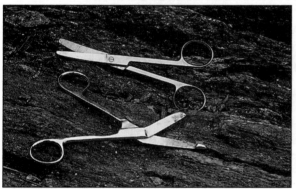

Small scissors like these not only have uses around the house but in the garden as well.

Stainless-steel surgical/medical scissors, often available in hardware store sale bins for a dollar or two, are great for fine pruning jobs on little plants and are always useful to have around. While you're at the bins, look for a couple pair of long tweezers, great for pulling hard to reach weeds in tight places and around hardy cacti.

Believe it or not, your old silverware will come in handy in 1,001 ways in your garden. Save it.

Now don't laugh at this one. What should you do with all that heavy-duty, miscellaneous, stainless tableware you're about to throw out or consign to the rummage-sale heap? Put it in your tool bucket. As finger tools, and for all the same uses as the others, they excel. Spoons and knives function in the soil much as they do on your plate. Forks make nice little rakes and cultivators for use in the rocks and containers. They are strong for the size and don't rust. As an additional plus, you already know how to clean them!

The Least You Need to Know

◆ There is an appropriate tool for every garden job.

◆ Except for finger tools, buy the best tools you can afford. You'll save money in the long run and have a better experience.

◆ Never use a tool for a job it was not designed to do.

◆ Always keep all tools clean and in A-1 condition.

◆ If small tools, such as trowels, are made of stainless steel they will never rust.

In This Chapter

- ◆ An easy rock garden on a slope
- ◆ A natural stepping-stone path
- ◆ A miniature rock garden in a trough
- ◆ A tufa tower rock planter

This miniature rock garden in a hypertufa trough can beautify any yard when done well.

Chapter 18

Basic Rock Feature Projects

By now, you should be itching to get to work. You've read all about the different kinds of rock and water features and learned what is needed to install them. Before taking on the bigger stuff, here are four easy rock feature projects that can get you started on revamping your yard.

You can do each of these projects relatively quickly and for nominal cost. Just plan carefully and then stretch those little-used muscles. Working with rock isn't always easy. Practice on these basic projects, and soon you'll be ready to move on to bigger things. Remember to ask for help with any rock project if you need it—especially if heavy lifting is involved.

An Easy Rock Garden on a Slope

Many rock gardens begin with a hillside and some rock already in place, often too big to be moved. Some yards don't have that luxury. Suppose you have a gently sloped hill planted in grass, on which you decide to create a rock garden.

To do this project, you will need the following materials:

◆ A sod-cutter, spade, shovel, and pick ax
◆ A rake
◆ A wheelbarrow
◆ A supply of course drainage material, such as broken bricks or small stones
◆ A supply of good soil, grit, and pea-gravel
◆ A supply of rocks of various sizes

This can be a good weekend project, and depending on the availability of rocks, probably will not cost more than a nice dinner for two.

Here's how you do it:

1. Mark out the area of your garden. Don't be overambitious. Remove the sod with a sod cutter and reserve it for later use.

Begin by scraping the turf from the area you are going to use for your new rock garden.

2. Pile 4 to 8 inches of drainage material or coarse builder's sand over the entire area. Be sure to create hills and valleys for topographical interest. Slope it down at the edges so it grades into the surrounding landscape. If your soil has very poor drainage, you might consider digging down to about 18 inches at the center of the garden and lining the hole with about 6 inches of coarse drainage material such as broken bricks or stones.

If you opt to dig a hole for better drainage, add a 6-inch layer of stones or broken bricks as drainage material.

Place the turf you removed from the surface over the drainage material, but invert it with the grass side facing down. This will keep the soil from sifting down into the drainage bed, utilize the soil from the sod (the best in your yard), and kill the grass. If you opted

to dig the hole for drainage, place some good-size rocks over the inverted sod to help support the surface rocks.

After inverting the turf over the drainage material, add some good-size rocks before filling the hole. They will help support the surface rocks.

3. Now add a number of good-size rocks to the top of the bed. Set them into the material so that, when you apply the last bits of soil and gravel mulch, they will be ½ buried.

4. Next mix the one part soil with two parts sand and grit (combine the sand and grit beforehand in equal parts). Wet the surface down well and then allow it to settle for a few days. After settling is complete, fill any low spots with the same mix.

5. Check rock placement and install any additional rocks. Place them at appropriate locations, as described earlier in Chapter 6. Dig ⅓ to ½ the rock into the ground, placed with their broadest sides down and angled so water will drain back into the soil.

After placing your surface rocks and wetting the garden down to check for settling, finish the top layer with your soil mix and begin adding your plants.

6. Add appropriate rock garden plants.

7. Mulch the planted garden with pea gravel or a similar-size stone, paying particular attention to lifting the edges of bun and mat-forming plants to gravel them and keep them off the soil.

This may seem like a different way to garden, but good drainage is one of the requirements for a successful feature of this type. Building up from ground level and using a free-draining soil will go a long way toward making your rock garden plantings thrive.

A Natural Stepping-Stone Path

A stepping-stone path can keep your yard from being worn out by foot traffic, give you a place to walk during rainy weather when the ground is muddy, and provide a way to walk through and weed your garden without stepping all over the plants. Installation is the same, regardless of the design parameters.

To do this project, you will need the following materials:

◆ A shovel and pick ax and rake

◆ A wheelbarrow

◆ Coarse sand

◆ A variety of flat, natural stones

◆ Plants, if you decide to use them

A small path is a project you can complete in 2 days. Depending on the availability of the stone, the cost is extremely nominal.

Here's how you do it:

1. Decide where you want your stepping-stone path and how wide you want it to be. As a rule, it should be wide enough for 2 people to walk side by side. Then mark off the area.

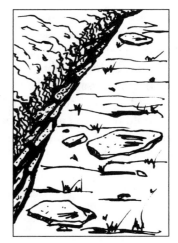

Here's a rough dirt path, partially overgrown, that would be perfect for the addition of stepping-stones.

2. Clear away any brush, weeds, rocks, sod, or other growth in the area. Rake the ground smooth.

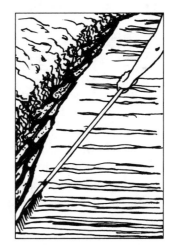

Clear the ground for your path by removing any weeds, rock, overhanging branches, and other obstructions, then raking the ground smooth.

3. Estimate how many rocks you'll need for the path and how you want to set them. Gather the rocks or order them from a garden center or nursery.

4. Choose the rocks you want to use and decide how you want to set them. Set them in the path area to see what they look like, just to be sure.

5. Dig out for each individual stone to be set. You don't have to make each hole perfect in the shape of the stone. Just make sure each hole is about 1 inch deeper than necessary. Add a layer of coarse sand to support the stone. This layer should be deep enough that the stone, when it is laid on it, will have its top flush with the ground around it.

Since the stones will be set at ground level, dig out for each individual rock before adding some coarse sand, setting the rock, and backfilling around it.

6. Begin setting stones in place. Put them in place and wiggle them around to settle them in the sand. Once they are all down, then backfill around and between the stones with sand so that the stones are solidly planted. Make sure each stone is in full contact with its layer of sand so that it does not tip or wiggle.

7. Water the path and allow the sand to settle. Refill to flush level as often as needed.

Once it's done, your stepping-stone path will be practical, add life to the yard, be a great place for plants, and have a character all its own.

There is a whole class of plants that is suitable for planting in an area where they may get walked on. We have discussed some starters in Chapter 19.

A Miniature Rock Garden in a Trough

The man-made, miniature rock garden is fast becoming a favorite feature all over the world. Those without the space for a rock garden in their yard will often opt for a trough garden, creating the same look in miniature. Some gardeners, with fairly formal, manicured lawns, will introduce a trough garden just to add a note of rugged beauty to an otherwise formal surrounding.

Trough gardens are fun to create and allow you to use your imagination, because you are really creating a landscape in miniature. In the 1930s, many English gardeners began turning old stone watering troughs into gardens. But with these natural resources dwindling, gardeners began making their own troughs from lightweight concrete.

There are companies that manufacture and sell these troughs. You can buy them in any size that will work for you, usually for a very reasonable price. You can even buy them pre-planted from some nurseries and garden centers. Or you can make them yourself, using a lightweight concrete mix called hypertufa.

To do this project, you will need the following materials:

- Portland cement—not pre-mixed concrete or mortar
- Sifted peat or a peat substitute, perlite, and fibermesh to complete the mix
- A wheelbarrow
- Two cardboard boxes of different sizes to use as a mold, or scrap pieces of 1-inch sheet building insulation with which to make a mold
- A sieve or screen
- Rubber gloves
- A stiff wire brush
- A dust mask
- A drill and masonry bit
- A sturdy, flat surface on which to work

You can do the initial stage of the project in several hours. Curing, however, takes several weeks.

Here's how to do it:

1. Have two cardboard boxes ready or construct boxes with the building insulation and duct tape. The larger the trough, the flimsier the cardboard alternative will be. If you're interested in a more free-form trough, prepare a pile of sand in a random shape. One box should fit inside the other, with 1 to 3 inches between the sides of the boxes. The bigger the trough you're going to make, the thicker the sides must be. Place a couple space fillers (e.g., empty film canisters, soup cans, etc.), into the bottom for extra drainage.

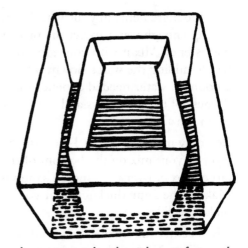

To make a rectangular-shape hypertufa trough, you can use two cardboard boxes of different sizes as your mold, placing one inside the other.

2. Mix your hypertufa. The mix, by volume, is two parts Portland cement, three parts sifted peat, and three parts perlite. You only use a small amount of fibermesh, only about a cupful for every 2 gallons peat and perlite. It should have the consistency of cottage cheese. To test for the right consistency, squeeze a handful of mix. You should see just a few drops of water fall out.

You'll know your hypertufa mix is the right consistency if you squeeze a handful of it and just a few drops of water fall out.

3. Mix the ingredients in your wheelbarrow, adding enough water to get the proper consistency. Mix it with your gloved hands, adding the water slowly. The amount of water needed depends on the dryness of the peat moss and the humidity in the air.

4. Begin by making about a 1- to 3-inch layer of your mix on the bottom of the larger box or over the random sand pile. Make it the same thickness that you will make the sides.

5. Then center the smaller box inside the larger box. Next pack the mix firmly between the sides of the two boxes. When you reach the desired height, smooth and level the top edge. If working free-form, pack the material on top of the pile until the preplanned depth and size are reached.

Using gloves to protect your hands, stuff the hyper-tufa mix firmly into the sides of your mold until you reach the desired height for your trough.

Now it's time for the cure:

6. For the first 36 hours, cover the entire mold with plastic. This makes the hyper-tufa cure more slowly, which makes for a stronger planter.

7. Test the hardness with your fingernail. If you can scratch it, the mixture is still too soft. Once you need a screwdriver to scratch the surface, the trough is ready for the second stage of curing.

8. Carefully remove the mold from the trough and smooth the corners and rough edges with a stiff wire brush. You can add texture by scoring it with the brush and/ or a screwdriver, but don't press too hard. Now leave your trough outside in a shady spot for about 3 weeks.

9. Next you must leach away the lime that is found in Portland cement because it can harm plants. You can do this by refilling the porous planter with water over 10 days, adding more when it is empty. Heavy rains will also do the leaching job for you.

10. Finally, you can additional holes in the bottom with a masonry bit, if needed, to give the trough additional drainage.

A standard soil mix for a trough garden is 20 percent compost, 30 percent loam, and 50 percent fine gravel or sand. This will give you the kind of drainage you need for dwarf conifers and alpine plants. If you need more drainage, increase the amount of sand/gravel. Landscape the top of the trough with rock and gravel if it will be in the sun and wood pieces and compost if it will reside in the shade.

After you finish your trough and let it cure the right amount of time, you can plant it and create a beautiful rock garden in miniature.

There are other ways of using hypertufa. You can use nearly anything of any size or shape as a mold. Some people use plastic containers or Styrofoam for their molds, but these materials must be lined with plastic for the hypertufa to stick. Others use a bucket as a mold to make a round container, but you must line a metal bucket with plastic as well.

A Tufa Tower Rock Planter

A tufa tower is an unusual rock feature made for rock garden plants. The trick is to assemble a number of these rocks so they look like a natural formation. This feature will open eyes and have your friends and neighbors wondering just how you did it.

To do this project, you will need the following materials:

◆ Three, four, or five slabs of natural tufa or lava rock, both of which are soft and porous and can be obtained at garden centers

◆ A drill and masonry bit or hammer and cold chisel
◆ Safety glasses or goggles
◆ Gloves
◆ An aluminum rod or masonry-reinforcing rod called rebar.
◆ Soil and plants

Here's how to do it:

1. Once you have your slabs of tufa, take a good look at them and decide how you want to stack them so that plenty of planting pockets will be available and "good faces" will face forward. They should not be stacked one directly on top of the other.

2. Mark the spots where you want your planting pockets, then wet the rocks and drill them out with a masonry bit and/or a hammer and cold chisel. The pockets don't all have to be the same diameter and should be between 3 and 6 inches deep. Don't forget to use the gloves and safety glasses.

Once you have your tufa slabs, decide where you want your planting pockets and drill them out with a masonry bit or use a hammer and cold chisel.

3. After you drill out each slab, turn it upside down and shake the dust out, reserving the chips, etc.

4. Once the planting holes are in place, drill a hole in each slab at the spot you want to attach them.

5. Take your rod and drive it into the ground. Go down deep enough so that the rod will support the feature. Measure carefully because the rod should not extend over the top of the final stone.

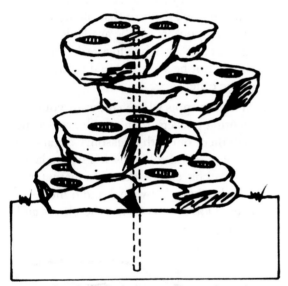

Once the planting pockets are set and you know how you want the slabs to sit, drill a hole through each in the appropriate place and link them together with an aluminum rod or masonry rod and drive it firmly into the ground.

6. Stack the drilled-out slabs of tufa over the rod, one at a time, adjusting them into the position you want. When the last slab is in place, make the final adjustments so that the feature is stable. As with a dry-stone wall, the slabs should fit together at the point where they are joined.

7. Begin planting at any time, using a porous soil mix, adding fine gravel and leaf mold to the soil. You can use the same combinations of plants you would use in planting a rock wall. Once the plants are in place, the feature will look very natural and unique.

Once your planter is in place, fill the pockets with soil and set a variety of plants. Once planted, you will have a unique feature that is full of color and looks like a natural formation.

All the rock features described here are fun projects, won't take too long, and don't cost a lot of money. Yet each is special in its own way and will enhance the look of your yard. And that says nothing about the priceless feeling you get from doing it yourself.

The Least You Need to Know

◆ With some careful planning and work, a sloping hillside can be adorned with a beautiful rock garden.

◆ Natural stepping-stone paths should be wide enough for 2 people to walk side by side.

◆ A well-designed rock garden in a trough is like a landscape in miniature and a great addition when space is tight.

◆ The well-constructed tufa tower looks like a rock formation created by nature.

In This Chapter

- ◆ Creating a do-it-yourself waterfall
- ◆ Making a miniature half-barrel pond
- ◆ Creating a bog garden
- ◆ Installing muddy ledges on the bank of a pond

This large container water garden, fully planted and set on a patio, is one example of a fine-looking water feature you can easily create.

Chapter 19

Basic Water Feature Projects

It's time to get your hands dirty again. In the last chapter, we outlined some basic rock feature projects. Now you'll learn about a few easy-to-build water features for your yard.

Each project is simple, can be done in a weekend, and isn't too costly. The basic installation methods are the same, but you can alter the features to suit your own individual purposes.

A Do-It-Yourself Waterfall

Until now, we've talked about waterfalls that flow downhill over a series of rocks. This one is a bit different, a single cascade of water that you will be able to manipulate in several ways. It gives you yet another option and way to create a waterfall.

You will need the following materials:

- ◆ A spade and maybe a pick ax
- ◆ A wheelbarrow to remove dirt and sod
- ◆ Concrete mix and a supply of bricks
- ◆ Flexible pond liner
- ◆ A submersible pump and length of outlet hose
- ◆ A selection of natural rocks

You should be able to complete this project in 2 days.

Here's how you do it:

1. This installation works best on a slight slope. Draw up a plan for an upper and lower pond and mark out the design on the ground. The lower, or main, pond should come right up to the bank over which the water will fall. At the top of the bank, dig a smaller pool or pond.

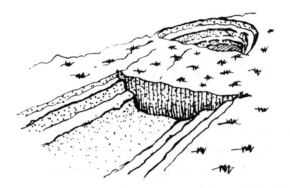

To begin the project you must dig out 2 pools—a lower pool and a smaller upper pool to feed the falls.

2. Between the 2 ponds, pour a shallow concrete foundation. Next, construct the brick wall against the bank, again using concrete to hold the bricks in place. The top of the wall must be at the same level as the water in the upper pond. Leave 1 brick out in the middle of the top row, creating a chute area for the water to flow through.

The brick wall should be constructed between the 2 pools using concrete for a foundation and to hold the bricks in place. Remember to leave the center brick out in the top row for your spillover.

3. Now it's time to install the liner. If the ground has any sharp objects, remove them. Lay a cushion or a layer of sand in each of the pools. With this kind of waterfall, line the lower pond first, bringing the liner up over the wall. Next line the top pool and allow a generous overlap to hang down over the wall into the lower pool.

When you lay the liner, the piece from the lower pool should drape over the wall into the upper pool. Then the liner in the upper pool should drape down over the wall into the lower pool.

4. Place a piece of cushioned underlay on the chute area and then cement in a 2-inch-thick slab of stone or concrete so that there is a slight overhang to the lower pond.

5. Next, get to work with your rocks and cover the top of the wall and the exposed liner with stone.

Now cover the outline of your feature with different-size rocks, building them up around the feature so they don't look like a necklace. Also cement a flat stone into the gap on the top of the wall as an over-hang for the water.

6. Place your submersible pump in the lower pond and either bury the return line or camouflage it with rock as it runs to the upper pool. The water should enter the pond from beneath a rock.

Add a submersible pump to the lower pool, running the outlet hose outside the feature and secure it under a rock in the upper pool. When the pump is turned on, the water will begin to flow.

Now dress the feature with additional rock and plants. Be sure the liner is hidden from view and that the plants you use complement or accent the stonework and the water. A grouping of rocks in the lower pool will deflect the falling water, heightening interest. Water plants and marginal plantings are the finishing touches. If the lower pool is designed deep enough, you can add fish.

This is just one way to construct a waterfall. We discussed many different styles and sizes in earlier chapters. This version is perfect for yards that don't have a lot of space.

Use your imagination and get creative.

Making a Miniature Half-Barrel Pond

The half-barrel pond or pool is a water garden in miniature, the equivalent of a trough garden for rock garden plants. This is a feature you can put into a conventional flower garden, at the base of a rock garden, or alongside a patio. If you're desperate for a water feature and don't have room for a pond or stream, check this out.

To do this project, you'll need the following materials:

- A wooden half-barrel (purchase at a garden center)
- Several water plants set in pots for under-water planting
- A burlap or Hessian sack

You can do this project in an afternoon, as long as the staves of the barrel are swelled and not leaking. It is very inexpensive to complete but can still bring the water gardening experience to your backyard.

Here's how you do it:

1. Before you begin you must be sure the barrel, which may be dried out from sitting in a garden center, does not leak. If it does, you must swell the staves, the individual boards that make up the barrel. As an alternative, you could line the barrel with a lighter-gauge pond liner.

2. To stop the leaks, place the burlap or Hessian sacks around the inside and base of the barrel. Now pour water over them, soaking the sacks and keeping them wet until the staves swell and the barrel becomes watertight. Then remove the sacks.

If your wooden barrel leaks, line it with a piece of burlap or Hessian sack and keep wetting it down until the individual boards swell and the leaks stop.

3. Place the barrel in its permanent setting. Fill it with water to within 4 inches of the rim. Allow the water to stand for several hours to once again make sure there are no leaks.

Fill the barrel to within 4 inches of the top and make sure there are no leaks.

4. Put your water plants in lattice pots so the water can circulate freely. Line the pots with burlap or Hessian so the dirt will not escape into the barrel.

5. You can put the pots in at the necessary level by setting them either on the bottom of the barrel or on a brick to raise them up. Don't overcrowd the barrel. Use no more than three to five plants.

If there are no leaks, set the barrel in its final place and set the plants in pots. Use a brick or two where necessary to make sure the plants are at the right height. Then top off with more water, and you're done.

Despite the small number of plants, try to include plants from more than one of the water plant classes discussed in Chapter 20. This is a low-maintenance feature that still has the potential to give you great enjoyment.

As an option, you can include a small re-circulating fountain or aerator for sound and movement. This also makes it possible to include a fish or two.

Plant around the base of your barrel to give the feature more character. You can plant directly into the ground or use a grouping of potted plants to accent the barrel. Foliage plants usually go well, especially if you have flowering plants in the barrel. They'll support without detracting from the main feature.

This simple project can be very attractive and is suitable for many different locations. It can complement larger features or work as a stand-alone if space is limited.

Creating a Bog Garden

Bogs are wet, spongy, generally acidic grounds that occur naturally in low-lying areas, often near ponds or streams. Because of these soil conditions, only certain kinds of plants can thrive there. Bog gardens can be installed adjacent to a pond or stream to enhance the natural look of the entire area or be done as stand-alone features.

Bog gardens can be any size and shape. Irregular configuration rather than perfect circles or squares look best if you're trying to mimic nature. They should always have a sunny exposure.

You can do the basic construction in a day. However, you should allow the soil to settle before you plant the garden. Cost for a small bog garden (not including plants) is probably no more than a nice dinner for two.

To do this project, you'll need the following materials:

◆ Spade and pick ax
◆ A pitchfork or other sharp implement
◆ A wheelbarrow to transport and mix soil
◆ A flexible pond liner
◆ A perforated soaker hose
◆ Flat stones and plants

Here's how you do it:

1. No matter what the size of the bog, you'll need to dig a hole about 18 inches deep. Save the soil. Unlike the pond, there are no shelves in the bog garden.

When digging for a bog garden, the hole should be about 18 inches deep all around, no matter what the shape.

2. Though the bog is not a pond, it is still advisable to use a flexible pond liner. These come in various *mil* number designations. A 45 mil liner is substantial and should last many years. Once you set your liner, you will want to puncture it in a number of places so that excess water can seep into the ground. You are creating a moist area, not a pond. Allow your liner to drape over the edges of the hole just like when constructing a pond.

Backyard Lingo

A **mil** is a measure of thickness, with 1 mil equal to $\frac{1}{1,000}$ inch. Thus, a 45 mil liner is $\frac{1}{45,000}$ inch thick.

Lay the liner as you would for a pond. Only this time use a pitchfork or sharp implement to punch some holes in the bottom for drainage of excess water.

3. Next, fill the hole to ¾ of its depth with a mixture discussed in Chapter 20. Most bog plants are adapted to living in areas with very little nutrition available from the soil.

4. An optional step, but one useful for keeping the bog moist, is to lay a perforated soaker hose evenly but in zigzag fashion across the top of the soil mixture. Allow the end of the hose to curl over the lip of the bog so that an extension hose can be attached to it as a water source. Then fill the rest of the excavated area with additional soil. Mound the soil mix over the excavated area to allow for 10 to 15 percent settling.

After filling the hole with about ¾ of the soil, lay a perforated soaker hose zigzag across the feature. This will provide necessary moisture during dry periods.

5. Many gardeners prefer to allow the area to settle for several months. If you live in an area with a change of seasons, construct the garden in fall and let the soil settle over the winter months. In the spring, top off if necessary to bring the bog to ground level.

6. If your bog garden is too large to reach the middle from the edge, set a few flat stones through the center of the area to allow easy access to all areas for planting and weeding. Because the bog is soft and wet, you want to avoid walking on the garden surface whenever possible.

7. In the spring, add your bog plants.

The soaker hose need not be left on at all times. It won't be needed in winter or during periods of regular rain. During dry periods, allow the water to trickle in slowly. Scratch the surface. If the mix is moist underneath, your bog is in good shape. It's not a major problem if the top inch or three dry out from time to time.

Even bog plants can rot and die if there is too much water in the garden. Be sure that the liner isn't holding too much water. Plant roots need oxygen as well as water and can actually drown if they can't breathe.

In larger bog gardens you can lay a stepping-stone path in the center so you can plant and weed without stepping on the moist soil. Then add your bog plants and you have a great feature.

Installing Muddy Ledges on the Bank of a Pond

This unique feature enhances your pond with marginal plantings and creates an attractive new planting area along its banks. By putting in muddy ledges alongside your pond, you create boglike conditions for certain species of marginal plants, helping make the transition from water to land in a wonderfully environmental fashion.

Muddy ledges are almost a bonus. It's easy to install them at the same time you are installing your pond, a process described in Chapter 11. Simply purchase a larger liner than you need for the pond alone, one that extends beyond the pond's edges. Installing muddy ledges only adds a few hours to the total construction time for the pond.

The only tool you really need to add the muddy ledges is a shovel.

Here's how you do it:

1. When digging out your pond (with its various shelves and deep area), take the time to dig out some extra narrow, dish-shape ledges around the perimeter of the pond. Add as many as you like—just be careful that you don't overwhelm and detract from the pond.

Dig in your narrow, dish-shape ledges around the perimeter of the pond at the same time you dig the hole for the pond.

2. As you spread the flexible liner into the pond area, stretch it over the edge of the pond and into the dish-shape ledges.

When you lay your flexible pond liner, have enough to drape over the edges and also set it in the dish-shape ledges you've dug.

3. Once you secure the liner and before you fill your pond with water, fill the ledges with soil. Unlike the bog, you do not have to perforate the liner that sits in the ledges.

4. As you fill the pond, the level will rise above the inner wall and also fill the ledges. The inner wall of the ledge will prevent soil from washing into the pond.

Fill the ledges with soil, then add water to the pond, allowing it to rise above the liner and fill the ledges. Then add your plants to the wet soil.

5. Some gardeners prefer to plant the ledges before the water is added, while others will wait and plant after the pond is filled. In either case, planting should be done by hand and not with any kind of metal digging tool. You don't want to damage the liner.

Unlike the bog, which depends on moist soil, these ledges remain muddy, emulating muddy areas around natural ponds in which certain varieties of plants grow. Basically, you are keeping shallow water in a soil-filled planting area.

The Least You Need to Know

◆ The installation of a do-it-yourself waterfall works best on a slight slope.

◆ Be sure the staves of a wooden barrel have been swelled to prohibit leaks before completing a half-barrel water garden project.

◆ When you create a bog garden, you might want to allow the soil to settle for several months before planting.

◆ The creation of muddy ledges at the edge of a pond allows you to use marginal plantings to enhance the look of the entire feature.

In This Chapter

- ◆ A world of possibilities
- ◆ Ways to learn about plants
- ◆ Plants for your rock features
- ◆ Plants for your water features

A wide variety of colorful plants are highlighted in this large rock garden. There are many varieties to choose from for any feature.

Chapter 20

Plants for Your Rock and Water Features

Although this book is about the use of rock and water in the garden, a short discussion of some of the fascinating plants that inhabit these features is a vital and necessary part of making your vision come true. Rock, water, and plants are the essential elements of any garden. Without each of them, a garden is not truly complete.

You can use nearly any garden plant in a rock or water feature, as long as it is in scale with your construction. Despite this, nowhere in your garden are the wildflowers of the world more at home than in rock and water features. While many traditional garden flowers have been altered and enhanced by plant breeders, the naturally occurring species are particularly suited to these sites because most are meant to mimic nature's own features. Now that you've constructed your feature, it's time to dress it up with plants.

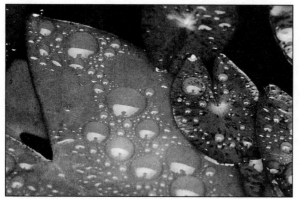

The ever-popular water lily takes on even more character as beads of rain sit on the floating plants.

A World of Possibilities

It's long been an axiom that rock gardens are a refuge for the finest wildflowers the world has to offer. Rock gardening as we know it was started to showcase plants that were being brought back from other parts of the world. Water gardening brings a whole different suite of plants to the gardener's palette. The world's wet spots, moist shores, and bogs are showcases of diversity.

Combining rock and water gardening allows you to use a bewildering array of plants in your backyard. There are thousands of plants from every corner of the globe, some common, some rare, some quiet and elegant, others brassy and unusual … and some are just plain weird.

Learning About Plants

By now you're probably up to your eyeballs with the continuing admonition to "do your homework," but there's really no substitute for research when learning about plants. The good news is: It's just as much fun as gardening itself, and you can do it all year round. The bad news: You'll never know everything you want to know. You're starting on a lifelong quest.

There are many sources of information on plants. You can read until you're blue in the face. Books by the hundreds, magazines by the dozens, plant society journals for nearly every specialty group, catalogues from more nurseries than you ever knew existed, and the Internet—a new and mammoth source of information—will fill as much of your time as you care to donate to the cause.

The Right Stuff

Looking for like-minded hobbyists to share your passion with? Consider joining one of the societies dedicated to your favorite plants. The North American Rock Garden Society (NARGS) is a first-rate source of information on rock gardening. It produces a quarterly journal, has local chapters—one sure to be near you—and has an extensive seed exchange offering the chance to pick up seed to start plants you won't find anywhere else. For information, contact:

> NARGS
> Jacques Mommens, Secretary
> PO Box 67
> Millwood, NY 10546

If water plants are your cup of tea, the International Waterlily and Water Gardening Society (IWGS) is the organization to join. It, too, has a journal and will put you in touch with (sometimes fanatic) growers. For information or to join contact:

> Paula Biles, Executive Director
> IWGS
> 6828 26th Street West
> Bradenton, FL 34207

There's no better way to obtain information on these exciting branches of gardening than to go to the experts.

Be aware of where this information is coming from. Authors from other parts of the country—and other parts of the world—will be sharing their experiences. For many reasons, the advice they give may not help. Differences in climate are often pronounced, and even subtle variations can have dramatic consequences for your plants.

Visits to public and private gardens and talking with other gardeners may be the best sources of information. You'll get ideas, learn from the experiences of others, and best of all, get information from close to home about what works best. Doing your research locally is the finest way to learn what plants thrive in your area and conditions.

Where to Find Your Plants

There are many places to find plants for your features. Start with friends. Fellow gardeners are usually generous with their excess, and especially so with common plants, which are great to learn on and stalwarts in the garden. Beware of wheelbarrow loads of plants offered by well-meaning neighbors. This many extras may indicate that the plant is invasive.

After friends, seek out your local nurseries and specialty growers. Not only can you visit but you can also hand-select the plants you'll take home. Because they're grown near you, you've got a better chance of success. Nurseries often sell several sizes of the same plant, usually in containers. You can buy larger plants and get instant results in the garden or pick smaller ones to keep the cost low and watch them mature. Selection can be limited and the prices slightly higher than other places, but there is no shipping involved.

There's no better place to get plants than from a good local nursery with a wide variety from which to choose.

Mail-order plants are the best bet for rare, hard-to-find selections. Many nurseries offering mail-order service are now online, and nearly all have printed catalogues. Be aware that plants shipped through the mail are generally smaller than those at your neighborhood nursery. This usually isn't a problem, because smaller plants still growing strong establish quickly and usually catch up to their larger relatives in short order. Sometimes plants are sent through the mail "bare-root" or out of their pots, wrapped in moist newspaper or another moisture-retentive medium. If you can't plant right away, you'll need to pot these up, so always check when you order whether your plants will be shipped in this fashion.

How to Choose Plants

Develop an eye for choosing healthy plants. Avoid dead and dying leaves. Look for a vigorous plant with clean leaves, true to color. It should be robust, filling the pot. If it looks like it's about to burst, however, look again. It may be root-bound. Roots should go to the edge of the pot, but not spiral round and round inside the pot in an endless circle. If you're choosing your own plants, don't be bashful about asking if you can tip the pot to check the roots. The other situation to avoid is a plant with no roots. Believe it or not, it can happen. Just tip the contents back into the pot, set it on the bench, and walk on.

The *Erinus alpinus* in this nursery flat are vigorous. Starting with healthy plants gives you the best chance for success.

Unless it's the only way to verify that you're getting a particular color in a plant that has a range of hues, it's not usually a good idea to buy a plant in flower. The plant puts huge amounts of energy into the production of its flowers, and it will have a harder time establishing itself after being planted.

The Right Stuff

No matter where you go to get your plants, you are likely to encounter hardiness zone ratings. These are numbers based on a map produced by the United States Department of Agriculture. It divides the country into areas based on average minimum temperature. Some gardeners take hardiness ratings as gospel. Use them to help you make your decisions, but realize that they are only guidelines and are intended to suggest the coldest region in which a plant is reliably hardy. Unfortunately, weather doesn't always cooperate. Extremes on either end of the scale will affect how well plants do for you. Zone designations are estimates. Use them as a rough guide. Don't rely on them when making your plant-buying decisions to the exclusion of other sources of information.

Plant Names

Scared off by crazy scientific names? *Buphthalmum speciosissimum*, *Ceratostigma plumbaginoides*, and *Cassiope lycopodioides* leave you tongue-tied?

Plant names can be confusing for the new gardener but are one of the great joys of the serious gardener. Scientific binomials don't need to intimidate the neophyte, so don't let them put you off. Scientific names are the *lingua franca* of the plant world. No matter where you go, people will know what you're talking about if you use them.

Don't let the scientific names of plants scare you off. These are *Ceratostigma plumbaginoides*—a tough name to pronounce, but a very lovely plant.

What about common names? The use of these unofficial monikers creates problems because of the proliferation of regional references to the same plant. Another problem is the use of the same common name for more than one plant. Is a "poppy" a *Papaver? Meconopsis? Stylophorum? Glaucidium? Romneya?* The name "bluebell" refers to *Campanula rotundifolia* in Scotland, *Hyacinthoides non-scripta* in England, *Campanulas, Polemoniums, Mertensias,* or *Penstemons* in the United States, and *Wahlenbergias* in Australia. Getting the picture?

Plant names are no more difficult to learn than the names of your neighbors. Like people, scientific names for plants are composed of two basic parts, genus and species. The genus name is the equivalent of our surname; the species name is like our first name. Sometimes a plant will have a name in single quotation marks following its scientific name. This is a cultivar designation and means that the plant is a selected plant that was chosen for a particular horticultural trait that makes it especially attractive to gardeners.

Scientific names are often descriptive, pointing out special features of the plants they belong to. Part of the fun of scientific names is learning to decipher their meaning and, by extension, learning more about the plants. But you don't have to know what the names mean,

just that they apply to one, and only one, kind of plant. If you'd like to learn what they mean, there are many sources to use to look them up.

Everyone's secretly afraid that they'll mispronounce these names because they look complicated. There's only one rule about plant names: Say it loud, and say it confidently. This is a written, not a spoken language. Everyone pronounces the names a little bit differently. As long as you get the syllables in the right order, people will know what you're talking about.

Even scientific names are not carved in stone. Plant taxonomists—the ones responsible for naming our little friends—are constantly researching the relationships of plants to each other and changing names, sometimes just when we're getting used to the old one.

Plants for Your Rock Features

Just as in the wild, plants in cultivation usually have a set of conditions in which they thrive. Matching their needs to the conditions you've created in your features is part of the great game of gardening. The better you match them up, the better they'll perform for you.

The starter plants suggested here will grow in most areas of the country, but you should always check with your local nurseryperson about how they'll do in your particular locale.

Plants for Walks and Patios

Plants for walks and patios generally share certain characteristics. They are small and usually creeping so that they fill the cracks between stones. Most important, it's a good idea if they can take some foot traffic. If you use your rocks as stepping-stones and avoid hitting the cracks between, many other plants can be used in your walks and patios. Here are a few good ones to start you off:

These *Erodium* are a perfect patio plant because they can grow in small cracks and tight places.

◆ *Mazus reptans.* This is a low-growing, mat-forming plant with adorable purple flowers. It spreads quickly and, although it loves the sun, can take some shade.

Mazus reptans.

◆ *Mentha requienii.* Corsican Mint is so short in stature it's like a sheet of cling-wrap on the ground. The flowers are very small, but this plant more than compensates by having a delicious minty smell when brushed or stepped on. It is not reliably hardy in all climates but usually comes back from seed.

◆ *Pratia pedunculata.* Another beautiful carpeter, this plant has starry, blue-purple flowers over tiny bright green leaves. It will be a beautiful addition to your patio planting in all but the coldest areas.

◆ *Sedum hispanicum.* This little sedum and its color varieties are adorable, even when not in flower. It is a succulent, and, when stepped on … well, it's not a pretty sight. Still, it does well between stones, will mind itself, and is great for sunny patios, but likes light traffic only. *Sedum sexangulare*, the Six-Angled Sedum, is a relative. This thick, flat, carpeting plant smothers itself in bright yellow flowers. Consider this one for your brick road.

Low-growing plants such as these are perfect for filling in small cracks between patio stones.

◆ *Thymus serpyllum var. coccineus.* This Creeping Thyme is an excellent deep red flowered form that lights up the cracks in your rock all summer long. Plant with *Campanula cochlearifolia*, Fairy's Thimble, whose white to blue/purple bells will grow right up through the thyme's mat of foliage in enchanting combination.

◆ *Veronica liwanensis, oltensis.* These are delicate lacy foliage less than 1 inch tall, studded with blue flowers. Both of these species are relatively new introductions from Turkey and are fantastic plants for paved areas or sunny steps.

Plants for Walls

Plants for walls should be able to thrive in small places with a minimal amount of soil. Because of this situation, they must be watered frequently and carefully so the soil doesn't wash out. Plants can soften and beautify rock walls, often cascading over the rock bringing life and color to the overall feature.

By planting in and around walls, you are softening the edges of the rock.

◆ *Aubrieta.* Purple Rock Cress actually comes in many colors and is an excellent beginner's plant. They look fantastic hanging from walls, awash in colorful bloom. Replace older plants with young when they begin to look woody and scraggly.

Aubrieta can smother themselves with flowers in the spring. Sometimes they'll continue to flower in smaller numbers throughout the season.

◆ *Campanula portenschlagiana.* A superb long-blooming rock garden plant, it flowers heavily in spring and then again in periodic flushes into November. This *Campanula* hangs down walls in billowing masses of foliage studded with upright-facing purple bells.

One of the mainstays of any rock garden, the *Campanulas* can be counted on for their wonderful bell-shape flowers in various shades of purple and blue. By carefully selecting the species and cultivars you plant, you can enjoy them all season long.

◆ *Erinus alpinus.* Alpine Balsam can be short-lived but it's worth planting. This tiny tufted plant puts out sparkling flowers of purple, but white forms also exist.

◆ *Haberlea rhodopensis.* A family relative of the African Violet, *Haberlea* has rosettes of dark green leaves, which dry almost to a crisp in hot, dry weather but rebound again when watered. The flowers are mottled soft purple and look like small gloxinias (another relative). This plant does best in shady portions of the wall.

The soft, delicate flowers of *Haberlea rhodopensis,* shown here, bely the tough nature of the plant in the garden.

- *Lewisia cotyledon.* This classic rock plant and its hybrids have absolutely stunning flowers in a wide range of colors. It does especially well in vertical situations because it cannot stand any water around the neck of the plant. Put it in a spot where it will get good sun. Better yet, put a flock of different colored ones in your wall for an amazing display.

- *Saxifraga.* There are too many wonderful Saxifrages to pick just one. With hundreds of different species and cultivars, there is sure to be one for every situation in your wall and elsewhere, and entire collections can be made with just this genus. Beautiful foliage and gorgeous flowers make these plants winners in flower and not.

Despite the toughness of their name, which means "stone breaker," *Saxifraga* have beautiful flowers.

Dwarf trees are equally at home among the rocks and are an integral part of the rock garden. Here *Tsuga canadensis* 'Cole's Prostrate,' a cultivar of Canadian hemlock, are shorter than 1 foot tall.

Plants for Rock Gardens

Purists insist that rock garden plants be less than 12 inches tall and come only from those areas above the timberline on the mountains of the world. However, most gardeners just can't exclude the rest of the world's small plants, and consequently, rock gardens today usually consist of small plants from anywhere that look good planted amongst the stones.

There is a dazzling array of rock garden plants, including every color in the rainbow and then some. Foliage, too, is infinitely varied and can be used to great effect to create a one-of-a-kind living work of art.

Entire libraries have been devoted to these plants. Here are a few to start you on your way to a lifetime of enjoyment:

- *Aquilegia.* Columbines are the spurred flowers of spring and early summer. Many gardeners are familiar with the taller varieties that get included in perennial gardens, but there are many tiny, dainty species that are 6 inches or less in height with flowers that seem impossibly large for the plant.

◆ *Dianthus*. Classics for among the rocks in your garden, pinks make spreading mats of prickly foliage above which float rafts of beautiful flowers in white and all shades of pink. These indispensable additions to the rock garden love sun and are sometimes scented.

Dianthus species and *cultivars* provide a wealth of opportunity to the rock gardener.

◆ *Gentiana*. Legendary alpine plants; if you pick the right species you can have spectacular blue flowers in your rock garden from April through October. A mat of gentians is one of the true gifts of nature.

Gentiana is a true alpine plant. There is no blue truer than gentian blue, but they also come in white and yellow.

◆ *Phlox*. The carpeting members of the phlox family are Creeping Phlox and the Cushion Phloxes. These compact plants come in a wide range of colors and slowly spread to form drifts of color in the garden. Best in early spring, they flower sporadically throughout the season, but after the initial show it's best to have something of interest close by.

Phlox subulata 'Tamaongalei,' also known as 'Candy Stripe,' provides a striking departure from the normally solid-colored flowers of Creeping Phlox.

◆ *Primula*. A large genus, the primroses offer something for everyone. There are tiny alpine species and taller, more formal-looking varieties. From early spring to midsummer you can have these beauties in your garden. They prefer a sunny, slightly moist position in the rock garden and are very useful near streams and ponds.

Primroses have special appeal to many people who grow them in their gardens and as pot plants.

Sedum sexangulare is a succulent plant, ideal for hot, dry places. Despite this less-than-plush living situation, it can smother itself with flowers, making a real splash in the garden.

◆ *Sempervivum.* Houseleeks, Hens and Chicks, whatever you'd like to call them, nothing is more descriptive than their name, *Sempervivum*, which means "always alive." There are many species and thousands of cultivars. Names are often confused, but it doesn't matter. Go look at a selection and pick the plants that appeal to you. Set into the rocks, they look like

jewels. The flowers are beautiful in their own right, but the plant form, a tight succulent rosette, is what most people grow them for. They often color even more deeply in late fall as they prepare for winter.

Popularly known as "Hens and Chicks," *Sempervivums* are easy to grow and should be a feature in every rock garden.

Plants for Your Water Features

Remember how we talked about the different categories of water plants and how by using all four you can create an ecological balance in your pond? Well, now it's time to talk about some of them and give you a variety from which to choose.

Let's get started.

Some nurseries specialize in water and marginal plants. They will have the best selection and can be a one-stop shopping experience.

The beautiful leaves of *Ludwigia sedioides* contract at night and expand again during the day.

Floaters

One of the primary functions of a plant's roots is to anchor and stabilize the plant. Floaters are among the few plants in the world whose roots don't provide this essential service. These wandering plants spend their lifetimes floating in the water, moving wherever the currents or the winds take them.

Floaters are valuable aids in the fight against excess algae. They help by shading the pond and by soaking up nutrients that would otherwise be used by the green scourge.

Fish benefit from the shade and also use the floating root system as spawning sites and as a nursery where young fish can escape and hide. The finny fiends aren't always appreciative, however, and often eat floating plants as a supplement to their diet. This usually isn't a problem, as most floaters multiply rapidly. Unchecked growth of floaters can be a problem for your pond and the environment. In some areas they are noxious weeds and threaten to choke waterways.

◆ *Lemna minor.* Duckweed often forms a skin of green over the water. These tiny green plants make a great salad if you have fish, but they can rarely eat them all, and once you've had it, Duckweed will always be around to help purify your water.

◆ *Azolla caroliniana.* Sometimes called Fairy Moss, *Azolla* looks like moss upon the water. It's crinkle-edge leaves color up maroon in the fall

◆ *Pistia stratiotes.* Water Lettuce is a fuzzy-leaf, rosette-forming floater that hangs long fine roots into the water. It, like the next species, is not hardy in cold winter climates—and can get away in warm weather ones. Be careful in the south to make sure this one doesn't get into natural waterways. It may be regulated as a noxious weed in some areas.

Pistia statiotes, or Water Lettuce, is beautiful but must be contained. In warmer areas it can become a noxious weed smothering the surface of the water. Check before you buy.

◆ *Eichornia crassipes.* Shiny green leaves with a bobber for a base, water hyacinth needs to be treated with care, like water lettuce. Reproducing like bunnies, water hyacinth has short-lived purple flowers and is not related to the bulb.

Oxygenators

Another ally in the battle against algae, oxygenators generally grow under the surface of the water. They are very effective at removing excess nutrients. In addition, they clarify the water, helping to keep it clear. Hiding places for young fish are often in short supply in backyard ponds, and these plants earn their keep by creating colonies on the pond's floor where fry can go to escape predators. Finally, there is the eponymous service they provide that benefits all the life in your pond and its water—they produce life-sustaining oxygen.

◆ *Elodea densa.* Anarchis (don't you hate it when the common name is just as strange as the scientific?) is more effective than most plants at siphoning nutrients from the water, stealing them from algae. Depending on how deep your pond is and where you live, Anarchis might make

it through the winter. To be sure, bring some inside in a bucket and grow it under lights. Its ecosystem services are too valuable to lose it.

◆ *Vallisneria Americana.* Jungle Val can grow up to 3-foot leaves that are less than 1 inch wide. It creates great fish habitat under the water and pumps oxygen out while cleaning up excess nutrients in the water.

◆ *Ceratophyllum demersum.* Hornwort is another interesting oxygenator. It has needlelike foliage and performs the same valuable services as the other plants in this category.

◆ *Myriophyllum aquaticum.* Parrot's Feather is a great-looking plant that will eventually reach the surface, raising its feathery, light green leaves above the surface. That doesn't mean it isn't doing its job below, but it's a beautiful addition to the floaters, its fine foliage providing needed contrast at the water's surface.

Rooted Floating Leaves

Hardly needing any introduction, Water Lilies and Lotus are the most popular of all water plants. Water Lilies have round floating leaves and stunning, starry flowers in nearly every color. It's no wonder that Lotus have religious significance in some cultures. Their flowers are the epitome of beauty and even the seed capsules are beautiful.

◆ *Nymphaea.* Water Lilies come in hardy and tropical varieties and miniature, small, medium, and large sizes. Tropical lilies shouldn't be put outside until water temperatures reach 70°F and need to be brought inside in the winter or they will freeze out. They prefer relatively still water, desire at least 5 hours of sun a day, and flower throughout the summer. Some tropical lilies are night-blooming. They can be huge and still need at least 6 hours of sun, but the flowers open when the sun goes down and don't close until morning—perfect for the after-dinner gardener. Hardy lilies can be kept outside through the winter. Their fantastic flowers open in the morning and close in the after-noon. Individual flowers last about 4 days, but the plants bloom from late spring until the end of summer.

◆ *Nelumbo.* Like Water Lilies, Lotus come in several sizes: large, dwarf, and teacup. Unlike their fellow floaters, Lotus leaves eventually rise up out of the water where they toy with passing breezes. The flow-ers are like peonies for the water—large, exotic, unimaginably beautiful. No matter how many you have, you'll want more. Be careful as these beauties are greedy—they'll take over entire ponds if allowed to spread at their will. Provide full sun for best bloom. Seed pods are decorative and will remain until late fall when frosts cause them to collapse.

Nymphaea come in many colors and in hardy and tropical varieties. Tropicals won't make it through the winter in cold weather areas and need to be brought in, so make sure to ask your nursery what you're getting when you select your plants.

Nelumbo flowers are among the largest for the water feature. When the petals fall, decorative seed heads provide season-extending interest.

Classic beauty for any water feature, *Nymphaea* are often grouped by size. There are miniature, small-, medium-, and large-growing varieties.

The leaves of *Nelumbo* are as striking as the flowers.

Marginal and Bog Plants

At the edge of your pond is a transitional environment where land meets water. In nature this is traditionally an area that extends from the shallow waters of the pond's edge to several feet into the shore. Plants that live here need to be able to manage with constant moisture at their roots. Those in the pond, also called "emergents" because they are rooted in the pond's bottom but grow and flower above it, have roots covered with water on a permanent basis. Those on land grow near enough to the pond that the ground is continually moist—but they must also be able to cope with seasonal flooding that may put them under for a time.

The use of liners in man-made ponds means this transition is more abrupt. If you choose to include a bog garden in your design, you will be creating the habitat you need to grow marginal plants.

◆ *Iris versicolor, fulva, pseudacorus.* These Water Iris provide the traditional spear-shape foliage of their border brethren, a valuable design element that is particularly effective pondside. They can be grown in shallow water or moist soil and will tolerate a bit of shade. Flowers are shaped like the iris of the perennial garden and come in about as many colors.

In addition to beautiful flowers, *Iris pseudacorus* adds its beautiful upright foliage to your waterside design.

◆ *Acorus.* Sweetflag has irislike foliage, often variegated with yellow or white stripes, and is wonderful for bringing light to darker areas around the pond. There are also dwarf varieties for use in areas where upright foliage is desired but other plants are small.

Acorus is another marginal with upright foliage, helping bridge the gap between water and upland areas.

◆ *Juncus effusus spiralis.* The screwiest plant around, the Corkscrew Rush has stiff, wiry leaves that twist and contort like its namesake. A wild addition to the water garden, it will grow in shallow water or the bog garden.

◆ *Sarracenia.* Many people's favorite bog plant, Pitcher Plants combine exotic flowers with beautiful, functional leaves—they trap, kill, and utilize nutrients from insects. Bright sun is preferred for flowering and best leaf color.

Sarracenia leucophylla, the white-topped pitcher plant, is carnivorous and relies on the insects it traps for nourishment.

◆ *Carex.* The sedge family is huge and confusing. No matter, their grasslike foliage creates green fountains in the bog and marginal habitats. Many cultivars are variegated. If you're choosy, you can have every shade of green along with white, yellow, blues, and browns. Important additions to the designer's toolbox, *Carex* are great for using between other featured plants and for knitting a designed water garden together.

◆ *Myosotis scorpiodes.* Water Forget-Me-Not combines lush green foliage with classic Forget-Me-Not flowers that bloom from spring to fall. This plant can become weedy, but its fast growth helps blend edges of water and rockwork. Just pull out any you don't want to keep it under control. It likes shallow water and can grow along stream edges where the water is moving.

Tropicals for Marginal and Bog Gardens

Big leaves, bold flowers, and tall plants are the hallmarks of the tropics. You can create a tropical look in your yard to transport you to another plane. All are dead if you let them freeze, so unless you like to start fresh every spring, make arrangements if you live in places where water freezes.

◆ *Alocasia, Colocasia, Xanthosoma.* Large elephant-ear leaves of these three genera bring the tropics home in a way no other plants can. Leaves range from green to deep purple, and the plants can grow as tall as an adult. You'll need to pull them indoors for the winter. Keep the plant moist and in front of a sunny window, and plant it back out when the danger of frost is gone.

◆ *Nymphoides geminata, N. cristata, N. crenata.* Water Snowflakes are like little water lilies with star-shape, fringed flowers of white or yellow. *N. geminata* has mottled leaves. These grow in shallow water.

Nymphoides geminata has mottled leaves and delicate fringed flowers. It's a tropical and will need to be brought in for the winter.

◆ ***Ludwigia stellata.*** Mosaic Plant splatters its groups of leaves over the surface of the water in tight concentric groups. Warm days of summer bring small yellow flowers, but it's the leaves that shine. Koi like this one for lunch, but grow it if you can.

◆ ***Hydrocleys nymphoides.*** Water Poppy is not a poppy at all, but is a beauty with glossy green leaves and bright sunny yellow flowers held over the leaves. Lots of sun and shallow water suit this one.

Some people treat tropical *Nymphaea* as annuals and replace them every year. Others bring them in from the deep freeze and return them to their water features when the weather warms.

◆ ***Zizania latifolia* 'Rubra.'** No plant list is complete without a plant that starts with "z." Grow Red Rice Plant in full sun to get the best red grass in the neighborhood. Arched golden seed heads add pizzazz to your *Zizania*.

◆ ***Cyperus papyrus.*** Yup, it's the real deal, Egyptian Paper Plant. It grows up to 12 feet tall but is generally considerably shorter than that. A great architectural plant for shallow water areas, it looks great in a large container on a patio, with it's great green stems and a head of graceful hair.

◆ ***Myriophyllum prosperinacoides.*** A smaller Parrot's Feather, this plant grows in bogs or shallow water and is similar to its larger cousin, just more compact.

◆ ***Canna.*** Another plant that needs hardly any introduction, cannas have been mainstays of summer gardens for generations. Combining large tropical leaves with flashy flowers, often in deliciously garish combinations, Cannas draw the eye wherever they are planted. Although most often grown in soil, they can be grown in the water and make great container subjects.

A green tree frog sits contentedly on a leaf of *Canna* 'Australia.'

The Least You Need to Know

- There is a nearly unlimited selection of plants available to rock and water gardeners.

- Take advantage of the wealth of information available about plants. Learn about what conditions you need to provide them in order to have success with your plants.

- It is better to start learning scientific names. Everyone will understand what you're referring to, and you stand a better chance of getting the plant you seek.

- There are many places to buy plants for rock and water features.

- There is a plant for every place, and a place for every plant.

In This Chapter

- ◆ Thinking you have done enough
- ◆ Moving on to the next level
- ◆ Bringing in a designer
- ◆ Doing everything you can do

This huge, elaborate rock garden can't be put in every yard. But even with a small yard, there are things you can do to further enhance your yard.

Chapter **21**

What Comes Next

You've built your first feature. After all the homework, studying, visits, discussions, books read, and warnings heeded, you took the plunge and did it yourself. Now you have a beautiful rock garden in your yard. Or maybe you've constructed a pond complete with plants and fish. Perhaps it's a small waterfall you decided to build, and it turned out great. The more adventurous of you might even have combined features, setting a waterfall in the middle of your rock garden or putting a pond near a planted dry-stone wall. In any case, you have taken the plunge into water and rock features.

What now? Are you happy to sit back and enjoy the fruits of your labor? That's certainly one option, one you undoubtedly deserve. Or have you been bitten by the bug? Did you love what you did so much that you want to do more? Many people can't resist the lure of rock and water. For them, once is not enough. Often, as soon as a feature is finished, another idea pops up. Rock and water features, with their beauty and character, can do that to you. In this chapter, we look to the future, to ways in which you can further use the skills you have learned and increase your enjoyment by changing, embellishing, or adding additional features.

Had Your Fill

Many people who install their own rock and water features find that they don't want to stop at one. They decide to build another, either appending it to the one they have or, if they have the room, making a completely new feature. Other people decide to embellish and enhance the one they have.

Builders of this wall have gone the extra mile. Built with special stone brought from Maine to New York, it's beautiful.

If you've got a pond, dry-stone wall, waterfall, or rock garden, and feel you cannot construct another major feature because of the limitations in your yard, there are still options. Many people are limited by space. Their pond or rock garden is set in a good place, but another feature would crowd their yard. The answer for them is to go miniature, work with small features—container water gardens, trough gardens, half-barrel waterfalls. These can all be incorporated into a small section of the yard, patio, or deck. Some people collect these smaller features and the plants that grow in them, and make them the focus of their yards.

Quick Tip

Literally thousands of small accessories are available at garden centers and home improvement stores to enhance your features. A wide choice of small fountains, statuary, lighting, even special fountainheads to make decorative spray patterns of the water thrown into the air, judiciously used, can allow you to change your approach from time to time.

Improving what you have is one of the best ways to keep yourself busy in your new hobby. Plants are an obvious area for future involvement. The world is full of things to try, and the most exciting part of gardening is that you'll never get to try them all. Experiment with new plants. Once you've got your hands dirty and have experience with the starter plants suggested here, seek out the rare and unusual. Play and have fun with design.

While the presence of the fountain has already enhanced the look of this large pond, the addition of this decorative log structure has taken it to yet another level.

The same goes for the rock in your garden. These gardens are made of stone, not cast in concrete. If you don't like a section of your rockwork, take the puzzle apart and rebuild it.

Open up a new world for yourself by adding fish to your pond if you didn't have them to start with. The enjoyment they bring you will far exceed the work necessary to keep them happy.

Quick Tip

If you still have the desire to build rock or water features but don't have the space in your yard, consider helping a friend or neighbor. Your own feature will undoubtedly become a topic of discussion with all who see it. It will spawn ideas for many of your friends and family. Your new-found expertise will be in demand, and your efforts much appreciated. You've done it once; it's always easier the second time.

Moving On from the Basics

Many people move past the basics to more complicated arrangements. Even during construction of your first feature, no matter how basic, ideas will begin to swirl in your head like the water in your feature. Areas for improvement, ways to do things better, and new planting opportunities will all come to you. This excitement is not unusual because once you know you have the ability to construct these features, it's natural to think of ways to use your new skills to build more complex and interesting installations or make your existing feature stand out even more. Space and life-style constraints still exist, but there is a way for everyone to continue on.

The Addition of a Second Feature

One of the more obvious ways to go beyond the basics is the addition of a second major feature in your yard. If you have the space and opt to do this, don't forget all the tips on design and planning that we discussed in earlier chapters. Installing a second feature just for the heck of it can actually detract from your overall decorative scheme.

By adding a set of stone steps going from a patio to a courtyard, there are now two rock features, both of which can be planted.

If you're not adding to an existing feature, consider putting your second at some distance from the first. Done appropriately, this will draw the visitor's eye from the first to the second and create a pleasing flow through the yard.

A Word of Warning

Don't simply lump features together. Avoid a "tacked-on" look by using stone in your new features that looks as much as possible like that in the first. If you can, get your stone from the same source so that it matches. Always make sure there's a plan, an overall goal in mind.

Accentuating the Positive

There are ways to go beyond the basics. Sitting/viewing areas, gazebos, and other garden structures can all add to the experience of your garden if designed and sited properly.

The addition of this gazebolike shelter overlooks the rock garden and is a great place for people to relax.

Another addition that works beautifully with water features is a small stone or wooden bridge. Again a relic of an earlier time, the graceful curve of the bridge over a small stream or waterfall is exquisite. It shows just a touch of the hand of man in your natural garden, connecting the wild with civilization. This type of addition is functional as well as aesthetic. Even the simplest, flat-stone bridge allows passage from one world to another.

There are many ways to go beyond the basics. These are the easiest ways. Just be sure you are adding, not subtracting. Sometimes your ideas will be bigger than your abilities. When that happens, it's time to call in the experts.

Hiring a Designer

Hiring a designer really takes you into rarified territory. Designers of rock and water features can do amazing things. They can plan and build beautiful features to fit any space and will work with you to achieve your dreams.

It takes a professional designer to create a formal rock wall like this one, but the result is well worth the investment.

If you have the space, the budget, and a special vision, a designer might be right for you. But always go back to school first. Do your homework. Visit with several designers. Look at their "books," photo albums of typical installations. Take a tour of several of their projects. Talk to references. Ask other customers how they like their new features and whether there were any problems in construction, financial matters, or post-construction operation of the feature. Discuss your vision with each, and assess whether they are capable of doing the job. Ask about price. It can vary markedly, but sometimes you get what you pay for.

This designed, formal fountain is sitting in a garden center just waiting to be installed in someone's yard.

When you decide to go ahead, make sure all the terms and conditions of the job are clearly understood by your contractor and you and that everything is in writing.

The Right Stuff

Designers today can do some amazing things. Swimming pools can be designed to look like natural ponds, surrounded by rock and plantings. Of course, chlorinated water will not be able to be planted or inhabited by fish, but the natural feel of such a pool is very desirable and relaxing.

Some designers will create a waterfall such as this one at the end of a natural swimming pool, giving it the look of being carved by nature.

A good designer will enjoy working closely with you. Your involvement may make the difference. Although you don't want to become a pest or make the job more costly than it is, the closer you work with your designer, the happier you will be with the results.

Another designer-created beauty, this set of stone steps leads to a formal, planted patio.

Coming Full Circle

This is almost the end of our journey. At the beginning, we introduced you to the world of rock and water features, how they have evolved and how they now fit into your modern world. Then we began to look at the things you could do to bring these wonderful pieces of nature into your yard.

If you've read this far, there's a good chance that you've already decided one of these features is right for you. By using the information provided here as a guide, you should be well on the way to completing your first project. Take your time, know what you want, plan carefully, have your materials ready, and you can install a basic feature.

Hopefully, you've learned even more. The installation of a rock or water feature is just step one. What you do after the basic installation is just as important. Planting rock and water features is an art form, but one that is well within your reach. While the feature itself is your canvas, plants are your palette, and the picture you create is all your own.

How's this for originality? It's a topiary replica of the Loch Ness Monster growing at the edge of a pond.

Another recurring theme throughout this book has been the duality between a return to nature and a more formal, measured look. Regardless of the style you choose, the addition of rock, water, and plants to your property will enable you to escape into an enchanted realm, relax, and find some tranquility in an increasing stressful world.

This is one of the rarest of water features, a water staircase running into a pool at the Villa Terrace Museum in Milwaukee. The entire structure and grounds are a replica of an Italian villa.

The Least You Need to Know

◆ Even if you don't have room for a second major feature, you can add to your yard by creating features in miniature.

◆ If you decide to add a second feature, make sure it complements the first and doesn't crowd the yard.

◆ Other garden structures can complement your rock and water features.

◆ If you hire a professional designer, do your homework, compare prices, and look for someone who shares your vision.

◆ Think of your feature as a gateway to a new world, a creation of your own that will give you years of enjoyment and pleasure.

Glossary

algae A nonflowering, stemless green water plant that can grow unchecked in water unless certain criteria are met.

Alpine plants Low-growing, colorful plants found above the timberline in mountainous areas around the world.

angle board A device made with three pieces of wood, one vertical, one at the desired angle, and the other to hold the two in place. The device is used as a guide to get the proper backward slope when constructing a retaining wall.

angle of repose The angle at which an individual stone is stable; usually with the broadest side down.

aphids Plant-sucking insect pests that can reproduce without sexual activity.

asymmetrical planting Plants grouped in nongeometric groupings to give the garden a random, natural look.

basalt A dark, volcanic rock that provides a pleasing background for plants.

biological filter Filters that contain layers of medium that harbor large concentrations of naturally occurring bacteria that break down fish waste and other organic matter.

bog garden A specialized garden in which the soil is kept constantly moist to fit the needs of the unique plants from that habitat.

bog plants Plants that thrive in the low-nutrient, constantly moist environment of the bog. Carnivorous plants and orchids are among the showiest.

boulder A large rock, usually blocky or rounded in shape.

burbler A feature with water bubbling out of it rather than being thrown into the air.

bypass pruner A tool for pruning plants whose blades have a scissors action and do less damage to plant material than other types of pruners.

container planting Any type of planting done in a container. They can be water- or soil-based gardens.

crowbar A heavy metal pry-bar used as an aid in moving rock.

deadheading The removal of dying or dead flowers from their stems.

deep-water plants Plants that have their roots in the bottom of a pond and their leaves and flowers floating on the surface.

drainage   The degree to which water will run through a feature or percolate into the ground.

dry-stone stacking   The art of putting stones together, without mortar, to create a feature.

dry-stone wall   A wall built of stone without the use of mortar or cement.

dwarf trees   Small or slow-growing trees that result from genetic inheritance, specialized maintenance, or hybridization.

ecological balance   A self-sustaining habitat in which the whole is maintained by the combination of its parts.

electrical cable   Cable used to carry electricity from one location to another. There is cable specially made to be run underground to a rock or water feature in the yard.

faux-stones   Fake or artificial rock.

fertilizer   A natural or man-made substance added to soil to provide nutrients and minerals to plants.

fingertip weeding   Grabbing a small weed at ground level between the thumb and forefinger and pulling it out.

flagstones   Large, flat, often rectangular-shape stones often used to create paths or patios.

floating plants   Name given to a variety of plants whose leaves and flowers float on the surface of the water and whose roots hang free in the water.

foliage   The leaves of a plant or tree.

formal planting   A style of planting in which even numbers and groups of plants are used and placed in rows and other geometric and/or symmetric configurations.

fountain   A spray or spouting jet of water used for decoration.

glacial erratic   A natural, large, irregularly shaped rock left when the glaciers of the last ice age receded.

gneiss   A layered rock usually of a striking gray color with lighter bands running through it.

Golden Orfe   A long, slender-bodied fish with a tubular body and snub nose.

goldfish   The most popular pond fish, capable of tolerating outdoor conditions and low oxygen settings.

granite   A hard and fine-grained rock that weathers slowly and is nonporous.

ground fault interrupter   A safety device at the outdoor power source that cuts power if a fault or surge occurs.

hardiness zone   One of 11 regions in North America as defined by the United States Department of Agriculture and based on average minimum temperature. The zones are used as a guide as to whether a particular species of plant can survive there all year-round.

in-line pump   Pumps placed outside a water feature in the line that re-circulates water from the pool in a feature back to its outlet.

koi   Large, colorful pond fish that can grow quite large and live for up to 100 years.

limbing-up   Pruning the lower limbs from trees or shrubs to increase the amount of light reaching the ground.

limestone   A common rock that is beautiful when water-worn, but not always the best choice for acid-loving rock garden plants because of small amounts of alkaline lime that leach out over time.

marginal habitats   Moist places along the banks of ponds and streams; a transition area between water and land.

marginal plants   Moisture-loving plants that thrive in shallow water, on moist banks, or in a bog garden or muddy ledge.

mat-forming plants   Thick, low-growing, often colorful plants with a matlike habit, useful in rock walls or along paths and patios.

mechanical filter   A filter that removes particles from water by trapping them in filter pads or similar medium.

mini-garden   Any replica of a full-size garden done in miniature, usually in a container or other very small space.

mulch   A ground covering such as straw, wood chips, leaves, or gravel around plants to help retain moisture, control weeds, and also beautify.

nursery   A place that sells plants and many other garden-related materials and supplies.

outlet   Name given to the part of a pump that returns water to the pond or waterfall.

overstock   Adding more fish to a pond than the ecosystem will allow. Overstocking can pollute the water and affect the health of the fish.

oxygenators   Plants that supply oxygen to a pond and help maintain the ecological balance.

pavers   Special man-made flat stones of various sizes often used to make walks and patios.

pH   A measurement of the acid or alkaline levels in water. Most fish will be fine with a pH between 6.5 and 8.5.

planting pockets   Bowl-like depressions dug into the shelves or bottom of a pond before the liner is set and filled with heavy garden soil and a layer of gravel. Water plants can then be removed from pots and planted in the "pockets."

"planting" rock   Term used for setting rocks, especially when the rocks are partially buried in the ground.

pond shelves   Flat areas below the surface of the pond and around its rim that aren't as deep as the center. Pond shelves provide places to put potted plants that don't need deeper water.

pondless waterfall   A waterfall in which there is no pond at the base of the spillway. The water filters down through a bed of rocks and is then pumped back up to the top.

preformed liner   Rigid pool liner made in a set shape from hard fiberglass with the shelves already built in.

pruning   The act of cutting a shrub or plant to a desired shape or size.

pruning saw   A saw used to cut limbs and branches from trees and shrubs.

pry-bar   A long-handled steel bar, which can weigh up to 40 pounds, used for moving and positioning large rocks.

rabbitting spade   A small shovel with a narrow blade originally used to dig rabbits out of their warrens in Europe. They feature a heavy, forged blade and are particularly useful in gardens with rocks and not a lot of space.

raised stepping-stones   Flat rocks used as a stepping-stone path but set on top of the ground as opposed to being dug in at ground level.

retaining wall   A wall constructed to hold back a hillside or sloping ground and keep it from eroding or collapsing.

rock feature   A functional and/or aesthetic construction built of rock.

rock garden   A type of garden that mixes rock and plants, usually made to look natural.

rock outcropping   A natural rock formation in which rocks are partly exposed by the natural erosion of the ground.

root rot   A fungal disease that can be caused by several conditions and is characterized by wilting, yellowing leaves, or a dying plant.

Rudd   A pond fish with a silver body and red fins.

sandstone   A light yellowish-gray to dark reddish-brown rock that is considered strong but still soft enough to weather into interesting shapes and porous enough to retain a little moisture.

scale Proper proportion; the dimensional relation of a feature to its surroundings.

scavengers Animals such as aquatic snails and tadpoles that help control the growth of algae in a pond and help create an ecological balance in the system.

scientific name The formal, horticultural name given to every plant; as opposed to common name.

shifting The involuntary movement of rock caused by natural forces or improper construction techniques.

skimmer Part of the filtering system that skims debris such as leaves and small twigs from the surface of the water in the pond.

slugs A common garden pest, slugs are a mollusk with no shell that emerge at night to chew tender stems and foliage.

sod cutter A garden tool with a long shovel-like handle and a sharp, bean-shape blade used to remove grass in sections.

spillway The part of the waterfall that water cascades over to a pond or gravel bed below.

spout A jet or column of water.

stagnant water Motionless, poorly oxygenated water.

stepped-back stone wall A formation used on slopes with the stones set deep into the ground.

stepping-stones Stones set into the ground to create a path.

stone borders Small walls used to set off a feature such as a garden or group of small trees or shrubs.

submersible pump A water pump that can be set underwater.

topiary The art of clipping shrubs and trees into ornamental shapes.

topography Term used to describe the physical features of a piece of property, such as a field or yard.

transplant shock The adverse reaction of plants when they are pulled from pots, root-pruned, and then put into new soil.

tropical plants Plants that thrive in a warm, moist climate and cannot survive cold, freezing weather.

trowels A small, spade-shape hand-digging tool.

tufa A soft, lightweight, porous rock formed by calcium carbonate left behind by evaporating water from springs and streams.

walled, raised bed A planting area contained by a wall.

water feature A functional and/or aesthetic construction involving water.

water garden A garden in which water is the medium for plants.

water plants Plants that grow specifically in water or in very moist, soggy soil.

waterfall A feature in which water falls or cascades downward into a pool or gravel bed.

weeding Maintenance procedure in which unwanted plants are removed from a garden.

West Nile virus A viral infection that began in part of Africa and has spread to North America. People can get West Nile if bitten by an infected mosquito.

widger A small, stainless-steel tool from England that is great for working in really small places in the garden.

woody plants Trees and shrubs.

Index

S